the Many Names of Robert Cree

the Many Names of Robert Cree

HOW A FIRST NATIONS CHIEF BROUGHT ANCIENT WISDOM TO BIG BUSINESS AND PROSPERITY TO HIS PEOPLE

Robert Cree
with Therese Greenwood

ECW

LIBRARY AND ARCHIVES CANADA CATALOGUING IN PUBLICATION

Title: The many names of Robert Cree : how a First Nations chief brought ancient wisdom to big business and prosperity to his people / Robert Cree with Therese Greenwood.

Names: Cree, Robert (Elder), author. | Greenwood, Therese, author

Identifiers: Canadiana (print) 20250228211 | Canadiana (ebook) 20250228246

ISBN 978-1-77041-830-1 (softcover)
ISBN 978-1-77852-497-4 (PDF)
ISBN 978-1-77852-496-7 (ePub)

Subjects: LCSH: Cree, Robert (Elder) | CSH: Cree—Fort McMurray #468 First Nation—Biography. | CSH: Indigenous leaders—Fort McMurray #468 First Nation—Biography. | CSH: First Nations Elders—Fort McMurray #468 First Nation—Biography. | CSH: First Nations—Alberta—Residential schools. | CSH: Cree—Education—Alberta. | CSH: First Nations leadership—Alberta. | LCGFT: Autobiographies.

Classification: LCC E99.C88 C74 2025 | DDC 971.23/2—dc23

Cover design: Jess Albert
Photos of the authors: Steve Bonisteel

This book is funded in part by the Government of Canada. *Ce livre est financé en partie par le gouvernement du Canada.* We acknowledge the support of the Canada Council for the Arts. *Nous remercions le Conseil des arts du Canada de son soutien.* We would like to acknowledge the funding support of the Ontario Arts Council (OAC) and the Government of Ontario for their support. We also acknowledge the support of the Government of Ontario through the Ontario Book Publishing Tax Credit, and through Ontario Creates.

Canada

Canada Council Conseil des arts
for the Arts du Canada

Ontario

ONTARIO ARTS COUNCIL
CONSEIL DES ARTS DE L'ONTARIO
an Ontario government agency
un organisme du gouvernement de l'Ontario

ONTARIO CREATES

PRINTED AND BOUND IN CANADA

PRINTING: MARQUIS 5 4 3 2 1

Get the ebook free!*
*proof of purchase required

Purchase the print edition and receive the ebook free.
For details, go to ecwpress.com/ebook.

For Tina Cree

CONTENTS

The Road to Reconciliation

*T*ansi. *Tawaw Niwaikoma Kank, Tamickiken. Nanaskomon Tatchinostatakwaw.* Hello. Welcome, my reader. I am honoured to share my story with you.

I had many names in my life. My mother named me Bobby Mountain and taught me traditional ways. I was a boy when my grandfather called me *Napikan,* "Great Man," for my spiritual curiosity. Residential school imprisoned me as Number 53. My people elected me Chief Cree to fight for our rights. As Robert Cree, I overcame trauma and addiction.

Now I am Elder Robert Cree, recognized by my people as a Knowledge Keeper. I am also *Kisikowasha Ka' Ki Kkawat,* "The Person with the Holy Child Within." That is the name the spirits gave me and which they recognize me by. By these names, I share Indigenous traditional teachings with my community, especially our youth. I also share my wisdom with members of the dominant culture. I share it with anyone who needs help as we walk the road to reconciliation.

For seventy years, I have been an eyewitness to Indigenous history. A lot of it was hard to see. But the wisdom of the ancestors warmed me as I travelled what was often a cold, hard road. It guides me today on a road of forgiveness and reconciliation.

I am often asked how, as a residential school survivor, I can forgive those who oppressed me. But that is how strong my people's traditional teachings are. They tell us life is to be lived in harmony with everything and everyone on Turtle Island. That is how Creator calls me to live and, for me, that means finding forgiveness.

In no way does that mean I expect Indigenous people to "forgive and forget." Reconciliation with the dominant culture doesn't mean erasing what was done to us. Those things happened over centuries, and some are still happening. My people know deep intergenerational trauma that will continue to affect us for a long time to come. There are many immense wrongs that must be properly addressed.

That is why we need the truth part of Truth and Reconciliation. I am called to bear witness and I thank Creator that I can. Many residential school survivors can't. It is too horrific, too heartbreaking, and they cannot speak without being overwhelmed. Other people can no longer speak because they passed over to the spiritual world. It is in their memory that I tell my story.

I was taught that it is the responsibility of Elders to preserve the past, but also to look to the future. It is our role to help people prepare for the challenges ahead. That's why I am telling you my truth but, more importantly, I am sharing the importance of the traditional teachings. Creator made Indigenous people the stewards of this knowledge so that we can help everyone Creator put on this Earth.

I believe that, with hard work, reconciliation is possible. As a Chief and Indigenous business leader, I have often walked with the dominant culture. I have seen racism and greed. I have also seen hard-nosed business people and veteran politicians moved by a traditional blessing. I have seen classrooms of non-Indigenous students wear orange shirts to acknowledge wrongs done to our children. I have seen newcomers to Canada upset to learn about the colonialist legacy casting a dark shadow over their new country.

Creator wants me to pray for them and for all of the people on Turtle Island so that we can live in peace and harmony.

I want that for you, my reader, whether you are Indigenous or not. I want you to know the beauty of the traditional teachings and the joy of letting go of anger and bitterness. I want you to feel the peace that comes from healing. I want you — Creator wants you — to live a good life of balance, with respect for one another and for this beautiful world that was gifted to us. That is why I am sharing my story with you.

It is also why I want to share a blessing with you as we start our journey together on the road to reconciliation.

When I do a blessing, I invite everyone to join me by praying with the words and actions of their own faith traditions. Creator gave all the people of the world the gift of prayer so that we could all pray in our own way. No prayer is better than another. Our prayers connect us with the many blessings given to us. When we pray by ourselves, we acknowledge those blessings. When we all pray together, we honour Creator and reinforce the blessing, making it even stronger.

I want us to pray together for reconciliation because it is time we all come together. Let's do away with discrimination, racism, greed, all the negativity that divides us. Enough is enough. We need to unite. We need to understand one another. It is time we come together to reconcile the fact we are all here to live together on Mother Earth. Let us join our voices together in gratitude for what we have been given.

We thank Creator for the gifts we share, for the four elements that make up everything in the world, including our physical bodies. We live in gratitude for the air that fills our lungs on the day we are born, that we breathe until the day we leave for the spirit world. We give thanks for fire, which fills our bodies with warmth, cooks nourishing food, and lights our way. We give thanks for water, which quenches our thirst, cleanses us, and makes up every human body. We give thanks for Mother Earth, which provides our food, our shelter, and gives us beauty to behold and nurture.

We thank Creator for the wisdom of the ancestors and the traditional teachings that have been passed down for centuries. We are thankful that we know how to live in a good way so that we can do the work that Creator intends for us to help others as well as ourselves.

We thank Creator for giving us all of these things to share in this wonderful world created for us.

Hiy hiy. This is what I have to say.

Kinanaskomitin. Thank you.

ROBERT CREE

CHAPTER I

A Cold, Hard Road

I always wanted to share the story of how my mum was brought into town by dogsled so that she could give birth to me in a hospital. She told me that story so many times I feel I remember the journey myself. Every bend in the river, the barking of the dogs, the sled bumping over the hard ice, the bite of the cold air. I see, hear, and feel it all, just the way she did on that freezing night when I was about to be born.

Stories are important to the *Niheyawak*, which in my Cree language means "the people." My people speak our own dialect unique to our geographic region, so if you are a Cree speaker you might find some words I use are said or spelled different from what you are used to. I use the words I was taught by my family and the Elders in my community. The *Niheyawak* have always shared our knowledge in an oral tradition. We hand it down from one generation to the next through our families, our Knowledge Keepers, and our community Elders. Elders are the most important people in our culture, greatly respected for preserving what we call our land-based teachings. Those teachings are based on centuries of learning about the land Creator gave us. They hold everything we need to live a good life, both for ourselves and for the world around us. I have always been part of that tradition, even on the night I was getting ready to be born.

It was around midnight in March of 1953 when my Uncle Norman Cree, my mother's brother, hitched his dogs to the sled. Uncle Norman had the fastest dog team in our First Nation. His dogs knew every twist and turn of the twenty-kilometre route that linked our small First Nations community in the boreal forest of northern Canada to the nearest small town, Fort McMurray, Alberta.

My father, Mike Mountain, helped my mother, Eva, lower herself into the basket of the dogsled. He carefully tucked a soft woolen blanket around her, then layered furs on top to keep her warm. He spoke gently to her in Cree.

"*Meoh pinpmoteck*," he said, wishing her a safe journey.

My father had to stay behind and watch over my two brothers and one sister, who were asleep inside the small home he had built in the forest. He was worried about my mum and me, of course. But he trusted his brother-in-law and the dogs to do their job.

It was a cold, hard road. My mum was exposed to the elements, travelling at top speed over bare, wind-whipped ice and pockets of deep snow, with no light but the moon and the stars. Temperatures on our reserve regularly reach minus thirty degrees Celsius, sometimes dropping by ten degrees overnight. A person could freeze to death in minutes.

My Uncle Norman was well aware of the dangers and he was prepared for anything. He had the teachings of our ancestors, whose knowledge had been passed down for centuries. He knew how to read the weather conditions, how to keep his passenger warm and secure, how to properly train his dogs. The dogs travelled the river's thick ice every winter, from November to May. They hauled pelts of *amisk*, beaver, and *wuchusk*, muskrat, to the old fur-trading fort in town. They came back to our community with salt, sugar, lard, flour, tea, tobacco, nails, and ammunition. They also brought medicine and were our reserve's only ambulance service.

Uncle Norman's dogs were strong and smart. They were trained to drag a sturdy, flat-bottomed toboggan heavy with the moose meat or firewood that the men in our family brought home to feed and warm their families. But that night they were pulling the lightweight sled that my uncle made from birchwood. It was built to go fast, and the dogs found the load light with just my mum, and me inside her.

My mother was a small woman, even nine months into her pregnancy. Her head rested below the handles that her brother gripped as he balanced on the sled's rear runners. Nestled under the fur, my mum held tight to a moosehide pouch she had sewn using moose sinew as thread. The pouch was part of the birthing tradition she learned from her mother and grandmother. It was to play a very important part in my life.

It took almost four hours for the dog team to arrive in town. My uncle pulled the team up in front of the two-storey hospital that had been built a dozen years before in Fort McMurray. Having a real hospital was a big deal in our isolated community hundreds of miles from the nearest city. Everyone was proud of it and boasted about the trained doctor, sixteen beds, and four bassinets for newborns. They knew how to treat mothers giving birth, and things did not take long after we arrived. I was ready to enter the world and, at a quarter past five in the morning, my mother delivered me. She named me Bobby Mountain, and I took my place in one of the bassinets.

I was a healthy baby, but in those days they kept new mothers in hospital a lot longer than they do now. We stayed a week before my uncle came back with the dogsled to take us home. It was still extremely cold, and the river ice was thick and safe. Tucked under the blankets again, my mum checked that the moosehide pouch, now filled with precious cargo, was safely nestled against her chest. After I was born, my mum had carefully preserved my umbilical cord inside the pouch, which lay cushioned between us as she held me in her arms all the way back to our community.

My mum needed to bring my cord home so that she could perform the birthing ritual that our women have followed for centuries. She had learned it while she also learned the practical things about feeding and caring for babies. She would wash my cloth diapers using water she heated on the wood stove. She would treat my baby coughs and rashes using traditional remedies. She knew everything she needed to raise a happy and healthy baby while living off the land, far from drug and grocery stores and all the things many young mothers now take for granted.

Most importantly for me, my mum knew the spiritual side of a baby's life was as important as the physical side. She was well prepared for the naming ceremony that would welcome me home. She knew our people's traditional protocols, like how to properly wrap a baby for the ceremony. She also knew how to prepare a traditional smudge, burning medicinal plants to cleanse us so that we could connect with Creator. She and my aunties had come together to sing the welcoming song for my older brothers and sisters. She was happy to be singing the song again, happy that I was a healthy baby who had been checked out in the hospital. She knew that when I smelled the smudge and heard the song, I would recognize the singers as my family. I would know who my people were and that I belonged with them on our traditional land.

When the singing and smudging were over, my mother went alone into a deep part of the boreal forest, which my people called *sakahk*, the bush. She found a perfect, welcoming place where she dug a hole in the ground. She filled it with sacred herbs and some moss and other greenery to make a soft nest and nestled my umbilical cord in it. Then she carefully filled the hole to cover it. After that she made an offering of tobacco and prayed in gratitude to Creator for the gift of her healthy baby boy.

By burying my cord in the ground, my mum forever connected me to the land Creator gave our people. She made that sacred connection happen to properly ground me. Because of her, I could walk the right path and accept Creator's many gifts. If my cord was not buried, if the proper protocol was not followed, I would not have that strong spiritual connection to our traditional lands. It would be easy for me to stray from the proper path and I could become rootless and lost. My mum made sure I was a part of the land and it was a part of me. Because of her, I would always be able to find my way home.

I am forever grateful to my mother for providing me with such a strong beginning. I thank Creator that she was blessed to receive knowledge from the Elders, and that she began preparing me for that spiritual connection before I was even born.

My mother and my family would give me the greatest gift I would ever receive, one that has shaped my whole life: my people's traditional wisdom. It gave me everything that is good in my life and helped me overcome everything that was bad. It is extremely powerful — so powerful that for centuries it has frightened the dominant culture into trying to strip us of it.

That is partly what my story is about: how I have had to fight for my people to preserve our culture, traditions, and our language.

To help preserve my people's traditional way of life, I have had to face many challenges and fight powerful adversaries. Luckily for me, my family and the traditional teachings of my people gave me everything I needed to be successful. I walked into boardrooms armed only with the wisdom of the ancestors and showed hard-nosed oil executives a better way to do business. I did the same thing with oppressive governments, convincing them that my people were the rightful stewards of the land Creator gave us.

Traditional teachings lit the path that allowed me to lead my people out of poverty so that we could walk in prosperity. They allowed me to travel even further. With powerful teachings of forgiveness, spiritual and physical wellness, and the interconnectedness of all life, I was able to bring together my people and those who historically oppressed us to begin the hard work towards reconciliation between our peoples. The wisdom of our ancestors is so strong that it has the power to help me accomplish all of these things.

First, I had to personally survive a brutal, racist system created to destroy all my people's traditional knowledge. As a child, I was stolen from my family and exiled from our traditional lands, institutionalized in what the government called "residential schools." I was beaten, starved, humiliated, and isolated. I had to find my own way back to the land that my mother so lovingly welcomed me to.

With the help of the Elders and the wisdom of the ancestors, I ultimately transcended years of pain and abuse. My people's traditional knowledge and spiritual teachings guided my way home to a place of forgiveness, healing, tolerance, and understanding. It was from that place that I challenged the outsiders who wanted to destroy our land and keep my people in poverty. In time, I became an Elder myself, passing my people's traditional knowledge to the next generation and championing a peaceful and just path to reconciliation in an angry and chaotic world.

But to get there, I had to travel a cold, hard road.

CHAPTER 2

In the Bush

I always felt lucky that my earliest years were spent in the most glorious place on Earth. Some people will be surprised to hear that. It might seem I grew up in poverty because we had no money, no electricity, no running water. We worked hard, from first light to sunset. Everyone in our family, no matter their age, had a job to do to make sure we had good food, warm clothes, and a cozy place to live. But we felt rich because we had one another. A loving family is the greatest treasure you can have.

Even more importantly, my family knew exactly where we belonged in the world. The Cree people had been blessed for generations, ever since Creator gave us everything we needed to live a good life. Even when I was a very little boy, I knew I was blessed to have been born Cree and part of Creator's great plan.

My family lived in what we call the bush, and what scientists call the boreal forest. The boreal forest rings the top of the world below the Arctic Circle and stretches across Europe, Scandinavia, Siberia, and northern China. In North America, it extends all the way from the Atlantic to the Pacific, from Newfoundland to the Yukon and Alaska. There are millions of miles of trees, mostly conifers like spruce, jack pine, and balsam. There are more than a million rivers, lakes, and wetlands. Thousands of plants, animals, birds, and fish. It is a worldwide, cold-weather forest full of life that can withstand frigid temperatures. I have heard that there are more trees in the boreal forest than stars in the Milky Way. Centuries ago, Creator made my people the stewards of this land and everything in it.

My people's traditional knowledge comes from generations of learning about this land that encircles Mother Earth. Today you hear people talking about the importance of the boreal forest in terms of climate change. Scientists tell us it helps keep our planet healthy, that it is the "lungs of the Earth." My people knew that long before the scientists did. We have studied this land for thousands of years. We have a name and a use for everything in it.

Ever since I was born, my parents raised me to nurture and honour the land that Creator gave us. My parents had a small house way out in the bush near the Clearwater River, the northern Alberta waterway that mingles with the Athabasca and Mackenzie Rivers and flows north to the Arctic Ocean. My people used the river for drinking water, food, and medicine. In winter when it was frozen, like the night I was born, we used dog teams to travel on it. In summer my people went up and down it to get supplies from town using rafts and skiffs we built ourselves. For centuries, it was our means of transportation, by dogsled or canoe depending on the season. But it was so much more than that. The river nourished and sustained our people, and in turn we nourished and sustained the river.

Every summer, after the spring spawning season, my father and brothers fished the river for pickerel and northern pike. We took only what we needed for our family, and we all worked together to do it. It was the same thing in the fall, when my father and his brothers-in-law hunted the ducks and geese that had finished raising their young and were on their way south. My mother and sisters plucked and cleaned the birds and cooked and smoked the meat. We did not hunt for sport. We took only what we needed. We lived as our people had for centuries, leading what is now a called a "sustainable lifestyle."

The water was pristine. We could drink water anywhere back then. When my dad and my uncles would go hunting, they did not have to carry any water when they went deep into the bush. They took salt and sugar to season the food they would get. They also took bannock that my mother made, a type of fried bread that my people first learned to make from encounters with Scottish fur traders. Then they would fill the bannock with fresh or smoked meat from game my father hunted. The food helped them keep their energy up for long hours in the bush.

In winter, my older brothers hauled our drinking water from a hole they chopped in the ice. In our cozy kitchen, my mother would use a tin ladle to scoop it from the bucket and pour it into the kettle and set it to boil. The cookstove was always lit, fired by the wood my father and uncles cut in the bush. Mum made tea and stews that bubbled all day so that we could help ourselves whenever we were hungry. She bathed her babies, washed dishes, and did laundry, all with water from the river.

When we fetched water in warmer months, we were careful to dip the pail around the oily, rainbow-coloured streaks that sometimes floated on the river's surface. The oil slick came from *kuskatew pimee*, black grease, a naturally occurring substance on our land that in English is called bitumen. Bitumen was formed when prehistoric plants and animals decayed over centuries, becoming a thick, sticky, tar-like sludge that was so plentiful, it leaked from the riverbanks and pooled on the water. Bitumen was another of Creator's gifts. Our people scooped it from the riverbanks to seal our canoes and make them watertight.

My family taught me about the river and how to use the many gifts it provided. I was taught that, if I felt a cold coming on, I should look by the river for the medicinal plant called rat root — so named because muskrats chewed on the roots. I could chew it or put it in a tea, and it would help fight off colds, coughs, upset stomachs, and fevers.

My mum also made sure I knew about the river's connections to the spiritual world. She told me that when she was a child, she played with the *mekwenescuk*, the little spirit people who lived under the riverbank. They were small spiritual beings who protected the river. They liked to play with children, but she had to be careful around them. If she wasn't paying attention to where she was going, they might lead her astray. If she fell in the river, the *mekwenescuk* could take her to the world of the spirits. Then she could not come back to the physical world and be with her family ever again. That was why I always had to pay attention when I was on the riverbank. I needed to make sure I did not go to the spirit world before it was my time.

My mother taught me that the river brought both good things and dangerous things. She had that knowledge from her parents, who had it from their parents, and so on back in time. If we properly respected the river, were careful how we behaved around it, and thanked Creator in gratitude for it, it brought us many gifts.

But it brought other things, too.

More than a century and a half before I was born, it brought fur traders travelling in the canoes that my people taught them to build. They were seeking beaver pelts that made warm, waterproof hats for wealthy people in Europe. For them, the river was a route to riches. They did not respect it as a gift from Creator and they did not treat it with gratitude. They hunted the beaver, the muskrat, and the fox until the animals were almost gone. They made their fortunes and left without giving thanks or replenishing what they took. By the time I was born, it required the expert skills of experienced woodsmen like my father and uncles to find animals to trap. Because they had that knowledge, they could feed and clothe their families.

When my family was teaching me, they could not know that safe-keeping our people's traditional knowledge would be my life's calling. They could not know that the bitumen they saw in oily streaks in the river was going to change everything. By the time I was a young man, oil companies would come from all over the world to capture it. Like the fur traders before them, they could not recognize a gift from Creator, something to be treated with gratitude and moderation. They scraped it out of the ground with huge, mechanized shovels and loaded it into dump trucks three times the size of our family's house in the bush. They treated the bitumen with stinking chemicals to make it flow into tanker trucks that travelled south to petroleum refineries. They chopped down thousands of trees to make roads. They sliced up centuries-old migration routes and tore apart hunting grounds. They drove away the *mekwenescuk*.

They had money, science, and the government behind them. But my people had one thing going for us. We had the teachings of the ancestors.

CHAPTER 3

You Have to Find Your Road

Right after my mother buried my umbilical cord in the boreal forest, I began learning the ways of our people. That meant learning about our land. Part of it was learning about our physical survival, how we fed and sheltered ourselves. But it was also a spiritual learning, part of my sacred responsibility as a Cree person. I knew from a very early age that Creator made my people the stewards of the boreal forest and that it was our spiritual duty to protect, nurture, and honour it.

Our traditional learning starts as soon as we are born, and it happens everywhere and all the time. There is no defined age when we start and we don't go to a special school for it or follow written lesson plans. Our traditional teachings are organic, not a separate thing done in a special building at an appointed time. Our teachings are part of daily life, a continual sharing of the wisdom of the ancestors that is integrated into every step we take on our traditional land. All family members share wisdom with children at every opportunity, using the land itself to illustrate the teaching.

One day, when I was a child, my dad came home from hunting and I saw he was chewing on something.

"What are you chewing, Dad?" I asked him in Cree.

"*Peiko*," he said. He took it out of his mouth and showed me a little cud of brownish, sticky tree sap. In English it is called spruce gum. My dad told me he scraped resin from under the bark of the spruce tree and chewed it into a gum.

"I look for it when I am out hunting," he said. "It helps keep me sharp and my respiratory system energized."

"Next time you go in the bush, Dad," I said, "can you please bring me some?"

Sure enough, the next time he went out hunting, he brought back little chunks of spruce resin for us kids. We had to chew it for a long time. At first it splintered into little pieces that got stuck in our teeth. Dad told us to keep chewing, and eventually it turned into gum. It was sticky and tasted strong and medicinal, a bit like cough medicine. We could swallow the juice, and it felt warm going down our throats. It was a real treat, and chewing it was fun. Dad told us that while it was fun, it also had a serious purpose.

"Spruce gum is very good for your breathing," he said. "Whenever I am in the bush on a long hunting trip and feel my energy start to dip, I chew it to build up my lungs." He told us spruce resin can be used to brew tea to relieve itchy throats and head colds. It can also be made into a salve for cuts.

"Creator knew we might get tired or injured after a long day of hunting," my dad told us. "So Creator put something in the forest to help our people while we are trying to feed our families. Every time we use it, we should give thanks to Creator to show that we appreciate this gift."

Then Dad taught us how to say a prayer of gratitude to Creator for putting that gift where we could find it when we needed it.

To this day, when I am out hunting, I still boost my energy with spruce gum. Sometimes I make spruce tea when I have a scratchy throat, or a spruce salve to help a wound heal. Whenever I do, I thank Creator for the gifts that are still here, if you know where to look and what to do with them.

Now you can use your computer to find out the chemical properties of tree resin and why it works the way it does. But my people figured it out centuries ago. We knew spruce resin was linked to healing because we saw how it worked on the tree, closing up wounds to the trunk and protecting it while the tree healed. It worked the same way a scab works on a wound on the human body.

The way my father taught us about spruce gum is an example of how my people pass on traditional knowledge through stories and demonstration, what in English is called an oral tradition. I asked my dad what he was chewing, and he told me what it was and where to find it. He showed me and my brothers and sisters how it worked. He also told us the right way to approach a gift from Creator. In English, this right way is called protocol, a process to make sure that we do the right things. Some protocols I can tell you about, and some are sacred to my people and I will keep them private. Overall, they have one purpose: to show respect. Even a tiny piece of gum needs to be properly acknowledged.

As a little boy I could see that it all made so much sense. Who wouldn't want to live like that? I wanted to learn everything I could about Creator and our traditional land.

A lot of learning went on in our little house. Every day I had many questions, because there was always something happening. My father and older brothers were always working to put food on the table and keep us warm in the winter. My mum worked the hardest of all. She never stopped all day long. She grew food in her garden and canned it for winter. She sewed and patched our clothes. She was always washing something — dishes, pots and pans, our clothes. My sisters helped our mum. From a very young age, I would help, too, bringing in firewood and fetching things for her.

Whatever else she was doing, Mum also seemed to be cooking all the time. Even though there were so many of us, there was always lots of good food. Mum baked, too. Whenever she made apple pies I would pester her to cut a little chunk of apple for me. Her hands moved so fast as she pared the skin from the apple, twirling the sharp knife around the fruit. She used to give me the peels.

"Here, eat these. They're good for you," she said. "They are the best part of the apple."

I did not know until I was grown up that science says the healthiest part of an apple is the peel, because that is where most of the nutrients are. That is the thing about traditional knowledge. It tells us things that science later shows. I did not know that when I was a little boy, of course. Back then I used to just grab those peelings and gobble them down while she told me not to tell my brothers and sisters.

"*Kinanaskomitin*," I would say. Thank you.

I still speak Cree fluently, and part of the reason is that I never talked to my mum in English — except for the one time I tried it when I was older.

"*Ke takosen na?*" she said. This means, "What's wrong with you? Are you sick?"

I switched back to Cree right away, and I always spoke Cree to her, out of respect.

It was the same with my dad. I always spoke Cree to him, too, for the same reason, even though he was well-spoken in English and was widely respected for that. He helped people when they needed to communicate with the bigger world outside our community. He spoke English because he had gone to one of the government's residential schools, up to Grade Nine. Some people thought he was a genius because he had that level of education. A lot of the adults in our First Nation had never been to school. I found out later that they were the lucky ones. My dad never talked to us about residential school; that was the one thing I had to learn for myself. When I was a little boy, I could not imagine any other type of education than the beautiful way I was being taught by my family.

I also learned from my *Mooshum*, my grandfather. He was too old to go out on hunting trips deep in the bush, but he still contributed to the physical work of feeding the family. My *Mooshum* taught me many practical things, including how to snare rabbits and other small game for my mother's stew, and how to collect eggs from wild birds for our breakfasts. He taught me spiritual lessons, too. As an Elder, my *Mooshum* was valued and respected for the vast amount of traditional knowledge he had to share. When I was a little boy I loved to spend time with him.

Mooshum told me that before my time there had been a little sawmill on a hill not too far from our reserve, but it had closed down. We would go up that hill and look for little pieces of board that had been left behind. There were lots of trees in the bush, but it was hard to get milled lumber, so we looked for things we could use. Nails were scarce, too, so we would gather up every single one we could find, even ones that were bent and twisted, and put them in a little bag. When we got home, *Mooshum* would pound them with a hammer to straighten them out and put them back in the bag for when they were needed. We were always looking for ways to reuse things, and there was no time limit on how long something could be useful.

Our family never, ever threw away anything. We used everything. It didn't matter if it came from the boreal forest, the river, or from the dry goods store in town. We never wasted a single thing we brought into the house. That was the right way to live with the gifts Creator gave us. But I was already learning that some people did not live according to this mentality.

"Why are people different in this world?" I asked my grandfather.

"When we are born we are given our own work," he said. "Before you were able to crawl, you were already given your work on this Earth."

"Creator meant for me to do a job?" I asked.

"Work is not the same as a job. A job is what you do. You could do anything. You could be a trapper. You could be a butcher. You could be a cowboy. You can do what you want."

"But how is that different from my work?"

"The work Creator gave you is for the good of the community," said *Mooshum*. "You are born with a gift you are supposed to use to help other people. It is up to you to find out what that it is."

"How do I do that?"

"You have to find your road."

"How will I do that?"

"You are already on it," he said. "Your family is helping you take your first steps."

That is one of the most important things that the Elders teach us. Each of us has to find our road. When my grandfather, my family, and my community were teaching me as a little boy, they were guiding me towards my road. It seemed like such an easy concept. Creator gave my people everything we needed to live a good life, so of course Creator also gave me what I needed to find my road.

CHAPTER 4

Napikan

My grandfather was right, of course. Even though I was still a little boy, I was starting to find my road.

I loved Creator's teachings. I thought they were perfect and I wanted to know everything about them. I asked questions constantly, and every answer I got led me to another question. I was always hanging around our Knowledge Keepers, the people in our community who may not be considered Elders but carry traditional knowledge and expertise in areas like trapping or hunting or beading. I also liked being with our Elders, especially my *Mooshum*, and was always asking about Creator. I wanted to know how we did something like set a snare to catch a rabbit or squirrel. But I needed to know why Creator wanted us to do it in a certain way.

That was what earned me my second name, what my people call my physical name. I was still very small when my *Mooshum* gifted me the name *Napikan*. In English it means "great man." It was an honour to get a name from an Elder like my grandfather, and it was supposed to follow me for my whole life.

"*Napikan*," my grandfather would say. "Be a great man."

Pretty soon my whole family called me *Napikan*. My mum had given me my English name, Bobby Mountain, in the hospital so that it could be written on my birth certificate. We were not allowed to register Cree names. It had to be an English name using the English alphabet. My mum called me Bobby at home but, once my grandfather gave me my physical name, she called me *Napikan*, too.

I asked questions about everything, including practical things I saw my father and uncles doing, like hunting, trapping, and fishing. But right from the beginning, the spiritual aspect intrigued me most. Instead of telling me I was too young for that, my family encouraged my interest in the spiritual side of things.

I was in the perfect place to learn. There was always spiritual learning going on in my home. My father was known in our community as a very spiritual man and was always expanding his spiritual learning. Elders would visit him and share their knowledge, something they thought would benefit him. That is the way of things with Elders. They share their knowledge with you according to what they think you need to know, but also when you need to know it. If they thought the time was right to share something with my dad, they would show up at the house, and he would stop whatever he was doing to be with them. The Elder would shake my dad's hand or give him a big bear hug. Then they would talk. Sometimes my dad and the Elder would go outside together and do a ceremony to keep building the spiritual element. After they finished my dad would go into the room he and my mum shared and come out with something, food or a gift of some kind. He would give that offering to the Elder for helping him with spiritual well-being, which helped him stay in good mental and physical health, too.

Sometimes I understood a bit of what my dad and the Elders were talking about, but most of it was too advanced for me at that time. They talked about something called the Medicine Wheel, and I knew it was very important and kept our world and our people in balance. I knew that as I grew older, deeper spiritual learning would come to me. I thought I had lots of time to learn. My father was always working on his understanding of the Elders' teachings, and I thought that it would be the same for me.

My father was teaching me, too. He was involved in different kinds of ceremonies, and he always let me watch and ask questions. I loved those ceremonies. Some of them took days but I never lost interest. I took notice of everything that was happening and how the ceremonies were performed. Once or twice a month, somebody would come and ask to use my father's sweat lodge, either for themselves or to help others. It did not look like the big, tall, well-lit sweat lodges you see in Hollywood movies. My father always built his sweat lodge in the same way, in the same order, according to our traditional protocols. First, he buried tobacco in the ground where he planned to build the sweat lodge and said a special prayer over it. Tobacco is a very important and sacred plant because it helps us connect to the spirit world. Then my father built a stone circle about two feet across and a foot and a half high, right over the top of the tobacco offering. It looked like a little round well.

Then, all around the stone well, my dad built a shelter big enough to hold several people. It was made of willow branches that he stripped of leaves and tied together with ribbons and sinew. He kept adding branches until the frame was strong enough to bear the weight of the two buffalo hides he kept for this purpose. He laid the buffalo hides over top of the branches and then piled wool blankets on top so that no light could peek through. A willow-framed sweat lodge is very strong and has no trouble holding up the weight.

There was an entrance for people to come in and out, but once you draped the hides and blankets over the entrance, it was pitch-dark inside. Outside, not too far from the entrance, my dad would build a firepit. There are protocols, of course, for building the fire and keeping it going as you heat the stones. A proper sweat lodge needs two people to run it: a Knowledge Keeper who knows the way of the sweat lodges and stays inside to make sure things run properly, and a helper who stays outside tending to the fire and warming the stones. When the Knowledge Keeper tells him to, the helper carries in the hot stones, usually on a shovel, and puts them in the stone circle. Then the helper goes back outside and makes sure the flap to the sweat lodge is shut tight so that no light gets in.

Inside the lodge, next to a wall around the hot stones, is a pitcher of water and a willow switch with some leaves still on it. The Knowledge Keeper dips the switch into the pitcher and uses it to sprinkle water on the stones to make them steam. The stones sizzle when the water hits them, and the spiritual connections start happening. Stones are very important. There is a lot of power in stones because they can also connect us to the spirit world. Sometimes I think they are one of Creator's most overlooked gifts.

A sweat lodge helps you mentally and spiritually, especially once the Elder starts praying. The Elder invites healing spirits into the lodge with song, sometimes also using drums and rattles. A sweat lodge is very healthy, balancing and cleansing you. It cleans your system physically as you sweat out all the garbage built up in your system over days, weeks, and months. This physical cleansing also helps remove your emotional negativity and increase your focus so you can be open to the healing message of the spirits. That is why people feel relaxed and comfortable when they come out of a sweat lodge. Every time I complete a sweat I go to sleep for two or three hours and wake up completely refreshed. I feel so light. I feel happy.

I also feel glorified, because the sweat lodge is a big part of the spiritual life of our people. It is a way to connect with Mother Earth and the natural elements of fire, earth, air, and water, things I was hearing about as a boy but did not yet understand. In a sweat lodge you'll see things spiritually, even though it's pitch-dark in there. Sometimes it's just a beautiful sensation because you're cleansing your body and spirit, wiping away all the filth. You're being connected. You're being grounded.

But you have to be ready for that type of power. Sometimes people go into a sweat lodge when they are not ready. Sometimes they have been drinking or using drugs, have a hangover or are in withdrawal, or are filled with angry or bitter thoughts. The spirits do not want you in the sweat lodge until you are in the right frame of mind, and they will let you know. Oh boy, will they let you know! I have seen people who tried to fool the spirits, and they ended up running out as fast as they could.

When I was about five years old, my father took me into his sweat lodge for the first time. I felt comfortable and relaxed. Now I know that was the spirits welcoming me in. They recognized me as *Napikan* and let me stay. But they knew that I was not ready for the full experience, so they made me very drowsy until I fell asleep. I slept through all of the activity, but when I woke up I felt great. I had a wonderful sleep. The spirits always let you know when you are welcome, just like they did when I was five.

I thought the sweat lodge was a wonderful place, but I noticed my dad was always quiet about it. When I was older I found out that, for a long time, he was forced to hide it because the federal government had outlawed sweat lodges. If my dad's sweat lodge had been found, the police would have come and torn it down. They could have arrested my father, too, and fined him or put him in jail. Two years before I was born, the government changed that law and sweat lodges were "legal" again. But he was still very private about it.

I am very lucky that my dad and people like him kept up the practice and built sweat lodges in secret even when it was illegal. If it wasn't for them, my people would have lost this traditional knowledge. There came a time in my life when I desperately needed a sweat lodge and the spiritual teachings of my ancestors. Without them I probably wouldn't be here today. I think that was why as a boy I was always asking spiritual questions. Creator knew I was going to need that knowledge to survive and to help others.

The fact that the federal government banned sweat lodges tells you something about the dominant culture. They did not try to understand the sweat lodge, but they recognized it had power, and that threatened them. They feared it, so their first thought was to destroy it. That pattern of fear and destruction was something I would see time and again, because finding my road was not going to be as straightforward as my *Mooshum* hoped when he named me *Napikan*.

CHAPTER 5

Transportation Is a Big Word

I was five years old when my parents moved us about 250 kilometres south of where I was born. We went to live at the Beaver Lake Cree Nation reserve, a First Nations community. We were still in northern Alberta, still in the boreal forest, and we still lived off the land. My father had relatives in Beaver Lake, and he knew everyone in the community, so nothing changed in the way we were connected to the land and our people. Our house was a bit bigger and had three bedrooms: one for the girls, one for the boys, and the other for my mum and dad. There was also a big living room and a kitchen. It seemed like a big move to us.

We were much closer to town. Now it was only thirteen kilometres to the nearest store. That sounds close but, in those days, it took a lot of effort to get to town. Nobody on the reserve had gas-powered vehicles. People still used dogsleds, and some had horses. My father and one of his brothers used a horse when they went out to cut firewood in the bush. Early in the morning on woodcutting days, my uncle would hitch his horse to a sledge, a flat, heavy sleigh with no runners used for carrying heavy objects like wood or hay bales. My father would carefully load his axe and the two-person saw onto the sledge, as well as the big lunch my mother made for both of them. Then he would hop on next to my uncle and they would head out into the bush, both men standing perfectly balanced at the front of the sledge. We kids would listen to the sleigh bells as they went farther and farther away until we couldn't hear them anymore.

I would spend all day listening for the sledge's bells to tell me they were coming home. As soon as I heard the jingling, I would run out to meet them as they pulled the horse over next to the woodpile. I'd watch them toss heavy pieces of wood off the sledge to my older brothers, who would stack up the woodpile. The new wood went to the back, behind what had been cut the previous year and left to season until it was no longer green and could burn without smoking in the stove. I'd also watch them care for the horse, which always did a good day's work. My uncle would unhitch it, feed it, and put a blanket on it to make sure it was warm and comfortable.

Then my dad and uncle would go into the house, where my mother would have something hot and delicious waiting for them. As they ate it up and drank a pot of tea, they would talk about what they had just done. They talked about the birds and animals they saw, the clouds, the way the wind blew. Every word they said was a teaching for me, for the days when I would go out into the bush and cut wood for my family. I could visualize every step they took. In my mind I was with them on the sledge, driving the horse and pulling over in a good spot, walking through the snow, swinging the axe, pulling at one end of the two-person saw, loading up the sledge. They would talk about the horse, too, and the work it had done.

There was a fellow named Gabriel Gladue who had a team of horses he hitched to an old panel truck whose engine had been removed, pulling it like a wagon. It was used as the school bus, and we kids called it a caboose. It was a big vehicle, all closed in, and he had outfitted it with a little stove. He kept just enough wood in there to throw into the stove and keep the kids warm until he got them to the school, which taught subjects the dominant culture thought important. There were no traditional teachings there. It taught what used to be called the "three Rs" — reading, writing, and arithmetic — the things we needed to know when we had dealings with the dominant culture. I was not quite old enough to go to school, so in the mornings I watched Mr. Gladue coming down the hill near our house with little wisps of smoke coming out of that caboose. I usually got a good look because, more often than not, the caboose got stuck.

Our community did not have paved roads. In fact, it had nothing you could really call a road. We had trails worn from the paths our people had followed for generations, and they were made for walking, not for vehicles. They looped around trees and rocks and were muddy, crooked, and full of ruts. So, every time Mr. Gladue tried to take his caboose up a hill, he got stuck. Everyone knew that, so there were always bigger boys watching for him. As soon as he got stuck, they would run over and push the truck up the hill. That was how our community worked. People were always pitching in where needed. No one had to ask. Mr. Gladue always had help, and soon the caboose would be moving again.

I really wanted to ride in the caboose, but I never got a chance. Our house was close to the on-reserve school, so when I started school I walked there. Once Mr. Gladue gave my brother a ride, just for fun. My brother told me all about it. The little stove was smoking, the caboose shook and bounced on the rough trail, and it was noisy and rattled as it moved along. My brother loved it. He was so happy he got a chance to try it out.

Mr. Gladue sometimes took his caboose into town for supplies, and sometimes he would pick up heavy goods for our family — fifty-pound bags of flour and things like that. But mostly when we needed something from the store, my mum walked all the way there and back. She always took some of us kids with her so that she could keep an eye on us and we could help carry things. Mum would start getting ready a day or two before we went to town. She always wanted us to look nice, so she would wash our clothes and lay everything out. Thick socks for the walk. A nice shirt. Clean pants with no rips. Mum used to sew and patch my pants because they always had holes in the knees. We were proud, and Mum wanted us to present ourselves well. Of course, not all of us could go with her, but I was one of the spoiled ones because she always took me. I loved those trips into town because she would talk to me all the way, telling me things about our people, why we did things the way we did. I asked her questions the whole way, and she never got tired of answering. It seemed to me like the thirteen kilometres there and back just flew by.

We used dogs for transportation, too. I can still picture one of the dogs we used for travel. It was part black Labrador and part Husky, and we called him Blackie. He was a very big dog. We kids used to ride him and play with him, but he also had work to do. My dad built a toboggan, and my older brother trained Blackie to be a single pulling dog, not part of a team. We used him for all kinds of things. We would put kindling on the toboggan and he'd pull it home, or he'd haul tubs of snow my mum boiled down for water. He was a good hunting dog, too. He brought in a lot of ducks and small game and helped bring the food home. He was well used and a nice dog.

Sometimes my brother would hitch up Blackie and they would take off in the morning and be gone all day.

"What do you do all day when you take the dog and go all over the place?" I asked my brother.

"A lot of guys from the community want to race me," he said. "We have races and we bet a little."

"Do you win?"

"Of course. Blackie is the fastest dog around."

One day I found out for myself just how fast Blackie was. Every time my brother hitched up the dog I would run after him, hoping to go along. My brother usually chased me back inside the house, but one winter day he said yes.

"Okay, *Napikan*," he said. "I know you want to see what it is like. You can come with me today."

I was so happy. I jumped up right away. Mum made sure I was dressed warm so I would not freeze. She helped me put on thick socks inside my winter boots. She put on my toque, my winter coat, my big mitts. My brother put me on the toboggan, and he ran along behind it.

It was a beautiful day. There was a big blue sky, the sun was shining, and the snow was so bright. It looked like a scene from a Christmas card, pristine with no footprints, snow weighing down the tree branches. We went down a little trail, the trees all flashing by. The toboggan made a crunching sound as it slid along, and I could hear the dog and my brother taking long, easy breaths. We were going fast, but my brother was easily keeping pace alongside, and I could tell Blackie was listening to him. I had a lot of fun as we followed the trail. It was a perfect day to be out on the land.

Then we left the trail, and my brother told the dog to go out on a little frozen lake where everything was wide open. Blackie picked up a little speed, but my brother still kept pace alongside us. Then the dog turned a bit, and I saw the cows. At least, I thought they were cows. I had never seen a cow before in my life. I saw a bunch of very big, reddish-coloured animals bunched together in one place. They were very strange-looking. They looked a bit like a moose but shorter and fatter, and I'd never seen a reddish moose. I shivered and it wasn't from the cold. *Uh-oh*, I thought. I kept trying to peek around the dog to get a better view, but I couldn't get a good look.

I was about to ask my brother about the animals when Blackie spotted them. He took off running straight towards them as fast as he could, way faster than we had gone so far. He pulled ahead so quickly that he surprised my brother, who tripped and fell over into the snow. There I was alone on the toboggan, and I could not stop the dog.

Think, I told myself. *What are you going to do?* When we moved to Beaver Lake, where there were farms, my dad had told me stories about cows, especially the bulls. Looking back, I think he did not want us bothering the farmer's livestock and was concerned about our safety as well. He had given me a good talking-to about cattle.

"Be careful around cows, *Napikan*," Dad said, "especially the bulls."

"Why?" I asked.

"Don't ever go near one because it's going to chase you and it will bump you with his head," he explained.

"Does it hurt?"

"There are horns on his head that could hurt you. You always need to be careful."

Even though Dad had warned me, I had not seen any cows until that day. I had no idea what might happen. Maybe they were all bulls! Maybe they would all chase me and bump me with their heads! There were a lot of them, and I would not be able to run away through the deep snow. I got scared and started hollering for my brother, and that made Blackie pick up even more speed. Every second we got closer to the cows. I looked behind me and saw my brother way, way back. *He'll never get to me in time*, I said to myself. If those cows come, they're going to get me first.

I jumped up off the toboggan and threw myself sideways down on the snow. The toboggan fell sideways with me and acted like a drag, slowing down Blackie. When Blackie realized something had gone wrong with the toboggan, he sat down. That was the kind of dog he was, very well trained when he got a clear signal. He sat there and looked behind me, watching my brother. I could see my brother running for all he was worth. Finally, he got to us.

"What happened, *Napikan*?" he asked.

"I don't know," I said. "I'm scared."

"What are you scared of?"

"I think those are cows over there," I said. "They might bump me with their head."

"You don't need to be scared. We will stay away from there."

My brother set the toboggan up straight and took Blackie by the collar, turning him around. He put me back on the toboggan and climbed on behind me. He had a little whip he used to make noise with. My brother never hit Blackie with the whip, it was for signaling. Blackie knew his trade, so when my brother cracked his whip, the dog flicked back his ears and trotted off for home.

Boy, talk about scared. Today, when I think about that wild toboggan ride, it is like it happened yesterday. That's what happens to some people who experience trauma. It keeps itself fresh, ready to pop out and startle you, even when you've buried it deep in the hope you will forget it. Back then, I did not know anything about trauma and how it stays with you for a long time. That was a lesson I still had to learn, and I would learn it over and over. Because changes were coming to the reserve, and one of those changes was about transportation.

It was not too long after the scary toboggan ride that there was a big meeting at the schoolhouse on the reserve, and a group of us boys decided to listen in. The reserve had its own one-room schoolhouse, but it was used for many things. It was the main meeting place for everyone, and community leaders met there to discuss ideas. We kids looked through the door and stayed quiet. We listened hard because it seemed like something very important was going on. My father was there, and my uncles, and Mr. Gladue, all the men from the community. They were speaking Cree, of course, but they kept using an English word, "transportation."

Wow, I thought. This must be important. Transportation is a big word. There were other words too, like "education" and "electricity." I did not understand the words because I was not in school yet and had not learned how to speak English. But I wanted to know about this thing, this transportation that everyone was interested in. It sounded like a really big deal.

It was more important than I could have imagined. The men wanted to build a road to improve access into and out of our community. Then we could get things like building supplies and roofing materials, and the electric company would have a way to bring power in. For once, I could not picture what they were talking about and how it would change the way we lived, how walking and horses and dogs would not always be the way we travelled over the land.

When I was a boy in the late 1950s, I could not know that transportation was going to work against my people, not for us. It would be linked to the oil companies coming to our traditional land. The more the world needed transportation, the more it needed vehicles, and the more it needed the oil under our ground. But it was so much worse than that.

Improved transportation gave the government better access to our communities. It was easier for officials to come and scoop children out of our homes and transport us away to residential school. That was what happened to me.

CHAPTER 6

Sixties Scoop

W hen I turned six years old, I started school right in our Indigenous community. My mum got me up early for my first day in Grade One. She made me a big breakfast so that I would have lots of energy for the day. She washed my face, brushed my hair, and helped me into the nice clean clothes she had laid out for me to put on. When I was ready, she sent me out to the schoolhouse, which we could see from our doorstep. She stood and watched as I ran off, making sure I didn't stray or mess up my clothes before I got there.

I thought school was going to be okay for me because it was not too far from my house. I could run there every morning. It turned out that running to school at the last minute was not a good idea, but I did not know that yet. I felt sorry for the kids who had to get up early to walk four or five kilometres, or those even farther away who had to ride Mr. Gladue's bus.

I was not sure what to expect on the first day I walked in. Our school was small, just one classroom with five rows of little tables and chairs all lined up — Grades One, Two, Three, Four, and Five, all in their own rows. One teacher taught all the grades. And holy smokes, all the kids I knew were there! They all sat down in those rows, and I was told to sit down, too. The teacher started talking to us, and right away he gave us the rule of law: Pay attention.

Then he started teaching us how to read and write, and that was when I started learning English. Before that, all we spoke in my home was Cree. The teacher showed us the alphabet and the big and small letters, starting with the letter *a* and all the way to *z*. After a few days of letters, he started showing us small words: *it*, *is*, *at*, *see*. We didn't start out with the big words, like *transportation*. Then we got into short sentences.

"Go to the lake."

"Run up the hill."

Finally, some people started to come into it.

"Jack goes to the lake."

"Sally runs up the hill."

At that school, all the kids were allowed to speak Cree while we learned English because the teacher was an Indigenous person, although he was not a member of our First Nation. I do not know where they got him from. Right away, all the kids in the room knew there was something wrong with him. We did not know exactly what it was, but we could tell by the way he acted and the way he smelled. When he entered the room, all the kids went dead quiet. When I was older, I realized that he liked his booze and would come into class a little tipsy. We kids could smell the booze on him. It didn't smell like a good thing, so we always quieted right down until you could hear a pin drop. We were afraid of what he might do. And with good reason, as I found out first-hand in another trauma I will never forget.

One day in first grade, I was a few minutes late for school. I came running into the classroom, dashing past all my friends already sitting at their little tables, and plopping myself down at my own. I watched the teacher get up from his big wooden table at the front of the room. He walked over and stopped in front of me.

"You're late," he said.

I did not say anything because he had not asked me a question. I just sat there looking up at him.

"You're late," he said again.

Then he gave me a big backhand right across my face. I went flying over backwards, my whole chair with me in it. I hit the floor hard. It scared me and the other kids, too. But I jumped right up. I did not say anything or make a sound. I did not cry. The whole room, all those kids, stayed dead silent as I picked my chair up and sat back down in it. He walked back to his desk and started teaching like nothing had happened.

Okay, I thought to myself. *This is how this works.*

Later on, when I was old enough to talk to him like a man, I saw that teacher a few times over the years. Every time I saw him, he looked worse than before. He kept drinking and going downhill. I learned that he had been to residential school, which must have been where he learned that a teacher could get away with something like that. But I never asked him how he could pass on that violence to a little boy after experiencing it for himself. I do wonder about it, even to this day.

Luckily, I only spent one year with that teacher, because I moved on after first grade. For second grade, I was bussed to a bigger school in the nearby town of Lac la Biche. That was one of the things the men of our community were talking about in that meeting about transportation. My community was always thinking about education, and the adults thought it would be an improvement to have a bus take students to the larger school in the town. They wanted us kids to be educated in the dominant culture as well as our own. They thought it would be an advantage for us to be able to read and write in English — like my father, who translated official letters and documents for community members. They also wanted us to learn arithmetic and other things needed in interactions with the dominant culture that ran the federal government and had so much power over us.

Of course, I didn't know that at the time. I was worried that I had to start all over again, make new friends, and figure out how the new school operated. I quickly learned it was the same thing all over again, the same rule of law about paying attention. When you were inside the four walls of a classroom, you were supposed to listen to everything that was said to you, to obey every command, to never ask questions. You sat in straight rows, you didn't look around, you didn't talk to your friends. You did not get up and move around. The teachers were very strict, although the second-grade teacher was okay.

It was a different story when I started third grade. One day, when we were playing outside during recess, I went running at full speed around a trailer that was on the school property. I was enjoying myself outside and have always loved running. I did not see another boy who happened to be running straight at me. I was moving fast and so was he. At the very last second, I saw him coming and threw out my arms, but I still hit him, hard. He fell down, knocked out cold. It happened so fast. I did not know what was going on. I did not know people could get knocked unconscious. I thought I'd killed him. I was so scared. I just stood there, shaking at the thought that I killed a boy. Then a couple of older boys came over and picked him up. He woke up, and it looked like everything was okay, but I was still shaken up. Then the break was over, and I walked back into class with everybody else, still in shock.

"Were you fighting?" the Grade Three teacher asked me.

I did not know what to tell her. I knew I had not been fighting, but I could not explain what had just happened. I wanted to talk, but I could not find any words.

"Were you fighting?" the teacher said again, louder this time.

I still could not answer. She grabbed my wrist and jerked my hand forward, palm up. She was holding a foot-long wooden ruler. She swung the ruler and hit me hard on my hand, over and over. *Whack! Whack! Whack!* Again and again on my little hand. It was very painful, and my hand was aching. Finally, she was done hitting me.

"Go sit down," she said.

I went and sat down. I was okay physically; there was no permanent damage to my hand. But I will never forget that day. That was the day I knew for sure that school was not a good place. It was nice to be with my friends, but the rest of it was not what I was used to. The adults were not going to be patient and kind like my parents, my grandparents, and my aunts and uncles. The teachers I met did not talk to me in a gentle voice and tell me why we did things a certain way, how it was connected to the land and the way we lived on it. They were not going to explain things with stories and examples, and they hated it when I asked a question. I never had a schoolteacher who explained why we had to learn these things or what they were connected to. The subjects were just hanging out there, unconnected to anything.

I hoped that if I did the things they wanted, kept quiet, and paid attention, I would be all right. My parents and my community were teaching me all the things I needed to know to be a good person. So, for the next few years, I was Bobby Mountain at school. I made my way through the grades. I learned English. I heard about the Queen and colonial history. I played with my friends at recess. I liked classes about math, which was the same in English or Cree. Things either added up or didn't. I liked science, too, especially things about the natural world. After school I was *Napikan* and learned traditional teachings from my family and our community. My road was still stretching out ahead of me, and it was beautiful.

But far away, in cities I had barely heard of, things were happening that would cause my road to take a dangerous turn. In the early 1960s, the Canadian government was doing something that ended up being called the Sixties Scoop. As a boy, I did not know anything about it, but I probably would have thought "Sixties Scoop" does not sound that bad. It sounds like an ice cream sundae. It does not sound like a federal government agenda to destroy the First Nations people's traditional way of life, to wipe our culture out of existence. But that is exactly what it was, and it started when Indigenous children were in the cradle.

The Canadian government scooped up Indigenous babies and took them from their parents, from their communities, from their traditional land. Federal law gave government workers the power to take any child. No one in the Indigenous community had to be told why a baby was taken — not the parents, and not the community officials who were supposed to be dealing with the government. It was not until the 1980s, twenty years after I started school, that social workers had to notify First Nations leaders when they removed a child from the community. When I was a boy, the government just scooped up babies and took them wherever they wanted. They were often adopted by non-Indigenous families who knew nothing of the traditional Indigenous way of life. How many babies were scooped up and adopted? Thousands, government records say. A lot of them did not even stay in Canada. Some were sent to the United States to be adopted by American families.

At the same time people were taking babies, government workers were scooping up older Indigenous children from their parents and sending them to residential schools, even if those children were already attending school in their own communities. It was official government policy, and the parents had no say.

A residential school was a religious education institution, part of a big, government-sponsored system established across the country to assimilate Indigenous children into colonialist culture. Residential schools were run by Christian churches and the Canadian government to convert my people to Christianity and assimilate us into Canadian society by erasing our culture and traditions. Residential schools were for one thing and one thing only, and the first prime minister of Canada told everyone what it was: "To take the Indian out of the child."

It lasted for generations. For more than 160 years, the residential school system was official government policy. Our people were powerless against it. If parents did not surrender their children, they were charged with a crime, arrested, and sent to prison. So, the choice was imprisonment for the adults, or for the children — because children were incarcerated in those institutions, treated the same way the government treated convicted criminals, but worse.

I tell you this as part of my truth and with absolute certainty. Because I was scooped up and taken to a living hell on Earth.

CHAPTER 7

The Knock on the Door

I was nine years old when, very early one morning, well before sunrise, there was an angry knocking on our door. It did not stop. It just went on and on, pounding and pounding. Everyone in my family was sound asleep, and the banging was so loud that it woke us all up. We kids could not figure out who it could be. No one ever knocked on our door. Everyone in our community just came right in, but no one we knew came in the middle of the night.

"Who is at the door?" my little brother David asked me. David was only six years old, so he was always asking me questions.

"I don't know," I said. "Let's go see."

We got up and peeked around the corner at the front door. We saw a Mountie, a Royal Canadian Mounted Policeman. He was in his brown everyday uniform, not the red wool serge you see in movies. He had a gun in the holster on his hip. Two other people were with him who were dressed in suits. My dad was talking to them in English, but he kept his voice quiet, and I couldn't hear what he was saying. He spoke for quite a while, like he was trying to talk them into something. He did not shout. He kept talking and talking, reasoning with them, trying to get them to see his point. But the police officer and the people with him were not listening. They did not smile or show any signs of agreement. The Mountie kept shaking his head. Finally, my father turned away from them and talked to Mum a little bit. Then Mum came into our room and got me and my little brother, and my two sisters.

"You guys have to dress up warm," she said. "You have to do it right away."

"Okay," we said. Usually, we would have asked her a hundred questions, but we were quiet because there were strangers in the house, and one was a police officer. We could tell that something was wrong, that Mum and Dad were upset. Mum was careful not to scare us as she helped me, David, and my two younger sisters get dressed. She made sure we had everything — underwear, socks, pants, shirts, all clean and tidy.

"I will make you a good breakfast," she said. We followed her out to the kitchen, where she put some kindling in the stove to heat it up because the fire had been banked for the night.

"There's no time for that," said the Mountie. "We have a schedule, and we have to get going."

I did not know what a schedule was but it did not sound good, especially if it was stopping my mum from giving us food.

"People are waiting, and there is no time," said the Mountie. "We have to go right away."

My mum got out our coats and hats. I put on mine while she helped my little brother button up his coat and lace up his boots.

"You're going to have to go with these people," Mum said to us. "I'm coming with you."

There was a van waiting outside the house and we all got into it — my mum, my little brother, my two sisters, and me. The strangers got in the van with us, but they did not introduce themselves. They did not say why they were there and why we were all in a van. They never said a word the whole time. In the house they had let the Mountie do all the talking. I never did find out who those people were. We kids were quiet, too, and still sleepy from waking up in the middle of the night, so after the van started moving we drifted off to sleep.

We woke up around six o'clock in the morning as we pulled into a town. I am not sure which one. We stopped next to a big bus parked on the street.

We got out of the van and stood there with our mum, who was holding David's hand while the strangers wrote our names down on little pieces of paper. They pinned our names to us with safety pins, like we were packages to be delivered. I did not know anything about what was happening to us. No one told us what was going on, where we were going, or why we had to do this. They just told us to get on the bus.

While I did not know what was happening, I knew it was not good. I could tell by the look on my mother's face when she hugged each of us and kissed us goodbye. She told us in Cree that she could not get on the bus with us, that we had to go with these people. She was trying to be brave, to not scare us any more than we already were, but we knew something was wrong. We had lived every single day of our lives with her and we knew when she was upset. But the look on her face was something we had never seen before. Our family was a happy one; all we had ever known was love and affection. We did not know until that morning that hearts could be broken.

The Mountie and the strangers did not get on the bus with us. There were just the four of us kids and the driver. He closed the door on my mother at the bottom of the steps and started to pull away. We kids were all crying, calling for our mum, and we rushed to the back window so we could see her as the bus pulled away. My mum was standing alone, dead still, tears streaming down her face as she watched us drive away.

I will never forget the sight of my mother, crying and helpless. She was our greatest strength as a family, the person we all turned to. She spent all her time caring for us, feeding us, clothing us, telling us stories, and teaching us the proper way to do things. She had buried my umbilical cord in the woods to connect me to the land, to our ancestors, and to Creator. It connected me to her, too. She had nurtured that connection every day of my life with her caring, her teachings, and her love. It was a sacred bond that should have been unbreakable.

It was that bond — to my mother, to our people, to our ancestors, to our land, to Creator — that the government people were determined to sever. They meant it when they said they were going to "take the Indian out of the child." The first step was taking us away from our loving family.

Of course, I didn't know that then. I didn't even know where the bus was going. As the bus pulled out of town, we started to question the driver in English.

"Where are you taking us?"

The driver said nothing.

"What is happening?"

We kept trying to find out where we were going, but the driver never answered. He did not even turn his head to look at us. He looked out the windshield at the road ahead and drove along as if he were all alone on the bus. He never once made eye contact, never said one word, not for the hours and hours we were on that bus. After a while, we stopped asking. After the first hour, we stopped crying. We drove over rough dirt and gravel roads, bouncing on the hard seats of the bus as if we were being tossed around in an old washing machine. We kept on like that for hours, bumping south, a long trail of dust stretching out behind us as we drove farther from our home, farther than we had ever been.

I looked out the window and watched the scenery change. I tried to memorize it, hoping I would be able to find our way back home if we got a chance to escape. At first there were lots of things I recognized: birch, spruce, and willow trees. Now and then we passed a stream or river. After a while there were different types of trees, greener with lots of leaves, not just needles and pinecones. We finally left the boreal forest behind, and there were longer stretches of green grass. I started to see farms with cows in the barnyard and big, ploughed fields.

The roads started to get a little better, too. It was still bumpy, but we were not tossed around so much. With every kilometre we travelled, I got more and more worried. It was way too far for us to walk back, especially with David being so little. Even if we did get away, the road was long and confusing, and there were no landmarks I could use to guide us home. We were a long, long way from everything we knew.

Finally, the bus stopped in a town. I am not exactly sure where, but it was hundreds of kilometres from where we started out. The bus driver parked the bus, opened the door, and finally spoke to us.

"Get off," he said.

When we stepped off the bus, we found more strangers waiting. I hoped they would give us something to eat or drink, at least some water. We were very hungry and thirsty. The Mountie had not allowed my mother to make us breakfast, and we had been on the dusty, bumpy road for hours. But they just marched us over to a different van, told us to get in, and took off again without telling us where we were going.

Think about that. They were able to organize three different vehicles to transport us and a police officer to take us from our home. But they could not arrange for a crumb of food or a drop of water. Later I learned what it was like to always be hungry, but all I could do that day was wonder if we would be fed when we finally got where we were going. I still had no answers when we started to move again. I kept looking out the window, but now there was nothing familiar for me to recognize along the road.

I do not know how to describe our journey that day, except that it was a very weird feeling, like having a nightmare while you are wide awake. It felt like something that could not be happening in real life, a bad dream that just kept going. I was not only hungry and thirsty but confused and frightened. I had been scooped up, taken from everyone and everything I knew and loved, and driven so far away that I had no idea where I was. Finally, when I was starting to think we would never stop, we pulled in front of the biggest building I had ever seen.

The Ermineskin Residential School in Hobbema, south of Edmonton, was more than five hundred kilometres from where I was born. It was a long building, three storeys high, with white wooden boards all along the outside and rows of windows along each floor. I knew right away it was not a good building. I sensed that it had a very bad atmosphere. Now, sixty years later, in front of that building there is a plaque with an eagle and a bear on it. There is writing in Cree and English that says, "1894–1976, Ermineskin Residential School, Honoring Our Survivors." There is an engraving of the building showing the little windows all in their row. The windows on the plaque look like cages, like bars on prison cells. Whoever made that plaque captured it well. They might have called it a school, but it was a prison.

I was being locked up in it for the crime of being an Indigenous boy.

CHAPTER 8

You Are Number 53

Right away, as soon as they marched us through the main doors, they separated us. First, they whisked away my sisters. It happened so fast that David and I didn't have time to realize what was going on before the girls disappeared through a door on the far side of the building. I did not know it yet, but the whole time we were there, all I would get were distant glimpses of the sisters I had seen every day until then.

David and I were led off in the opposite direction into a big recreation room with a lot of boys playing and running around. We were told to sit down on top of a table, so we perched there and watched boys play while a male supervisor walked around keeping an eye on everyone. I looked and tried to find someone I recognized. I saw David looking for someone he knew, too. It was a strange feeling, very disorienting. Our whole lives we had been surrounded by family and people we knew. Everywhere we went, we would know someone or be related to someone. Now we did not recognize a single person. My little brother and I sat together on that tabletop and looked around a room full of strangers, feeling a loneliness we had never felt before.

But we still had each other. They had taken away my sisters, but David was still with me. I could look after him like my mum always asked me to do. David was only six, the youngest of all us kids. I was nine, so my mum often asked me to watch him to make sure he didn't lose his mittens, that his shoes were tied up, that he was ready for dinner, that he was ready for bed. I would have to take care of my brother until I could figure out a way to get us home. I put my arm around him, and we sat there until, finally, the supervisor came over to us.

"You boys will be getting something to eat pretty soon," he said. "Get ready. If you miss this there is nothing until suppertime."

As soon as he said that, a nun came in from what I found out was the dining room. I had never seen a nun before and I was terrified by what I saw. She was in a big, black-and-white outfit that covered her from head to toe. She did not look like a person, all wrapped up like that, and I was not sure if there was a human being inside. I could not see if she had a face; it seemed to be hidden by the top of her strange outfit. I thought she might be some kind of a monster or spirit. Everything was covered except for her hands, which were carrying a great big wooden bowl of bread, the slices stacked up high.

As soon as the other boys saw her, every one of them raced over in front of her and started lining up. They were pushing and jostling one another until another nun came out and walked up and down the line with a wooden ruler. If somebody was pushing or out of line, they got hit, hard, with the ruler. They all settled down into a quiet line, and the nun used the ruler to check that they were equally spaced apart. I could not tell what was going on; it made no sense to me.

"You guys better get up there," the supervisor said to David and me, "or you're going to miss your food."

We were so hungry that I had to put aside my fear of the figure in the big black costume. I needed to make sure that David and I had something in our bellies to keep our energy up in case we got a chance to escape.

"Let's go," I told David.

We got up and went to stand at the end of the line, with David just in front of me. The nun was giving one slice of bread to each boy. There was nothing on that bread. No butter, no jam, no drippings, no nothing. It was just a slice of plain bread, but every boy who got one ran off to their own spot and gobbled it down as fast as possible. I found out later that was because sometimes the bigger boys were so hungry, they would go after the smaller guys to get their slice of bread. David and I went back to our spot at the table after we got our measly portion.

We were so hungry. I sat there looking at my slice, wondering if this was all we were going to get to eat after that long trip and if there was going to be anything to put on it, like butter or jam. David gobbled his bread down right away like he saw the other boys doing.

"Is there any more, *Napikan*?" he asked me in Cree.

"Here, David," I answered in our language, and I handed him my slice of bread. "Eat this one, too."

He grabbed it and gulped it right down. There was no more bread for anyone, just the one slice the nun had doled out to each boy. I was so hungry as we sat there, thinking, *Well, they have taken me away from my home, and taken away my sisters, but at least David and I are still together.*

That was when another nun came in and took David by the hand and started leading him away.

"Where are you taking my brother?" I said in English.

"He is going to be in the dorm with the youngest boys," the supervisor said.

"He can stay with me," I said. "I can look after him."

"That is not how we do things here," said the supervisor. He didn't explain anything, just watched the nun lead David away from me and through the door.

I didn't cry as they took David away. I didn't want to make it any harder for him. I was doing the same thing my mum had done when they bundled us into the bus. But my mind was racing. Things were getting more and more complicated. If I escaped, how would I find David? My sisters? If I did find them, how would I get them all home? My mind was churning. I was in a strange place on my own and there was no one I could turn to.

For the first time in my life, I was completely on my own. No parents, grandparents, or older brothers and sisters; no aunties and uncles, cousins, Elders, community members, or friends. No cozy little house, no traditional land full of fresh water and good food and healing medicine. I thought they had taken everything from me.

But it turned out I still had a lot to lose. Because that first prime minister was serious when he said he wanted to "take the Indian out of the child." In the decades since he said it, the federal government had designed a system to take everything from my people, one step at a time. It was very efficient. In just one day, they separated me from everything I knew and loved, everything that Creator had given me.

Then, on that very same day, they started to separate me from myself.

First, they made me take off all the clothes my mother had carefully picked out for me that morning. I do not know what happened to that warm, comfortable little outfit. They gave me a different everything — shirt, pants, underwear, socks, shoes. I got the exact same things all the other boys were wearing. They were not new and had been washed many times, and they felt scratchy against my skin from the heavy laundry soap. I was told we only changed once a week, so we had to keep those clothes clean until laundry day. I found out later that the only time they made us change is when we went out to church on Sunday. When the local people looked at us, we were all dressed up and looking clean and tidy. As soon as we got back to the residential school, it was "change your clothes."

After they took the clothes from my back, they started in on my body. I had long hair back then. A lot of kids did, even non-Indigenous ones, because it was back in the days of the Beatles and hippies, and long hair was the style. But my hair was long for a different reason. Now that I was nine, my mum wanted me to grow out my hair until it was long enough for me to wear braids. Then, Mum would have plaited it in our traditional way, honouring our ancestors who wore braids. While she wove my hair into the pattern, the same one we use for braiding sweetgrass and other important herbs, she would offer prayers of gratitude to Creator. She would thank Creator for giving her a son, for the gifts given to her son, and for her son's connection to his people and his land. My braids would have connected me to Creator, our people, and the land. As I grew older, I would have taken good care of my braids to show my respect for our traditions, as well as myself.

I never got to see that day. Right away, they sat me down in a chair and used a big electric razor to shave off all my hair, right down to a short stubble, what they used to call a brush cut. No one I knew had a haircut like that. I never got used to it. I always felt a cold wind on my head. It did not feel like the wind I was used to, a gentle breeze that tickled me as it blew my hair across my face. The wind did not feel right anymore. It felt like it was stabbing me. I always felt cold, the whole time I had to wear that haircut.

When they cut my hair, I thought that was it. They had taken my parents, my sisters, my brother, my clothes, and the very hair from my head. What else could they take from me? But still they were not done.

The next thing they took was my name.

"You are Number 53," said the supervisor.

"I am *Napikan*," I said.

Right away they got mad. "That is not a real name," they said. "We only speak English here."

"My English name is Bobby Mountain," I said. That was the name the teacher used at my school.

"Your English name is Robert Cree," the supervisor said, looking at a piece of paper. When I got a little older I realized that, when they pinned the name tag on me before putting us on the bus, someone mixed up my father's English name, Mountain, with my mother's English name, Cree. But nobody in that building — nobody in the whole residential school system — ever admitted they made a mistake. They just kept moving forward with the name someone scribbled down on a piece of paper. I did not know it then, but with one stroke of the pen, Bobby Mountain had completely vanished.

"I'm Bobby Mountain," I tried again.

"No you are not," he said. "Here you are Number 53."

"Why do I need a number?" I asked.

"So we can tell who you are. All the boys here have a number."

"Why?"

"It is a system," he said. "We do everything by numbers. Your bed is 53. Your dining room chair is 53. Your classroom desk is 53. That way you don't sit in somebody else's chair or sleep in somebody else's bed or work at someone else's desk."

"But why?" I asked.

"Because that is the way we do it here. No more questions unless you want to be punished."

That was that. I found out pretty fast it was not a place to ask questions. Asking questions got my ears twisted or my face slapped or my body hit with a ruler.

The other thing that was clear right away was that they didn't care if I was Bobby Mountain or *Napikan* or Robert Cree. They were going to call me Number 53 no matter what. That told me right away that the people who took me knew a name had power. I have told you a bit about the importance of names in my culture. When my grandfather gifted me the name of *Napikan*, he was setting me up to find my road in life. That name was supposed to follow me as I found the work that Creator intended me to do. By changing my name, they were trying to change me. By taking away the name of every Indigenous child in the school and replacing it with a number, they were changing our people. They were trying to send us in a new direction, away from the road we were meant to walk.

Not once, for the six long years I was a prisoner of the residential school system, did they see me as a person. They did not care that I was a nine-year-old boy who spoke Cree and knew how to respect the Elders. That I knew how to trap a rabbit, gather wild bird eggs, and build a sweat lodge from willow branches. That I knew how to properly thank Creator for the many gifts to our people.

I was the person who lined up in the Number 53 spot. That is all I was.

That night I lay under the Number 53 blanket in the Number 53 bed, the bed I was supposed to make perfectly the next morning and every morning after that. The bed was in the junior boys' dormitory, a huge institutional room full of metal-framed beds lined up in rows, each bed equally distant from the next. I was used to sleeping in a room with my brothers, but this felt completely different. It didn't feel safe and cozy. It felt sad and dangerous. I could hear other boys breathing and tossing and turning. I could hear someone having a nightmare. I could hear someone crying softly. I did not sleep that first night. I lay there all night, wide awake, going over and over everything in my mind. All night long, think, think, think. *How am I going to get out of here?*

How am I going to get home?

CHAPTER 9

You Will Never Be Late Again

The next day, when we were lining up to go into the dining room, I saw my younger sister. I was so happy to see her. She had been with me every single day of her life. As soon as I saw her, I ran to her, threw my arms around her and hugged her. She did not have time to get her arms around me before I felt a terrible pain in my ear. One of the nuns had grabbed it and twisted it to pull me away from my sister. The nun kept twisting it as she turned me around to face her.

"*Ow! Ow!* You're hurting me!" I squirmed around, trying to get away.

"You cannot talk to any of the girls," the nun said, and she twisted my ear harder until I stopped struggling.

"It's okay," I replied, even though I was crying now. "She is my sister."

"No! No! No! No!" the nun said. She made a clucking noise like *tch-tch-tch*. She did not let go of my ear, and she gave it an extra twist. "Talking to girls is never allowed. No exceptions."

I didn't understand what she was saying. I had talked to my sister every day since she was born. Why was it a bad thing all of a sudden? But my ear hurt so badly that I pulled myself together, stood still, and tried to stop sobbing.

"You're not allowed over on the girls' side," she said, finally letting go of my ear. "Get back to your side of the room right now. Don't ever come back to the girls' side again, or I'll have to take you to a priest."

I didn't know what that meant, being taken to the priest. But if it was worse than dealing with the nuns, I wanted to avoid it. I went back to the other side. Years would pass before I would hug my sister again.

I soon found out that the only time I got a glimpse of my sisters was when we ate, and only for a few minutes. The dining area was divided, boys on one side and girls on the other, and between us was the kitchen, where we would line up to pick up our little bowls. Three times a day, for breakfast, lunch, and dinner, we picked up a bowl or plate to take to our numbered seat. That was when all of us boys would try catch a glimpse of our sisters. If none of the nuns or supervisors were looking, we would do a small wave to let them know that we saw them. I figured out quickly that I better not get caught waving, or someone would hit me or strap me with a piece of leather.

After lining up in the kitchen, all the boys had to sit down in our numbered spots in the dining room. We had to stay there in silence, not fidgeting, with empty plates in front of us while we waited for the priests, who had their own special spot in the corner of the dining area. There was a wall between us, but the wall had a huge window cut into it so that they could look out at us at any time. They wanted to be set apart from us, but they also wanted to see what we were doing because they always had to be in control.

We kept our eyes on that window to see when the head priest sat down, because he was always served his food first. When he was late, we all sat in silence and waited, no matter how long it was. As soon as he sat down, the nuns rushed in and put delicious food in front of him and the other priests. They didn't eat the same thing we did. A meal was always specially prepared for them. A nun would bring in a bowl of creamy mashed potatoes and put it down in front of the head priest. Then a bowl of carrots. Beans. Chicken. Beef. Gravy. Fresh bread. Butter. They would bring in platter after platter to lay before him, while we sat and watched. The platters would be hot, the steam rising off the food, and all the kids could smell delicious aromas coming through the window cut into the wall. It smelled like my mum's kitchen.

As soon as the head priest took the first bite, the nuns would start coming around to where we kids sat in silence at our tables. We weren't allowed to talk while they slopped something into our little bowls. Whatever they dumped in the bowl was what you got, and what an awful thing it was. The food was tasteless and lumpy, usually a brown-grey mush. Mostly we could not tell what we were eating. Even with that terrible food, we still could not take a bite until we got permission.

Of course, before anyone ate, one of the priests had to say a prayer first, in English. It sounded a bit like a prayer to Creator, but the way the priest prayed was very rigid and always had to be said the same way. We had to memorize it. After we said it, we still had to wait for the command to start eating. We would look down at the grey slop in our bowls and try not to think about the delicious food the priests were eating. When the command came, we ate every bite of that slop because we were so hungry. All of our food was portioned out by the nuns, and the portions were very small. There were no second helpings. We were always hungry, but the worst thing you could try to do was get more food. If they ever caught you stealing or hoarding food, you got the worst punishments they could think of.

That was another reason none of us boys wanted to get caught waving at our sisters and be taken out of the lineup in the dining room, because you would not get any food until the next mealtime, or even the meal after that. It was very risky to be caught even glancing at my sisters in the lineup. So, after that one little interrupted hug, I hardly saw my sisters at all and I never, ever spoke to them. With its school, the government was trying to turn us into strangers. Strangers to one another, but also to everything we had shared, everything we'd been taught, everything that nurtured us.

Another thing they did to separate us from our families was to make sure that everything was in English. We were not allowed to speak Cree to one another. If we forgot, if we said one word in Cree, we were punished right away. We were slapped in the face, or lashed on the hand with a strap, or punched with a fist, whatever the person punishing us felt like doing.

Speaking Cree was punished violently because they hated not being able to tell what we were saying. Cree, the beautiful, gentle language that my mother and father spoke to teach us the ways of our people, did not exist in that place.

Speaking to our sisters, trying to get food, and speaking in Cree were the three biggest crimes in that school. That was clear right from the start. There were many, many other rules, too, and breaking any of them got you a slap across the face, or worse. No one told you the rules, of course. You found out about them when you broke them.

One of the things I struggled to understand in my early days at the school was something called a timetable. A timetable was printed on paper and it said what had to happen and when. Every day we had to do the same things at the same time, and there were a lot of things to do. We had to get up, make our beds, get dressed, get to the dining room, go study, go back to the dining room, go do chores, go to the dining room again, do recreation, go to bed. No matter what you did — sleep, wake up, eat, study, work, play — you had to do it exactly when the timetable wanted you to do it.

One time I was a bit late and went running into the recreation room, where I was supposed to be.

"Late," said the supervisor by the door. That was all he said. One word. *Late.*

I knew from my Grade One experience that this was not going to go well for me, but I was still surprised when he punched me in the head, hard, with his fist. He was a grown man, and I was a nine-year-old boy, and he sent me flying. I landed with a crash on the hard floor. I just lay there. I was not quite unconscious, but I was dazed and my ears were ringing. I could not get my arms and legs to work to get up again. He came over and picked me up and put me on my feet.

"Get going," he said.

As soon as he let me go, I fell down again. I did not know someone could punch you that hard, could give you such a bad head injury that you couldn't get up, could not stand on your own feet.

"Get up," he said and picked me up again. I was still dizzy, and I fell down again.

"Remember this," he said, picking me up. "You will never be late again."

Finally I managed to stay on my feet and stagger away. But I never completely got over that punch and hitting the floor. To this day it affects me. I have a problem with my balance and my hearing.

That was just one punch, one example of the violence we faced every minute of every day. They made us speak English, but the real language they used was violence. They tried to train us the same way a bad person trains a dog, reinforcing what they wanted by isolating us, withholding food, withholding affection, slapping, kicking, punching, and worse. There was nowhere for us to turn. No one in authority we could go to. No one to show any compassion or kindness.

One of the very first things that happened to me in my early days at the school was a scuffle I got into with a bigger boy. I forget what it was about, and he didn't hurt me. There was a little pushing back and forth between us. But I was upset, still being a young boy, and if I had been at home I would have gone running to my mum. I wanted a hug and someone to tell me I was okay. After the boy and I tussled, I saw a nun come walking in and I went running to her. I threw my arms around her and hugged her around the waist. I thought she would hug me back, pat my head, say nice things to comfort me like my mum did.

But I didn't feel comforted. I did not feel anything coming from her. It was like there was no person there at all. All I felt was cold. Those outfits they wore, the big black-and-white uniforms, I don't know what the heck they were for, but they were made of hard, scratchy cloth. There was no softness to it when I put my arms around it. But it was more than the rough, hard feeling of the clothing. There was no emotion coming from the person wearing the outfit. None of the love and caring I knew from the women I grew up with. There was absolutely nothing. I felt a big blank wall. Then she grabbed my ear, pulled it hard, and used it to turn me around. Still holding my ear, she pushed me out at arm's length so that I faced her.

"You're not supposed to touch me," she said. "Never, ever touch me."

I just stood there.

"What are you standing there for?" she said. "Go play."

I ran away from her. I didn't know what else to do. But I knew right there and then there was something wrong with those people. I didn't know what it was. They didn't show any emotions, any humanity. They showed nothing but coldness, pain, hate, and anger. They forbade my own sister to put her arms around me, to comfort her brother. Now I knew no one was going to comfort me in that place. No one was going to show me kindness. No one was going to help me.

CHAPTER 10

Christmas

The first official break after I got to that school was at Christmas. I heard from some of the other boys that kids were sent home to be with their families during the Christmas holiday. I was so happy. I didn't care that it was going to be a long and bumpy ride home. I wanted to see my mum and dad and my siblings. I wanted to sleep in my own bed again, and I wanted to eat my mum's delicious food. I secretly hoped that if I got there, maybe I could figure out a way to stay.

The end of December is very dark and cold in northern Alberta. There are only about six hours of daylight, and the temperatures are always below freezing. But it was always warm and snug in our house. We had a tree that made our little house smell like the forest, and we kids covered it with homemade decorations.

We did not have much money, but my mum worked hard to make Christmas a nice time for our family. She and my father had been baptized, which was not unusual for our people at that time. Some were baptized by choice, and most of them by the powers-that-be in the dominant culture. My parents were not conflicted about it. This may sound odd to you, but my parents believed that all prayer was good. My parents taught me that all cultures were given their prayers by Creator, and that all prayer has value.

Today when I am asked to do a blessing at a large gathering, I ask everyone to pray along with me using the prayers they have been taught in their own cultures. There is nothing Creator loves better than to hear our voices joined together as we ask for a blessing. My parents strongly believed that everyone who prays in a genuine way is praying to Creator, who made everything and everyone. It does not matter what language you pray in or what name you call Creator. It matters that you have balance and harmony in your heart and that your prayers are sincere. Creator is above the bad things that some people do in the name of religion. That is how my parents saw it. I believe that, too.

My parents did not see anything wrong with celebrating Christmas. It was a time of prayer and did not contradict anything they believed in. They also thought it was a wonderful family time, a feast to bring everyone together, and a chance to spoil their children a little. Christmas was a beautiful day in our home, a big celebration. My parents saved up all year so that each of us kids would get a toy from the store in town on Christmas morning. The gifts were never anything big, certainly not by today's standards, but we were happy with what we received. I remember one time I got a little toy gun and I loved it. I played all day with it.

After everyone opened their presents, our house would be nice and warm from our wood stove because Mum would start cooking a huge meal. We never had turkey; she used to cook either pork, a roast, or a ham, and there were all kinds of vegetables, too — potatoes and carrots and beans — and of course Mum's apple pies for dessert. The smell of delicious things would fill up the house. Our mouths would be watering as we thought about all the wonderful food waiting for us.

While she cooked and we played with our toys, people from our community would come to visit. Everyone was welcome and, if they wanted, they could stay for dinner. There was always enough for everyone. When it came time for dinner, we ate like crazy. After all that eating and playing and visiting, when we were ready to go to bed, we just crashed. We fell asleep right away, and when we woke up the next morning, we still felt wonderful because we'd had such a good celebration the day before. I remember that even as a little boy, I felt uplifted celebrating Christmas with my parents and siblings.

I could not wait to get home for that along with David and my sisters. We would eat until we burst! We could have something delicious any time we wanted! And I could see my sisters and hug them and talk to them. The very first thing I was going to do was give my mum a great big hug and feel her familiar arms around me, hugging me back. It was going to be wonderful.

But when the other boys started getting ready to go home, I was told that boys like me, from very far away, had to stay at the school. It was too much trouble to send us all the way back to our families. They organized a trip in the middle of night to scoop us up from our homes, but they couldn't be bothered to send us home for a break. Instead, they kept us there and made us have Christmas with the nuns.

I cannot think of anything sadder than my first Christmas in residential school. It was a horrible time. Even though my siblings also had to stay there over Christmas, they still kept us separate. Most of the boys in my dorm were gone, so it was extra quiet, almost spooky. I was very, very lonely.

Things looked up a bit on Christmas morning when the nuns gave me a gift-wrapped present. They saved the wrapping paper, so I had to open it carefully without ripping it. But it was worth it because inside, there it was: a toy plane! It was the only toy I got since I arrived there, and I played with it non-stop. I also played with some of the other boys who had been left behind. They got presents, too — toy cars and stuff like that. We also got extra food and a little piece of cake on Christmas Day, although the priests still got served first and still got the tastiest food. And at the end of the week, before the other boys returned from their homes, a nun came and took back all our gifts. There was no explanation. She gathered up all the presents, piled them into a box, and took them away.

The next year when Christmas came, we still had to stay at the school. It was the same routine all over again. I got a gift-wrapped present with a different gift. I saw that plane from the year before and now somebody else had it. That year I was not surprised when they came to take away our toys. It was the same thing every year. We were never allowed to keep anything.

Everything had to be stripped away from us, even the things they pretended to give us.

CHAPTER II

Nobody Said Anything

As the weeks and months went by, I got to know a few of the other boys in my dorm. Once I made a few friends, I started to feel a little less alone. My brother David was still off on his own most of the time, but sometimes I saw him when all the boys were sent outside at the same time for recess. I saw he was making friends with the other little guys. Once we got to know the other boys, things were a bit more bearable.

Some of the boys already knew one another because they were local. They were in what was called day school and they got to go home to their families at night. But there were a lot of boys like me who had been taken from homes farther away. No matter where we were from, we all followed the same timetable in the classroom. That included time they scheduled for us to be outside for recess or sports. All the boys liked being outside, partly because that was when we could talk to one another. If the nuns were around we still had to speak English. But if they were far enough away, we would risk saying a few words in Cree.

As the first winter wore on, it seemed to me it was much colder at residential school than my home in the boreal forest. The temperature could drop to minus twenty-five degrees Celsius or lower, so cold that at home our parents would not have let us go outside. But the timetable said it was time to go outside, so outside we went. It was hardest on the little guys who were David's age. They would stand shaking beside the snowbanks that surrounded the school's skating rink, huddled together to keep warm and cut down the wind. They would be crying, tears coming down their little faces. An hour is a long time to be out in that cold. It made me sad and angry at the same time to see them freezing like that, and one day I could not take it any longer.

"We've got to do something," I said to some of the boys my age, "or the smaller boys are going to freeze."

"What can we do?" one of them asked.

"We need to make some kind of shelter that will break the wind," I said. "Then we need to get them moving so they stay warm."

My mother's brothers, Joe and Jimmy, were respected as great hunters by our community. They knew how to survive in the coldest weather by building shelters under trees and in snowbanks. My father and his brothers also knew how to survive in the bush in any type of weather. I had listened carefully to the men when they talked about their hunting trips. I asked them questions, and they answered by sharing their traditional knowledge, so I had a good idea of what to do. I told the other boys that if we hollowed out the snowbanks by the rink and made some tunnels, the little guys could go inside and play until they warmed up. The other boys agreed, so we started to tunnel into the snowbanks around the rink, along the side hidden from view by the school. We did not have any shovels or tools, so we used our mittened hands to dig snow and pile it farther away. Pretty soon, with all of us working together, we'd made some good-sized tunnels. Then we got David and all the little guys and brought them inside and played with them, wrestling and moving around. We all started to sweat and soon we were all laughing and playing. When the bell rang, we brought the little boys out of the tunnels, and they ran into the school, happy and smiling.

Of course, the nuns looked at them and wondered what was going on.

"Where were you boys?" the nuns asked.

Nobody said anything. Not even the littlest guys. Everyone knew that anything good we told them about would be taken away.

"How come you're sweating?" they said.

We said nothing. We would not even admit we were sweating.

"How come you're smiling?"

Imagine being in a place where your smiles make people want to find out what you are doing so that they can stop it. But we well knew to tell the nuns nothing. They never knew we made those tunnels on purpose to help the little boys. It never occurred to them that we had our own skills and could work together to help others. They never imagined that our fathers and uncles had shared their traditional knowledge with us and showed us how to survive in the cold. We'd been taught how to read the weather, how to look around and figure out what needed to be done, how to build a shelter with just our mittened hands. We'd learned what to do if we got caught in the bush in bad weather, how to survive cold and hunger until we got home safe. That was the knowledge that the government wanted to take away from us, and yet that was what we needed to survive their school.

We used that knowledge every chance we got. The older boys were sometimes allowed out on the grounds around the school, including a wooded area used for things like cross-country running. It was far enough away from the school and heavily treed enough that it was hard to keep an eye on us every minute. A few times my friends and I took advantage of that to try to build a sweat lodge. We were not building it as an escape from the cold, like the tunnels we made in the schoolyard. I told the other boys about my dad's sweat lodge, how it made you feel good and helped you release negative energy. We tried to build one seeking spiritual warmth and a connection to our culture. We had to build it in secret just like my father had done for years. While the government had changed the law so that sweat lodges were now legal, they were still a great crime at that school. If we had been caught trying to do a sweat, we would have received the worst punishment they could dish out.

But still we risked it, gathering and stacking willow branches and using our coats to cover them. We tried to get our hands on tobacco, too, although if we had been caught stealing the priest's cigarettes the fallout would have been horrible. A few times our sweat lodge was discovered, but we said we were building a fort for fun. They believed it, as our sweat lodges were poor imitations of the real thing, just a pile of branches with coats on top, and they fell down all the time. But being inside, even for a few minutes, made us feel better. Anything connected to our traditions gave us a little bit of peace.

The other way we used our traditional skills was to find food, because we were always hungry. Like me, the other boys had been taught to trap small game, and hunt "chickens," the English word we used for the wild birds we caught. We knew how to skin game and build a cooking fire. It didn't happen often, but sometimes the other boys and I would try to catch and cook small animals in secret. Every now and then, the school had some program that meant we had to be outdoors for longer periods of time and were scattered around and harder to supervise. We would find a way to set a few snares and come back the next day to check them. If we caught something, we would build a fire and cook the game on sticks. We also knew what berries we could eat and what to stay away from. Eventually the nuns and priests would find out what we were doing. They would forbid us to go where the wild game was and punish us in whatever ways they could think up. Sometimes they made us skip meals, making us even hungrier.

Food was part of their power over us. They used food to punish us, taking away meals when we did not follow the rules. They also used it to bribe us. The same way they knew that a name had power, they knew food had power, especially for growing boys forced to do physical labour. They never paid anyone to come in and do work at that school if they could make one of us do it for free.

I remember one time I was asked if I wanted to flood the skating rink, making a smooth ice surface for the boys who played hockey.

"When you flood the skating rink, you get an apple and a couple of cookies and a glass of milk," the supervisor said.

That was a big treat. We never got anything like that. "Yeah, I want that," I said. "I will do it."

Of course, no one told me that I would have to do it in the middle of the night. That night I was sleeping and, all of a sudden, I was woken up at two o'clock in the morning by the supervisor, who was shaking me.

"Come on," the supervisor said. "You have to go flood the skating rink."

There was no way he would let me go back to sleep. He kept shaking and shaking me.

"Okay," I said, and I started to get up.

"Don't make any noise," he said. "The other kids are sleeping."

Because the beds were lined up right next to one another, I had to be extra quiet. I got up quickly. The air was cold, so I hurried and dressed warm, and then the supervisor led me out to the skating rink. It was a bunch of boards placed like a fence around a flat piece of earth. There was already ice on it, because it was the middle of winter, but the rink had to be resurfaced every night. First, I had to shovel off any snow because it would make bumps in the fresh ice. That took a little while, but the work warmed me up and I was glad. It was a freezing cold night.

After the shoveling, we started the actual flooding.

"Here, hold this," he said and handed me what looked like a fire hose. It was huge, and there was a lot of water pressure. I struggled to get a good grip on it.

"You have to slowly swing it back and forth," he said, showing me how to do a sweeping motion that sent the water flowing out evenly across the ice surface. "You need to make it smooth, no ripples, for people to skate on it."

"How long do I have to do it?" I said.

"About two hours," he said. "I will come out and get you when the time is up."

For the next two hours, I moved around that rink and swung that heavy hose back and forth. I kept adding layer after layer of water to build up the ice so that it was smooth. The water dripped from the hose onto my woolen mitts until they were frozen solid, and my hands were like icicles. Every so often, I would take off my mittens and put my hands next to my skin inside my coat, like my father had taught me. I think that is the only reason I didn't get frostbite. By the time the supervisor came to tell me I could go back inside, I was shivering non-stop. Even after I went into the warm building, I could not stop shaking from the cold. Now I know that was my body's way of trying to generate heat because my internal temperature had dropped and I was in serious danger of hypothermia. When I went inside, though, no one said anything about my shivering or tried to do any first aid. But I got my reward for my hard work. A nun gave me a glass of hot chocolate, an apple, and two cookies.

To heck with the cold, I said to myself. *I'm eating something good here.*

I had something to tell the boys the next day.

"Guess what I had last night?" I said.

They tried, but they did not guess it was food.

"I had an apple and two cookies and a cup of hot chocolate," I said.

"Really?" my friends said. "How did you get that?"

"I flooded the skating rink last night. If you flood the rink, you get a treat."

After that, everybody wanted to go flood the skating rink.

It was like that every day. We were always being asked to do physical labour and were never paid for it with money, but if we were lucky we got a little food. I remember quite clearly another time when they asked us if we would like to do some kind of work in exchange for treats like potato chips and candies or apples and oranges. I went with some of my friends, and we found out we were going to catch mice. We went into a big field and turned over bales of hay. Field mice would run out from under the bales, and we would hit them with little sticks and throw them into a bag that we were supposed to bring back to the school, where they could be counted. No one told us why they needed the mice. I started wondering if we were eating them, if that was what was in the grey slop in our bowls. I was so worried about this that I took a chance and asked what the mice were for. I was told it had something to do with a scientific study, and they needed hundreds and hundreds of mice for it.

I have always wondered what that science work was. Science was one of my favourite subjects and was one of the things we studied when the timetable told us to. When we weren't working, we did schoolwork a few hours every day from Monday through Friday, studying different subjects, all of them in English — things like geography, art, and of course colonial history. The studying was no different from that at the school I had been in back at home. I still liked science and math the best. Math was straightforward. It did not matter if I was doing sums on paper in English, or in Cree in my head. The answer came out the same.

I liked science because it was about the natural world. It talked about the land in a different way, but I could see elements of traditional teachings in there. The school wanted to erase all my traditional knowledge and replace it with science, but that was never how I saw it. I always saw traditional teachings and science as interested in the same things — what makes a plant grow, what makes a fish spawn — but coming at them in a different way. I never thought it had to be one or the other. Right from the beginning, I felt that the two types of learning could respect and learn from each other. The older I got, the more strongly I believed that.

My biggest interest while I was at that school was astronomy. I read anything I could find about it in the school library. Astronomy amazed me then, and it still does. The universe is so vast. There is so much out there, and there is so much about it we haven't grasped yet. Now, with space exploration and huge telescopes that reach out into the cosmos, we are learning new things every day. We hear scientists saying "we just discovered this" and "we just discovered that." But we haven't even scratched the surface. We will be discovering new things for generations. Light from exploding stars is still making its way through the universe. We have not seen it yet, but that doesn't mean it is not there. It will make its way to us some day. I knew from my *Mooshum* that Creator started this eons ago, and it is still unfolding. It all has a purpose, and we will learn that purpose as time goes on.

Astronomy brought me great comfort when I needed it. It told me that our universe was so much bigger than one residential school in one town in one province in one country on one world. My imagination could go on and on in a universe so vast. At night I would lie in my bed and think about the universe and the wondrous things in it. I prayed silently in Cree to Creator every night for the strength to survive the school. But I also tried to pray in gratitude for the gifts Creator gave us, the gifts that I knew were out there even though I could not see them yet. I tried to remember all the teachings I had in my nine years, going over them in my head, so that I would have them when I needed them. When I finally escaped, I would find my road again and I would need Creator's many gifts to do what I was born to do.

But in daylight, things were different. I could dream all I wanted, but in real life I was going to have to do something. That is the only real lesson I learned at that school. You can't dream all the time. Doing something is the thing.

CHAPTER 12

Keep Your Head Up

Some of the better days, the easier days, were the days we played sports. When we boys were at home with our families, we were always physically active and spent most of our time outdoors. At residential school we were mostly indoors, sitting in our numbered spots and doing what the timetable said. We played sports any chance we got, it didn't matter if it was football, baseball, basketball, whatever. We did anything to stretch our muscles and use our energy, especially if it meant we could be outside. During sports we could also talk to each other while we played — in English, of course.

We were in Canada, so hockey was our biggest sport. That was the main reason we had a big outdoor skating rink at the school. Our hockey team was a big deal, and we had talented players who were very fast skaters. Our team played games against all types of schools around southern Alberta, and we did very well. When I laced up my skates and went out on the ice, I was fast, too. I liked being out on the rink. I liked the clicking sound of my skate blades on the ice, feeling the cold, fresh air on my face, and hearing the boys calling to one another and laughing. It was a good feeling.

But I will never forget the first time I found myself in a hockey game in an official competition with another school. The coach came up to me a few days before the game and asked if I wanted to play with the junior boys team. This was a big deal because the team had top-notch players. I was a little smaller than the other players, so I thought carefully about it before I committed. But I knew I was fast, and I believed I could keep up with them.

"I'll play," I said.

"Are you sure?" the supervisor said. I must not have sounded sure, because he asked me that a few times.

"Yeah, I'll go," I said. "If the team needs me, I'm there."

As the game approached, I thought, *If I am going to do this, I want to do it right.* The star forward on our team was my friend Howard, one of the boys I got to know while I was settling in. Howard was a very fast skater and a big goal scorer, and he always ended up with the puck. I was going to play defence and I knew I was quick enough to score some points, so I set up a plan with Howard.

"Buddy," I said, "you know I'm fast."

"You are very fast," Howard agreed.

"If I can get that puck coming towards me," I said, "I know I can get it in the net."

"For sure. I know you can do it."

"Can you watch for me to be in the clear? Then pass me the puck so I can score?"

"I'll keep an eye out for you," Howard said.

The day of the game came, and when they dropped the puck at centre ice, Howard was right in the middle of the action. I was doing okay. I had no problem following the play and keeping up with the players on our team. As the game went on, Howard and I were both keeping an eye out for my big chance. Sure enough, the time came when Howard got the puck, and I saw an open spot, so I took off for it.

"Howard, puck!" I shouted, and he passed it towards me.

Howard was a very good player, and it was a solid pass. The puck came straight to me and I got it on my stick. I had what hockey players call a breakaway, which means there were no players between me and the other team's net, no one who could stop me or take the puck away before I shot it at the goalie. I was flying down the ice, from our team's defensive zone through centre ice and past the other team's blue line, and was heading for their net. The goalie was there, but he was out of position and the net looked wide open.

The crowd had started cheering, really loud, like a roar. It was deafening, and I could not make out what they were saying. I thought they were saying, "Stop! Stop!" I found out later that it was "Go! Go!" But the noise was so loud that it shook me up and I could not think.

I looked for Howard because I thought he was going to join the play, but he did not. He was letting me do what I had asked, leaving the puck to me so that I would have a shot on net. I saw the goalie was still leaving most of the net open, and I could have scored a goal very easily. But I just froze. I froze because everybody was still yelling. It was thunderous, but I could not tell what the crowd wanted. I skated right past the net and never took a shot, and the crowd groaned, "Aww!" It was louder than cheering had been, and I was even more afraid. My first breakaway and I refused to take the shot.

Afterwards, the other players kept asking me, "Why didn't you shoot the puck? What stopped you?"

"I don't know what to tell you," I said. "It was my first time. I wasn't ready for it."

I still like hockey and I watch games on television. I have an autographed photo of Frank Mahovlich. He was a star player in the National Hockey League and one of the best hockey players of all time. The photograph shows him and some of his teammates, and none of them are wearing helmets. Even the goalie has no face mask. That is how they used to play, years ago when I was a boy. They were rough and tough. Now, the players have all types of gear to protect them. All these years later, when I think about this protective gear, I understand what was creating my fear and holding me back that day I had the breakaway. I knew that if I was in the wrong place at the wrong time during the game, I could get seriously hurt. I had seen guys get hit in the head with a puck that was moving at 150 kilometres an hour and they dropped to the ice surface, out cold. Things could get dangerous on the ice.

The truth is, even though hockey was our big sport, I did not much care for playing it. I never liked the roughness of it. Hockey is a very aggressive game, and especially was back then. I don't just mean the bodychecking — players using their hip or shoulder to smash into you, trying to jar you so that you lose control of the puck. In those days, the whole game was about intimidation and aggression. You could be skating along, and if the referee was not looking your way, somebody might hit you right in the gut with their stick. Some of those games could get very rough. And that was my problem.

There was enough random violence in my daily life, enough fists coming at me from out of nowhere to knock me down, to hurt me, and to muddle my brain. The last thing I needed was more brutality. I was afraid of the violence that was part of hockey; I was always expecting pain to explode in me at any moment. That is what living with violence every day does to you. It makes you fearful. You always have an eye out for it because it can come out of nowhere. That is what I was experiencing, and I could not get past it on the ice, although at the time I did not realize that was what was holding me back. There were other sports at residential school, football, baseball and the like, and I tried them all. Whatever I played, I always put all my energy forward and tried to be the best player I could be. But I was never really into playing against other teams. At some level, I was always afraid of violence.

After a while, I figured out I preferred individual sports, where I could challenge myself. Gymnastics was something I particularly enjoyed. We boys would go to the gymnasium and practise, pushing ourselves to do better. We would do stretches to get ourselves prepared, then do all the things you see at the Olympics — vaulting, pommel boxes, the whole thing. We especially liked doing routines using the rings that hung down from ropes. You needed a lot of upper-body strength to pull yourself up, and a lot of control to do a proper routine. We would jump up to grab those rings, pull ourselves upright with our arms, and challenge ourselves to see how long we could stay up. We would hold the position until our arms started shaking. We would also do routines on the trampoline, jumping as high as we could and doing somersaults.

It was fun and freeing, and part of me was enjoying myself. But I was also learning about control and about pushing myself to achieve something.

I was able to learn these things because gymnastics was the one area where we had a very good instructor who was supportive of us and gave us a lot of encouragement. He was a good man. There was no random violence with him, no cruelty. I felt safe in gymnastics class, so my fear lessened, and I was able to concentrate on the sport. As I learned more about it, I learned about myself, too.

The first time I looked fear in the face was when the gymnastics instructor asked us to climb up long ropes that hung from the ceiling. There were four ropes in a row, and each one had knots tied all along its length and a little bell at the very top. Four boys at a time would climb their ropes all the way to the top, ring the bell, and come back down again. Back in those days, there were no safety precautions — no spotters, no hooks you clipped on to prevent a fall, no nothing. You had to know how to use your hands and legs to keep yourself safe, or you fell all the way down to the hard gym floor below.

At first, I was scared. I did not want to climb my rope.

"I know you can do it, Robert," the instructor said. He never called me by my number, but he also thought my name was Robert Cree. That was what my student record said. I had long ago given up trying to correct anyone about my name, even the kindly instructor.

And faced with that climb, I could not say anything at all. I just stood there in silence while the bottom of my rope swayed a bit, set in motion by boy who had climbed it last. The instructor could tell I was frightened, but, unlike the other adults in that place, he did not enjoy my fear.

"You don't have to be afraid," he said. "This is something you can do."

I reached out my arms, took hold of the rope, and lifted my head to look up at the top.

"That's it. Just keep your head up," the instructor told me. "You don't want to look down. Keep your eyes focused on the task you are doing. That makes it a lot easier."

"Okay, sir," I said.

I decided to give it my best try. What the heck, everybody else was doing it, and they were getting up and down okay. I was in very good physical shape, so once I started using my arms and legs the way the instructor suggested, I quickly made my way to the top of the rope. I saw the bell and reached out and rang it. So far, so good. But then I stopped. Going up was the easier part. It was going down that scared me. But I kept my head up and did not look down. I looked straight ahead at my rope, made sure my legs were wrapped around it the way the coach said, and then started back down, bit by bit. It seemed to take forever, but the instructor was encouraging me the whole time. Finally, I made it down in one piece. That was the first time I ever acknowledged that fear was holding me back from something. I found out I could face my fear, take charge of myself, and conquer it.

The other boys and I kept working at our gymnastics training, pushing ourselves further and further, and soon we were competing at a top level. The school officials liked to show us off, so they would put us on the bus and take us to Red Deer, Calgary, Edmonton, all over the province of Alberta, to compete with different schools. When we were competing, we boys were serious. We made no bones about it — we were there to win.

I wanted to win but I needed to improve my performance. Another friend of mine at school was very good at gymnastics, and he regularly took first-place medals. At first we were about equal, but he had gotten better than me. I had grown a bit since I was on the hockey team, and he was a lot smaller than I was, so I blamed my height for why he beat me.

"You're just the right size for gymnastics," I said to him. "Me, I'm too tall now."

"There's no such thing as being the right size," he replied. "You are not doing your preparation properly."

"What do you mean?" I asked. "I do all the same physical training as you."

"It's not your body that is holding you back, it's your mind."

"My mind? How can my mind hold my body back?"

"You can't see yourself winning," he said. "If you can picture what you want to achieve, you can go ahead and do it."

What he said made a lot of sense to me, so I decided to take his advice. The next time I competed in a gymnastics meet, I sat down before my turn came up. I relaxed my body and thought about my upcoming routine.

I created a vision of myself doing the flips and cartwheels, jumping over the pommel boxes, doing a somersault, and landing on the floor mat. I saw these images over and over until they took hold. Then I went out and did the routine exactly as I saw it in my head. My friend was right — I had to see what success looked like before I could go out and achieve it. It was a very important lesson for me. I kept it up as I participated in more tournaments, and soon I was coming back with medals and ribbons.

My gymnastic experience was very important to me. It taught me about self-confidence and control, about setting goals and how to achieve them, and about working towards success. It was not long before I realized that this idea applied to everything in life, not just athletics. If I wanted to achieve something, to reach a goal, I needed to be determined to do it. I needed to concentrate on it until I could visualize all the steps needed to make it happen. Later in my life, I found out it is the same thing with business. When I wanted to reach a business goal, I focused in on it. I planned it out in my mind until I saw myself being successful. Then I would go out and get it done. The sooner I did it, the better. I did not slack off or waste time. I focused my mind and left the bystanders and naysayers behind.

Because I was also learning that if I slacked off or was not paying attention, a new obstacle would be put in my way. Then someone else would get the gravy, and I would be left with the crumbs.

CHAPTER 13

Living Ghosts

I wish I could tell you that my athletic successes were the turning point in my life and that everything got easier from there on. But athletics taught me another hard lesson. No matter how many medals I brought back, nothing changed for me. No matter how physically strong I was, no matter how successful I was, I was still at the mercy of the people who ran that school. They could find all the busses and drivers they needed to drive hundreds of miles to a tournament where I could make the school look good by winning ribbons. But they couldn't find a bus to take me and my siblings home to our family at Christmas. All the cruelty and violence was still there. Even star athletes were not safe from it.

I still remember the day I learned that lesson. Our regular gymnastics instructor was away, so we had a substitute. I can't remember if he was punishing me for some infraction or just being cruel for no reason. Probably both. Whatever the reason, the substitute instructor threw me down on the hard gym floor and dragged one of the thick, heavy gym mats we used for tumbling and flung it on top of me. Then he ordered the rest of the boys to jump on top of the mat. They all piled on, and they were heavy — hundreds of pounds. The weight was too much for me, and I was pressed hard to the floor, unable to move. I struggled to draw my breath, but there was too much weight on my chest and no air under the mat. I could not make a sound, could not yell for help. It went on and on until I thought I was going to suffocate. I thought I was going to die there in darkness on that cold gym floor. I don't know how long it was, but I was on the verge of passing out from lack of oxygen.

Then I felt the boys getting off the mat. I heard the instructor walk over and peel the mat off me. I could not get up because there was no air left in me. I lay there dazed and gasping for breath like a fish reeled into a boat. Finally, the instructor picked me up and set me on my feet. When I finally caught my breath, I sat down on a bench. I do not know how long I sat there alone. No one came and asked me if I was all right, not even the other boys, who were too scared of the instructor.

While those types of assaults happened all the time, I remember that one in particular because everything about residential school felt like that. All those years I was trapped there, I felt like I was suffocating under a heavy weight. I felt pinned down, powerless, unable to cry for help. I felt like I would never breathe freely again. Random violence. Cruel tricks. Never knowing where a punch or kick would come from. We could be hurt at any time. We could die at any time. There was no one there to stop it.

Yet I still feel lucky that it wasn't worse.

The whole time I was there, I knew there were special boys who had to be left alone. None of the nuns slapped them or beat them with wooden rulers. None of the supervisors punched them in the face or the kidneys or the gut. None of us kids were allowed to roughhouse with them — no pushing or scuffling, no games at all. Nobody was allowed to touch them or even go near them. Sometimes they got extra food. Sometimes they got called away from whatever was happening in the timetable. Sometimes they got woken up in the middle of the night.

Those were the priests' "special boys," and none of us envied their special treatment. We felt terrible for those boys. If adults could punch you in the face right in front of everyone, what terrible, unspeakable things did they do in private? We knew those boys faced incredible pain and suffering that most of us could not even imagine.

We were also a little afraid of the special boys because their great suffering changed them into something else. They were more like ghosts than boys. They were there but not there. They were pale all the time, and their skin looked cold and clammy. Sometimes they threw up. They were always tired. They wet the bed. They had terrible nightmares and called out in the night for their mothers. They cried in their sleep, and sometimes while they were awake. They were always staring into the distance and seeing things the rest of us did not. Physically, it was like they were in a constant state of shock. Spiritually, it was like someone had reached inside them and pulled out their spirit. All that was left was their physical shell, which still had to walk around the school like it was alive.

Sometimes, one of these special boys would disappear, and we would ask where he was.

"Don't ask," we were always told. "It's not your business."

There was one night when I thought I was going to become one of those special boys. I was sound asleep in bed number 53 when I was startled awake by someone grabbing me. Before I could sit up, my arms and legs were pinned down. Someone put a blindfold over my eyes and tied it around the back of my head. I was in total darkness, but my other senses opened up fast to compensate for the fact I could not see. I heard them breathing and could tell right away that there was more than one person by my bedside. None of them were talking, not one single word, but I knew there were at least five different men — four of them holding down an arm or a leg, and another one at my head. They picked me up out of my bed and I could sense that they were taking me towards the door. I struggled the whole time they carried me down the stairs and into a hallway, where I heard the door to the recreation room open. I thought they were going to take me through the room and into the kitchen, but they stopped halfway across. Then they turned me upside down, my legs up in the air and my head down towards the floor, and lowered me headfirst into freezing cold water.

I did not get a chance to take a breath before my head went under, so I swallowed water as I tried to take in air. I started thrashing and kicking for my life. I thought they were drowning me, that they were going to murder me. They could do it; there was no one to stop them. I kept kicking and fighting, but there were too many of them. I could not break free. They kept dunking me, lifting me out for a few seconds, and then plunging me back in. I could never catch my breath before I went down again.

Just when I thought it was the end, that I was going to die, they let go of my arms and legs, and I dropped hard to the floor. I lifted my head and the first thing I did was grab that blindfold and pull it off. I looked up to see I was surrounded by grown men, priests and supervisors. They were standing around a metal tub full of water and chunks of ice. They were laughing and clapping their hands while I stood there shivering and crying from the cold and the shock.

"You are moving dorms tomorrow," one of them said. "You're going to join the older boys."

I found out later that this was what they called an "initiation" and they did it every time they moved a boy to a new dormitory. I was getting older, so they were transferring me to a different room with different boys. They took me hostage in the middle of the night and tortured me because it was time to sleep in a new bed.

"Go to bed" was the only thing they said to me as I slowly walked out, still crying.

Yeah. Go to bed. I did not sleep for three nights after that. I lay in my new bed and waited for them to come back. I was wide awake and peering into the dark, listening for any sound of them coming for me. Their cruelty haunts me to this day. I still cannot sleep in the dark. I have to have a light on every night when I go to bed because of what they did to me.

I don't know how I escaped becoming one of the special boys. It might have been because I was a little bigger and harder to subdue. Or because I could speak English and could have told someone. But who knows what motivates an evil monster to choose his victim? They had hundreds of boys to choose from. They could take anyone they wanted at any time. If a priest had decided to sexually assault me, no one would have stopped it. I still pray in gratitude that I was not victimized in that way.

These days you hear about the Truth and Reconciliation Commission that the Canadian government set up to find out what happened in its residential schools. The commission went across the country gathering stories, witness testimony they called it, about things that happened to the boys and girls who were scooped from their families and locked away in those schools. All of those stories are now filed away in Ottawa in the federal government's archives. There are thousands of files and millions of words, and every word is true.

I saw it all. I am telling you: Every word is true.

CHAPTER 14

The Little People

O ne day when I was thirteen years old, I was told to pack up my things and head down to the main entrance of the building. There was no explanation, but they did not have to tell me twice. I quickly gathered the few possessions I had, mostly my sports ribbons and medals, and headed to the front door. I was so happy when I saw that David and my sisters were there waiting for me. We had been kept apart for four years, and all of sudden they brought us together. We were still inside the building, so we did not dare hug one another, jump up and down in joy, or say anything in Cree. But the four of us were very excited. We thought we were going home.

They put us all in a van, and for the first time since we arrived at that nightmare of a place, we were sharing the same space. It was wonderful to be near them again. We sat together and talked, and we could even hug one another and hold hands. We could show our affection because, once again, the driver paid us no attention. He might as well have been driving an empty van bumping along the road that led north.

David sat by me the whole way. He was nine years old and had grown in the four years we had been there, but I was thirteen and still his big brother. We talked about how happy our parents would be to see us, how we would sit down together at our kitchen table and eat our mother's delicious food until we were ready to burst. That night we would sleep in our own beds, and then in the morning we would wear nice soft clothes that our mother picked out for us. *We're free*, I thought to myself. *It is finally over.*

It is hard to describe the sick feeling in the pit of my stomach when we turned off the main road. I knew it was far too early, and that we were nowhere near home. There were no signs of the boreal forest's trees, plants, or birds, and no landmarks that told me we were home. They had not given us anything for a long trip, no food or water, but I thought nothing of that because they had not given us anything on the morning they took us away from our home either. Soon we were pulling into the driveway of a huge, brick, multi-storey building. I could feel its powerful negative energy sweep over me as we pulled up in front of the unwelcoming concrete steps leading to the front doors. The driver opened the door, and this time we did not have to be told to get off. We gathered up the little bundles that held our few possessions and, heartbroken, we stepped out of the van.

Our nightmare was not over — they were just moving us to another school, Blue Quills at the Saddle Lake Reserve near St. Paul, Alberta. They moved us around for their own reasons, on their own timetable, and they did not need to tell us why. This time we did not ask any questions because we knew there were no answers. As soon as we walked through the doors, they split us up. My sisters were taken in one direction, and David and I went to the other side, where they wasted no time taking David away from me. The only difference this time was that none of us said anything. We knew the consequences of asking questions.

Nothing was different in the new school. The food was awful, the nuns were mean, and the priests were cruel and dangerous. Everything was done by timetable and the number they assigned us. I missed the friends I made at our first school, especially the other athletes. I was alone and starting all over. But now I knew what I needed to do to survive. Be quiet. Be on time. Tell them nothing. The days dragged on, and I sometimes caught glimpses of my siblings in the dining room. I played sports as much as I could. I prayed to Creator silently when I lay in my bed in the dark at night.

I was fourteen years old when I finally got to go home for a visit. Somebody somewhere decided I was old enough to take the train alone, and one morning I was told to pack up a few things because I was going back to my parents for the summer break. I was worried they would change their minds, so I wasted no time getting ready. Before the day was out I was on the train alone, heading north to my home.

I was so excited. I could not believe I was actually on a train and going to see my parents. But I was also trying to manage my expectations. I was told before I left that I had to come back to the school in September because I could not officially "graduate" until I was eighteen years old. If I did not return, the Royal Canadian Mounted Police would come get me. That would be very bad for my parents, who would be charged with a crime and could end up in jail. I knew it would be very bad for me, too — I would be brutally punished when they captured me and returned me to the school. I would also never be allowed to go home again. I was also worried that, when my siblings were old enough to go home for summer break, they might not be allowed because our family could not be trusted to return them. Right from the start, I knew it was a round trip and I had to go back in the fall.

The government had an easy time tracking me while I was home. In every Indigenous community there was someone called an Indian Agent. The Indian Agent was a white man who worked for the government. He had absolute power over every Indigenous person on the reserve. He implemented all of the government's policies and controlled the purse strings for our community and our day-to-day lives. If I tried to stay with my parents, he would tell the government, the school, and the police. He would know right away if I did not go back when I was supposed to, because he was also in charge of the train tickets. At that time, Indigenous people were not allowed to ride the train without the Indian Agent's permission. We had to get a special ticket and could not board a train without it. He would be tracking me to make sure I had my ticket and was on the train back to residential school.

Even though the Indian Agent knew everything that happened in our community, he did not bother to tell my parents I was coming home. When I stepped off the train there was no one to meet me. It was a strange feeling as I walked alone to the home I had not seen for years. Everything was so familiar and yet so intense. As I walked past the plants and trees I knew so well, their shades of green and brown seemed more vibrant. So did the cool, fresh air tickling my face, the soft sound of my footsteps on the dirt road, the gurgling croak of the ravens passing their messages to one another, the distant buzz from the sawmill where my uncles worked. It was real but it felt like a dream. It was hard for my brain to adjust to the fact that just a few hours before, I was in an institution making my assigned bed and eating in silence in my assigned seat. Suddenly, after years of hoping and praying, I was now walking up to my family home.

I automatically headed for the back door, which everyone in the family used. We never went in by the front door, we always stepped directly into the kitchen where my mum spent so much of her day. I opened the door without knocking, like I always had, and found myself stopping as I passed over the threshold. It was such a big, important thing to do, to walk back into our home. I was suddenly overwhelmed to see my mother. She looked a little older and sadder, but otherwise she was just as I had pictured her so many times, sitting at the kitchen table, her hands busy preparing food for our family. She looked up at the sound of someone walking in and saw me standing there for the first time in years.

"My dear boy," she said in Cree.

I knew it was the day she had been praying for ever since we were scooped out of her arms. I knew she would never stop thinking about us, never stop hoping we would come home to her. She would have waited forever. But, after all those years of waiting and hoping, the government could not bother to tell her she was going to see one of her sons. When I walked through the door she had a big shock. For a moment she just looked at me, as if she wasn't sure I was really there. But then she jumped to her feet, and the emotion I felt coming from her was pure joy.

Now I can imagine some of the things that must have been going through her mind. I had grown so tall since she last saw me, when she had stood in the middle of the road crying and waving goodbye as the bus taking us away disappeared in the distance. The last time she saw me I was a cheerful nine-year-old boy who ran into her kitchen bubbling over with questions about the physical and spiritual worlds. Now I was lean and muscled from all the sports I was playing. I looked more like a man than a boy. I also stood on the threshold of my home in silence, the way the school had trained me to do. The change in me must have been a horrible reminder of everything she missed during those important years as I started to grow into a man. But all she showed me was love and joy.

"Come in, come in!" she said in Cree as I stood there in the doorway. She ran over and wrapped her arms around me, and it felt wonderful. It was exactly how I remembered her hugs, but even more intense and lasting much longer. I thought she was going to hang on to me forever, but finally she led me over to the table and sat me down in one of the chairs. She had tears in her eyes as she kept looking at me. Over and over she touched my arm, my face, my leg, as if making sure I was really there.

"You are too thin," she said.

"I have been playing a lot of sports to keep myself in shape," I answered in Cree.

She shook her head. "Too thin," she said again.

She was right. I was too thin. All the kids at the school were thin. But I didn't want to tell her why. I didn't want her to know how horrible the food was or that it was used as a way to control us. I had to go back, and I didn't want her to worry.

"You are going to eat something good today," she said.

"I can't wait," I replied.

Right away, she got busy at the stove cooking me up something to eat. It was part of her instinct as a mother to feed me, but it is also my people's tradition to welcome someone with food. I sat down at the kitchen table and watched her familiar movements as she boiled the kettle for tea and put her cast-iron frying pan on the heat. I breathed in the wonderful smell of her cooking. I felt like I was dreaming, and for the first time in years, it was not a nightmare.

It wasn't long before she carefully put a big plate piled high with food in front of me and sat down to watch me eat it. I ate it so fast the food seemed to disappear into the air. Right away she went back to the stove and fixed me another plate, and I finished that in record time, too.

While I ate, we talked to each other in Cree. I had eaten horrible gruel in silence for so long, I had forgotten how good it felt to enjoy delicious food cooked with love while freely speaking my language. It felt liberating to speak Cree out loud in full sentences, not the whispered words my friends and I exchanged when we hoped no one was looking.

But I also found myself holding back when she asked how my education was going. Though I had pictured myself coming home many times and always imagined joking and laughing with my family, I had never thought about what I was actually going say to them. My father had been to residential school, but he never spoke a word about it to my mother or any of us children. He worked hard to put that part of his life behind him and be a good husband and father. But my mother had never been to residential school, so she did not have a picture of it in her head. When she asked me questions about the school and what I was learning, I realized I could not bring myself to tell her what it was really like. For one thing, my three siblings were trapped there and going through that brutal reality every day. If I told my mother everything, it would make her burden even heavier.

I never lied to her because I could not imagine telling her anything that wasn't true. Instead, I talked about my sports achievements and tried to make it sound like I was learning a lot of useful and important things. I told her that at Blue Quills I looked for opportunities to challenge myself, to keep working on my self-discipline. I told her about gymnastics and my prizes, and also that I was now taking swimming lessons. I described my lessons, which were very big on water safety and had a series of levels that you had to pass. They never took us out to a river or lake; we did them all in a swimming pool. I advanced through the program, attaining one level after another. How to prevent accidents. How to save yourself. How to save other people. I passed it all, got all the certificates. I was proud of what I'd accomplished and told Mum all about it. She listened to all my stories but did not say much. Then she got up and carefully took down a picture she had tacked up on the wall.

"My boy, I received this in the mail," she said. "Is it yours?"

"Yes, I painted that," I said.

"I thought it was you, but I was not sure. There was no letter with it."

"It was me, Mum."

"You did a good job."

"How long ago did you get that?"

"It was a few years ago," she said.

A few years earlier I was in an art class where we drew and painted, making little pictures they sometimes let us send back to our parents. We were allowed to write home, and I had written some letters but never got an answer back. My mother's words confirmed what I'd always suspected, that they were never mailed. The nuns made us write in English — which my mum could not read — so that they could review every letter before they mailed it. They did not want us to say anything about wishing we were home, let alone the real horrors that happened every day. I had always thought they put all my letters right into the garbage can. Sure enough, my mother had only received that one thing from me in the mail over the years.

My picture had nothing to do with residential school, so it was safe for them to send. It was a painting of two collie dogs. I worked hard to get their ears right, really concentrating because I wanted to make something good for Mum. It turned out quite nice. Then the nuns mailed it off to her without a note saying which of her children painted it. She treasured it, putting it up on the wall in her kitchen where she could see it every day. Imagine how many times over the years she looked at that painting, the only message from her beloved son.

The whole time I was home, Mum did not want to let me out of her sight. She wanted me beside her all the time. But I was young and after a while I wanted to see people my age. I started spending time with my older siblings, my cousins, and my old friends. We hung out, doing the usual things kids did in those days before the internet, cellphones, and cable television. We spent most of our time outdoors, looking for things to do. My mother always asked where we were going and what we were doing. I was always honest with her, but I was no longer the talkative boy she had known. My answers were short and lacking detail. There was a wall between us — she kept showing me her concern, and I pretended I was fine.

I am sure my saying so little worried her terribly. All during my childhood I was *Napikan*, the curious boy who pestered her non-stop with questions. She would answer me patiently, even though she was busy all the time. She never stopped what she was doing, whether it was peeling potatoes or frying bannock or making oatmeal, because she had a lot of mouths to feed. While she worked she told me beautiful stories that included a traditional teaching, something important I needed to know. While I sat in her little kitchen, she told stories about the ancestors and about herself when she was a little girl. One of my favourites was about the Little People, and I asked her to tell it over and over.

My mum told me that when she was a small girl, she would go down to the river and play with the *mekwenescuk*, the Little People, who lived near the banks of the Clearwater River. When she got to the riverbank, she would hear giggles and whispers if she paid close attention. Then the *mekwenescuk* would come out from their secret home under the water and ask her in Cree if she would like to play. Mum was not afraid of them because they were even smaller than she was, just about two feet tall, with tiny arms and legs and hands and feet. She could see them, but she could not touch them because they were spiritual beings. She never saw their homes or where exactly they came from, but when they appeared she would play with them along the riverbank until it was time for her to go home.

My mum liked playing with the Little People. They were happy because Creator gave them everything they needed and they could live the same life in their secret underwater home that they had for thousands of years. The *mekwenescuk* did not appear every time she went to the river. Sometimes they would come out, sometimes not. But she knew they were always there. They showed up when they wanted to play with her. They did not appear for just anyone, and if someone else happened to come by, the *mekwenescuk* would disappear again under the water.

She had been told by her parents and the Elders to watch out for the *mekwenescuk*. They were tricksters who would try to get her to follow them and take her where she would not want to go. The Little People did not want her to go home. They wanted her to stay with them and go to the spiritual world. Sure enough, sometimes the *mekwenescuk* would ask her to go underwater to try to find something for them, but she knew it was a trick. She took care to stay on the riverbank when she played with them.

She also made sure to watch where she was going so that she did not fall into the water, where they could take her.

My mum knew she was not meant to be with the *mekwenescuk* in the spiritual world. She belonged in the physical world, on the traditional land of her people. But even as a little girl, my mother knew she was supposed to respect the *mekwenescuk*, because Creator made them, too. It was an honour they chose her to play with them, and she had the wisdom of the ancestors to keep her safe.

But despite these pleasant memories, things still weren't the same. Even back in my old bed and surrounded by my family, I did not sleep soundly at night. I could not sleep at all without a light on. I know my mother noticed the changes — my insomnia, my periods of silence, my evading her questions. I'm sure she saw other signs, too. But I continued to tell my stories of sports triumphs and lifeguarding classes, and closed the door on her questions.

One day I was hanging out with one of my sisters and some of our cousins when we decided to go down to the river. I was telling them about my swimming lessons and the fancy pool with chlorine that kept the water clean and clear. It was nothing like a river, I told them. You could open your eyes underwater and see everything. You also had to wear a bathing suit, not an old pair of shorts, and there were all kinds of rules about how to behave for safety. It sounded exciting to them because I told it the way someone would describe a resort vacation. They thought it sounded wonderful to swim laps in a bright, clean pool compared to dog-paddling in a river full of fish, logs, and debris.

I didn't want them to know how I suffered in that school. I wanted to act like I was an ordinary teenager, not a prisoner of a racist government. I wanted to hang out and get up to mild mischief, which on that day meant going down to the river to skip rocks. We made a game of how many times a stone could bounce before it sank. The flatter the stone, the better it skips. Searching for the right stone, I climbed a ledge above the riverbank and had a good view of everyone below. I saw my sister bend down to pick up a rock and slip off the mossy green edge of the riverbank, fall in, and quickly disappear under the water.

I ran down to the riverbank and dove in, clothes and all. I swam to where I had last seen her. I dove into the water, and right away I saw her. I caught hold of her arm and pulled her back up. She was panicking and struggled with me, pulling me down. At first I thought everything was okay, because my training allowed me to stay under water without air for quite a long time. I was able to drag her back up to the surface, where I took a breath. I thought she would take a breath, too, and then we would head for the shore. The river's current had moved us out a little farther, but I thought I could make it. But she kept panicking and was fighting me. We went down again, and this time she held me down, keeping us both under the water. That was when the real struggle started. I was able to grab her wrists and get her to the surface. Then I pushed her as far as I could towards the shore. My cousins were making a human chain by linking their arms together and waded out far enough to catch hold of her and pull her out.

I was weakened from struggling with her, and I sank back down under the water. This time I kept sinking. The river was so much murkier than the pool where I practised that I felt disoriented. I looked up and saw the sunlight on the water's surface, but it seemed very far away. I knew which direction was up, but I felt so weak that I worried I would not make it all the way. I made a huge effort to get to the surface. As I came up I took a short breath, but right away I went under again.

The river was deep, and I kept sinking. I did not think I would ever reach the bottom. When I finally felt my feet touch something solid, I looked up and saw the sunlight was a lot farther away. I gathered all my strength and used my legs to push off the bottom to go as high as I could. I could not get my head above water, but I managed to get my arm up just enough so that somebody grabbed my wrist. I thought at first it was my sister and I got ready to fight her before she pulled me down. But it was my cousin, and he pulled me up so that the human chain they had made could bring me to the shore.

They dragged me to the riverbank, where I collapsed. I felt sick, and all the water I swallowed came back up. It took quite a while to get rid of it all. Finally, I came back to myself and sat there shaking and trying to recover. It was quite a while before I could stand and walk. I was shivering and soaking wet as I made my way home, where I found my mum standing by the door.

"Mum," I said. I stood there shakily, my wet clothes dripping on her clean floor.

"Yes, my boy?"

"I just about drowned."

"How many times do I have to tell you to be careful around the river?" she said. "How many times did I tell you about the *mekwenescuk*? Why don't you listen to me? How can I help you if you won't listen?"

She spoke very gently, but sadly. I felt a terrible shock as she said those words. She had talked to me about the river since I was a little boy. My whole life she had told me to be careful by the water, that it was dangerous. Over and over, she told the story of the *mekwenescuk*. I loved listening to her stories, but I did not remember them when I went down to the river that day. I had filled my mind with swimming pools and safety courses and forgotten the teachings of my own mother. That put my sister at risk, too, and my mum had always counted on me to look after my siblings. I should have reminded my sister to be careful, to stay away from the edge. I should have kept a closer eye on her and made sure she stayed safe. Instead, I focused on the wrong thing, on school lessons about daring rescues, when I should have been concentrating on being safe in the way my mother taught me.

Right then and there, I made up my mind that I would always listen to her. If she wanted something done, I would do it. If she told me not to go somewhere or not do something, I would not do it. When she shared her traditional teachings, I would follow them to the letter. Because it came really close. That school was working — it was taking me away from the things my mother had told me, all the lessons she taught me. Forgetting her teachings had almost got me killed, and my sister, too.

CHAPTER 15

Seventy-Three Ways
to Use a Moose

After my mum guided me back to the traditional teachings, something wonderful happened. My older brother August offered to take me on my first moose hunt. I had been learning about moose since I was a small boy. Now that I was fourteen years old, it was time for me to put what I'd learned into practice.

The biggest rite of passage for an Indigenous boy is his first moose hunt. It took years to gain the knowledge I needed for that day, but it did not come in a classroom or at an appointed time. It came from my father, uncles, and older brothers, who had the deep knowledge of hunters feeding their families. It came from the Elders, who passed on the ancestors' wisdom that the moose was one of the greatest gifts from Creator.

My learning began when I was five years old. My *Mooshum* began taking me into the *sakahk*, the bush. He taught me to make a snare to catch small game for the family stewpot. In the spring, we walked to the lake to collect wild duck eggs, gently placing them in tin pails that held lard from the store in town. We took what we needed and left the rest to hatch. At home, he showed me how to skin the game, prepare the meat, and store the eggs. After our work was done, *Mooshum* asked me to take the lard pail and fetch water from the *maskek*, the muskeg, flat wetland covered with a spongy layer of moss and grasses. My mum boiled the water and steeped the tea. *Mooshum* would take the warm mug in his hand, close his eyes, take a slow sip, and smile. I thought it must be the most delicious tea in the world. Then *Mooshum* would tell a story about the ancestors or Creator. I would hang on every word.

My father and uncles told stories, too, when they came home in their laden canoes after days away hunting *moswa*, the moose. They sat down at the kitchen table for a bowl of the stew always simmering on my mother's wood stove. Like *Mooshum*, they spoke in Cree as they described in detail what they saw, heard, and felt. How they paddled the fast, deep river. How they set up their hunting camp on the shore. The bird calls they heard from *kakao*, the raven, and *wiskachans*, the little grey songbirds the English named whisky jacks. They talked about all the animal tracks from *moswa* but also *meschakanis*, the coyote, and *mahkesis*, the fox. They talked about the spiritual aspects, too. As soon as they took the *moswa*, the hunters stopped to thank Creator. Only after they'd finished their prayer did they begin to field-dress the animal. Then they carefully loaded everything into the canoe to bring home.

The meat was shared with the community, and the best parts — tongue, heart, liver, and kidneys — were saved for the Elders. Even before the Elders ate, my father carved small slices to cook over the sacred fire he specially prepared. The slices were consumed by the sacred flames, their essence rising with the smoke as an offering to the ancestors. Then the men sang an honour song, playing drums covered with moosehide from previous hunts. The tribute honoured the spirits of the ancestors and showed that their teachings were remembered.

Now, despite everything residential school had done to me, I was getting the chance to put my traditional learning into action. Back then our community had a rule that no one under the age of fourteen was allowed to touch a firearm. We were taught from a very young age that firearms are dangerous when not properly handled. We had to respect them and be responsible around them. Even at fourteen I could only hunt with someone experienced like my brother. I was not allowed to go alone.

August took his responsibility seriously, and before we set foot in the bush, he reviewed firearm safety with me. He warned me about the bad things that can happen when people are careless.

"Never carry your gun on your shoulder," August said. "If someone is carrying their gun that way and they fall, the gun can fire and hit somebody."

"Why would people carry their gun like that?" I asked.

"I don't know. It's a bad idea," August said. "We don't do that. We always carry a firearm on the side."

There were other rules my brother reviewed, mostly about safeguarding the people with you. "Always think about other people," August said. It was the same message I had received from my father and uncles over the years. It was a good message. I have been hunting for more than half a century and have never had an accident.

That first time I went hunting, I really wanted to get a moose. It is a rite of passage because it marks the day you start providing for your family and your community. I felt on the cusp of something big, but I was also enjoying the day. I was happy to be walking deep in the bush with my older brother. The tall trees kept us shaded and cool. The light breeze on my face brought the still-familiar scent of plants and wildflowers. We travelled downwind so that we would not be detected by any moose, who have great big noses they use to continually scent for danger. August and I walked in silence, and we heard the croak of ravens, the call of magpies, and the whistle of white-throated sparrows. I kept my eyes peeled for any sign of movement amid the earthy browns and restful greens that make up the bush, because motion might mean a moose.

I was trying not to let my mind wander, to stay alert and focused on the job we were there to do. I was rewarded when I saw gentle movement on the left-hand side of the trail. I stopped right away, turning to peer into the trees where I had noticed it. I heard the sound of something big moving around, and then it came into clear view.

"There's a moose over there," I said.

My brother shushed me fast and made a gesture that meant it was my moose because I saw it first. I raised my weapon, but in my excitement I moved too fast, and the moose noticed me. It was getting ready to run, so

I cocked the trigger, aimed, and fired. For a second, time seemed to stand still, with the crack of the gunshot echoing eerily through the forest, the sharp smell of gunpowder drifting around me. I was almost surprised when the moose fell down with an enormous crash, crushing saplings and undergrowth as it hit the ground.

"I got him!" I yelled to August.

"You think you got him," my brother said. "Now make sure you did."

"I got him," I insisted.

"You don't want him to come to himself and jump up," August said. "He will suffer if he runs away injured. You have to go over there and make sure."

I remembered the lessons about carrying firearms, so I moved carefully and safely. As I got closer, I knew my brother was right because I could hear the moose starting to thrash about. I had taken it down, but it was still alive and trying to struggle to its feet. I got close enough to the animal that I could not miss and carefully lined up my second shot. I fired and another shot echoed through the bush. That was it. I had my first moose.

The first thing my brother and I did was show our gratitude, the way our father taught us. We said a prayer in Cree to Creator in gratitude for the gift of the moose. We also thanked the moose for giving itself to us. August had brought tobacco to use for this, and we buried it in the ground by the moose. I gave extra thanks for receiving the gift of a moose on my very first outing, especially because in a few weeks I would be going back to residential school. I would take this experience back with me and it would give me power to sustain myself when I lay in bed at night and thought about the sacred teachings.

As soon as we finished praying, we started skinning. August was already experienced at field dressing, and he watched over me. He gave me tips about how to hold the sharp knife and quarter the cuts so that they were small enough to fit our packs. We had to pack everything back through the bush because it was late summer, so we could not use a sled. There were no such things as all-terrain vehicles then. It took about two hours to finish up, and then we started our hike back home. Even though we lugged heavy packs, I felt light on our walk to our community. I felt part of Creator's plan again.

When we got back, there was a big fuss over us. The meat was shared with everyone, and the Elders got the choicest cuts. Everybody was happy. I was ecstatic. It was my first moose and my whole community was sharing it. It was one of the best days I ever had. It unfolded just the way I had pictured it when I was *Napikan* and first learned that my people had seventy-three ways to use a moose.

I heard that number a lot while I was growing up, from my *Mooshum*, my parents, my uncles and aunties, the Elders, and people in the community. Everyone said we knew how to use every part of the moose. We never threw anything away because it was a gift from Creator and we had to honour every part of it. It was also because for centuries we needed to use everything to survive in the northern climate.

Let me give you some examples of the many ways we use the moose. We scrape the marrow out of the bone as a delicacy that helps our older people stay in good health, keeping their bones strong and minds sharp. We thoroughly clean out the smaller part of the intestine so that we can stuff it with meat and other spices and dry it into a very tasty sausage. These days our people generally store moose meat in modern freezers, but we have a traditional way to make it into *pemikan*, which lasts for months if you make it properly. We render the fat (we call it *pemi*) from the meat to make grease. Then we mix the grease with meat we have dried and pounded down into a sort of powder.

There are big cuts of meat on a moose, which the Elders sometimes call the fixings. There are many different textures and tastes because it is an active animal. Its meat is strong and muscled and can be tough in some parts of its body. The softest, tenderest meat is along the backbone, so if you want to try moose meat for the first time, you should go for that. My people use the harder muscled part for stew meat, and we also use the ribs.

Not all the uses given to us are for food. We know how to take the moose's stomach to make a nice bag for hauling water or storing berries. We clean it out and put grass inside it to keep it stretched out. Then we tie up one end and hang it to dry. After it dries, we clean out the grass and there is a nice receptacle waiting to be used.

We also use the hooves to make a nice basket for storing or carrying things. We remove the four legs near the knee joint. Then we take the four pieces with hooves on and sew them together. The hooves make a solid bottom to rest on the ground.

We take other bones from the moose's leg and lash them together with pieces of its sinew to make a scraper. We use that to remove flesh from the inside of the hide. We need a strong scraper because moose are so big, it takes at least a full day to flesh one hide.

Bones can also be used to make knives, or a clip to hold shut the flaps of tipis. Some can be used for sewing needles. It takes hours of work to make tools out of moose bone, but they are solid. I still have bone needles made decades ago. We thread the needle with the moose's sinew to sew clothing out of the hide. We make pants, vests, and tunics. We make winter mitts, boots, and hats, all of which we trim with the fur of different animals. Moose mittens with fox fur are very warm.

We also use the hide and sinew to make two kinds of drums. The first are the small drums we use for our Round Dances, which are for community celebrations. In the old days we had a Round Dance to celebrate things like the return of a hunting party. When the hunters brought back their harvest, there would be a community feast that lasted an entire night. Everyone danced in a circle to celebrate their safe return and to thank Creator for the bounty. The small drums, we call them hand drums, bring people together in the dance. We still have Round Dances for important community events, and hand drums are an important part of that.

We also make large drums for Powwow dances, which need several drummers to gather around and play together in unison. These are very powerful drums for sacred dances that tell stories of our spirituality and our culture. Powwows last for days and have many dancers who tell different stories. There are many types of dances and traditional clothing worn for each one. In English we call our Powwow clothing "regalia." Each dancer has their own regalia, which represents both the individual and our culture. Regalia is considered sacred to the dancer and takes a lot of work to create. Today's regalia is made from the hides of moose or deer and adorned with beads and eagle feathers. It is just beautiful. Moosehide is also used for the moccasins that all the Powwow dancers wear, as well as moccasins for daily use.

To properly harvest a moose, my people respectfully follow every step. The hard physical labour of hunting and butchering. The commitment to using every piece and taking only what is needed. The show of respect to the Elders and ancestors for passing down wisdom. The expression of gratitude to Creator for the gift of the animal. It is all connected, all part of the right way to do things. The gifts of Creator and the teachings of the ancestors cannot be neglected. If they are, the world becomes unbalanced, and the spirits send warning signs — just like they sent me at the river when I was ignoring my mother's teachings.

When I was a boy of fourteen learning to hunt, learning to share with my community and honour the spirits, I never thought that a dozen years later my community would elect me Chief. I did not know I would be making choices for my community about how to balance traditional things like moose hunting with things like the multinational oil industry coming to our land. But by the time I was Chief — just twenty-seven years old, one of the youngest Chiefs in Canada — I had seen first-hand the way that the dominant culture looked at a moose. And they did not have seventy-three uses for it, the way my people did. But that was years in the future. When summer ended, I was back on the train to residential school.

CHAPTER 16

I'm Good Here

Nothing had changed when I returned to residential school in the fall. It was just as brutal and cruel as ever. But I was getting older and I saw other boys turn eighteen years old and age out of the institution. After their birthday they were given a set of clothes and sent off on their own, like convicts who had finished their prison sentences. I knew residential school had to release me, too, when I turned eighteen.

I just had to make it through four more years of merciless, timetabled days until then. I continued to focus on athletics, self-discipline, and secretly nurturing my traditional knowledge. I kept quiet and tried to avoid anything that brought negative attention. But as I got older things were changing for me in the eyes of the people who ran the residential school.

Partly due to my mother's good food over the summer, I had shot up in height. I was almost six feet tall, lean, and muscled from my athletic pursuits. I don't know if my size discouraged anyone in power at residential school from attacking me. As I learned on the night of my "initiation" into the older boys' dorm, they could easily get together a large group if they wanted to overpower me. But my growth spurt caught the eye of someone in authority at Blue Quills. When I turned fifteen, they decided to move me out of the main building and keep me a few miles away in a nearby foster home they operated like a boarding house.

I lived there with other Indigenous boys around my age, mostly from the Saddle Lake community. They called us day students. On weekdays they bussed us to the residential school building. Most of the day students came from local families and were allowed to go home on weekends because we were in farm country, and they were needed to help with chores. It was a lucky day for me when one of them invited me to go home with him for the weekend. I was allowed to go because I would be helping on the farm and it sounded like I would be working hard and not having fun.

I still thank Creator for that invitation, because soon I was able to join other boys going home to help on their family farms. I still had to follow all the rules, of course. It was like being a convict on day parole in that I had to tell them exactly where I was going and be back at an appointed time to check in. If I did not do that, or if I was late, I would lose my privileges and not be allowed to leave the next time. I was also worried that if I violated their rules, it would blow back on my friends and get them in trouble for inviting me.

I am sure the nuns thought it was good for me to be doing hard labour that "built my character." But I never told them how much I loved the work. If they knew I enjoyed it, they would have found something more "character-building" for me to do. Whatever that was, I was guaranteed not to like it. When the nuns questioned me about what I did on the weekends, I never smiled and just gave yes or no answers, so they could not tell how much I enjoyed it. It didn't feel like work at all. It felt like freedom. I happily helped bale hay, cut wood, mend fences, whatever they needed me to do.

Those weekends were wonderful. One family had some very nice horses, and when the work was finished, my friend and I would ride for fun. Sometimes we raced each other, and sometimes we just loafed along and enjoyed the day. There was one little mare I especially liked and I always got to ride her. Some weekends I would be on horseback most of the day, helping to check fences to make sure there were no gaps that the cattle could escape through. If they did get out, it was our job to round them up and get them back into the field. My little mare was well trained at this. Sometimes a cow would start to stray from the herd, and she would see it before I did and jump after it. A few times I was relaxed and daydreaming when that happened. The mare went one way, I went the other, and I tumbled to the ground. One time I hurt my wrist, but I didn't tell anyone at the school about it. I didn't want to say anything that could risk my weekends away. It only took a few days before everything was healed up, and by the following weekend I was ready to ride again.

I also had some really nice meals on the weekends, which was a very big deal for me as a teenage boy who was always hungry. Most farm families back then had a big home-cooked dinner at noon on Saturdays and Sundays. There would be a roast of beef, pork, or chicken, with lots of potatoes, vegetables from their garden, and delicious milk from the cows. I ate everything in front of me, and the mum of the family was always scooping more onto my plate. We went back out with our bodies full of fuel and worked until the end of day. Then we headed back inside for more nice food. To go with our after-supper tea and coffee, there would be a home-baked dessert, usually cake or pie made with whatever fruit or berries were in season. I could eat as much as I wanted, just like in my mum's kitchen. But, at the end of the weekend, I had to go back to the school.

I thought this taste of freedom would make things better for me. But somehow it made things seem worse. I was on an emotional roller coaster, happy and excited when I left the school for the weekend, miserable and restless when I came back. My brain was starting to send me signals that my trauma could not stay buried forever, but I tried hard to ignore it. In those days we thought that when something was over, you just made up your mind to get past it. That's what I thought I would do in three years when I turned eighteen. I would leave and put residential school behind me and never think of it again. Now I have learned about post-traumatic stress disorder and the long-term effects of institutionalization. I know that getting closer to leaving was stirring up everything I had been repressing. All I knew then was that every time I went home with another friend, it got harder and harder to go back to school. One day I realized I just could not do it anymore.

Finally, one morning I described what I was feeling to one of my friends whose family, like mine, lived too far away for him to go home on weekends.

He was feeling the same way, and we made a spur-of-the-moment decision to run away from Blue Quills. There was no big incident that pushed us, although I had never gotten over my disappointment when, instead of taking us home, they were just shipping us to a different school. I was tired and fed up, and so was my friend. We'd had enough and thought, *To heck with this, let's try to find our own way home.* We had no plan. We agreed to head north and figure it out on the way. We knew that whatever dangers we met along the road, whatever happened to us, could not be worse than the things that happened in the school. We snuck away with just the clothes on our backs.

We walked for hours on a dusty gravel road, travelling north. It was getting close to midday, and we were hungry and thirsty. We came to a farm where we saw the farmer outside in his yard, and we quickly decided to ask for work. We walked up to him and offered to work for food and the chance to sleep in their barn. I think the farmer, who was non-Indigenous, knew we came from that school and pitied us. He didn't even ask us why we were walking along the road or anything like that. He told us he needed some help right away and sent us out into the field to pick vegetables, adding that we could come in for a meal at lunch time. He offered to pay us, too, real money for our labour. He was honest and also gave us a huge meal. The farmer and his wife spoke nicely to us and we were happy staying there. We slept in the barn for two or three days before people from the school tracked us down and took us back. My friend and I did not put up a fight. But we did not tell anyone that he had paid us money, so we got a free ride back with money in our pockets. Later we slipped away to a store and bought some treats to eat.

Of course, there were repercussions after they brought me back, but punishments were having less of an impact on my thinking. I knew what to expect — the beatings, the starvation, all of it was the same. I also knew I could handle it now I was bigger and stronger. But I could not settle back down to the daily routine in the school, and nothing they did discouraged me from trying to escape again. I ran away a few more times, now by myself. I still did not have a plan. I just headed north and started to hitchhike, although I had no problem walking all day if I had to. There was only one route north, though, so they were always able to catch up to me.

I was not discouraged by my unsuccessful attempts. Instead, I decided to approach my escape like I had gymnastics. I visualized how to do it, rehearsing the moves over and over, both physically on the roads around the school and also in my head. Every time I ran away, I learned a little more about the road and how far I could expect to travel. I started to analyze what I had going for me and how it could help me escape for good. I knew that when I could finally visualize step by step how I would successfully escape, I would have a plan that worked.

You might wonder why, when I was doing all this planning, I never considered stealing a horse or a car so I could travel farther and faster. Thievery never occurred to me. My parents did such a good job teaching me Indigenous values that even residential school could not turn me dishonest. I am very grateful to my mum and dad for giving me those values. Not only is it the right way to live, but it also kept me out of more trouble with the dominant culture. If desperation had driven me to become a thief, I might have been caught and sent from residential school straight to youth jail. It would have been easy for me to get caught up in a justice system that to this day discriminates against Indigenous people. I might have never made it to freedom.

After several unsuccessful attempts, I had a good grasp of what was working against me. My parents were hundreds of kilometres away, and it would take at least a week of travel for me to get all the way back to them. They did not have a telephone, so I could not get in touch with them to ask for help. Even if I had money, I could not take a train home without a pass from an Indian Agent. The road home was so long that school officials had lots of time to catch up with me, usually around the third day. I could not visualize a way to make it all the way home without being caught. Then I realized I needed to change my thinking. My goal had always been to make it home, but what if I started smaller, with the goal of not getting caught and taken back?

That was when I realized I had two things to my advantage. The first was that Blue Quills was farther north than my previous residential school. It was closer to my home, but it was much closer to where my Uncle Lawrence, my father's brother, had a farm. If I caught a ride, I might be able to make it to him in one day. The second advantage was that my uncle was a very smart man. He had been to residential school, but managed to find a way to keep his sons at home. I hoped he could help me, too. I decided that on my next escape attempt, instead of heading home, I would head for Uncle Lawrence.

One day during morning recess, I saw a chance to slip away when the schoolyard was crowded and the supervisors busy. It was early enough that there was lots of daylight left for travel, and the weather was good for walking. It was the perfect day to try my new plan. But it was also the day I had to face the hardest thing about running away, something I had pushed out of my mind during my visualizations: My brother David was at the school, too. We had been in residential school for six years by then, and he was almost twelve. He was in the schoolyard that day and saw me heading towards the edge of the school property, so he came running over to me.

Of all the terrible things that happened to me at residential school, this is the hardest for me to tell you about. I had wracked my brain for six years trying to figure out a way to get me, my brother, and my sisters out of there. I was never able to come up with something that would work, no matter how hard I tried. Mentally, I knew I could only successfully escape if I did it alone. But emotionally and spiritually, I will always carry the burden of the conversation David and I had that day.

"I know you are running away," David said. "Please take me with you."

"I wish I could, David," I said. "But you are too young. I can't take you with me out on the road."

"Please don't leave me, brother. I can keep up."

"I am sorry, David, but I can't take you. I have to do this on my own. Go back and play with the other boys."

As David turned away from me, my heart broke. It is still broken. I knew I had a much better chance of not being sent back if I was alone. I was getting close to the age when they had to let me go, and I was hoping that my uncle could figure out a way to convince them it was not worth their while to take me back. But David was so young that, even if we made it to my uncle's place, they would insist on taking us both back. I would still have to escape by myself later.

I never got over the guilt of leaving David and my sisters behind and saving myself. It was the hardest thing I have ever done. I know it was the government's fault I was placed in that situation. I know it was nothing David or I did. But I will always feel a knife in my heart from having to leave him behind. No decision I ever made after that, as Chief, as a businessman, or as an Elder, was as hard or as heartbreaking as the choice I made that day.

I left immediately, trying to focus on my plan. I got lucky because not long after I made it to the road and started hitchhiking, someone stopped who gave me a ride all the way to my uncle's place. I don't remember much from that ride. All I could see in my mind was David's face when I told him to go back. And every time a car passed us, I was anxious that it might be someone out looking for me. But it was the farthest and fastest I had gone in one day, and after only a few hours the car pulled in front of the laneway to my uncle's place. He was alone in the farmyard when I walked up to him. Even though he must have been surprised to see me, he made me feel welcome right away.

"Nephew, it is good to see you," Uncle Lawrence said in Cree. "Where did you come from?"

"I ran away from the residential school," I said.

"I thought you might have," he said.

"I've had it. I've had it with the nuns and the priests. I can't deal with them anymore."

I did not have to say more or ask him for help. He had been to residential school, so he knew exactly why I was there.

"Well, you better stay here with me instead," he said.

"They always track me down," I said. "They always take me back."

"Nobody's going to touch you here. I will make sure of that."

He took me into the house, where my aunt was busy in the kitchen.

"Our nephew has left residential school," Uncle Lawrence said to her. "He is going to stay with us for a while so we can make sure he doesn't have to go back."

"That's good," my aunt said. Then she gave me a big hug and started making up a plate for me, just like my own mother would have done.

There was no debate between my uncle and aunt about whether they would take me in and help me. They did not ask a single question about why I had left. Uncle Lawrence knew what residential school was like from his own experience. I don't know what he told my aunt about it, but she had seen him do everything he could to make sure their sons Philip and Tommy did not have to go. That night my aunt set a place for me at their table as if I had been eating there every night. My cousin Tommy, who was a real chatterbox, would have peppered me with non-stop questions, but Uncle Lawrence told him to hold off and give me a chance to settle in.

After dinner, my aunt made up a soft, warm bed with clean sheets for me. I thought I would fall asleep right away, but I was too anxious. I tossed and turned worrying about the school officials tracking me down. My uncle seemed confident he could deal with them, but I could not figure out how he was going to keep me safe.

The next morning, after my aunt made the whole family a wonderful breakfast, Uncle Lawrence wasted no time before telling me about his plan. It was both simple and radical.

"Nephew, I am going to go into town this morning and meet some officials," he said as he sipped a cup of coffee. "I am going to find out everything I need to do to make sure you can stay here with us."

"Then what, Uncle?" I said.

"Then I am going to do it," he said. "I will put everything in place so you don't have to go back to that place."

It seemed like a simple plan, but it sounded radical to me. Uncle Lawrence was going to do something I had never seen an Indigenous person do. He was going to change something the dominant culture did not want changed. Every time I saw someone try that, like my father trying to talk the Mountie out of scooping up his children, it ended in failure. Decisions by the dominant culture seemed to be written in stone.

I had always lived apart from that culture. I grew up in the bush and my first school was Indigenous-run. In residential school the lines between Indigenous and non-Indigenous people were clear and never crossed. I knew very little about the dominant culture, except I should be quiet and try not to draw its attention in the hope they would leave me alone. That was the strategy of most of the Indigenous people I knew, to stay under the radar and hope that kept you safe. But Uncle Lawrence seemed confident about his different approach. He had been able to keep his own sons at home, so I let myself hope.

My uncle lived in a farming community and he had to deal directly with the dominant culture to sell his livestock and his harvest. He knew some of the non-Indigenous farmers quite well and spoke English with them. He respected all farmers, Indigenous and non-Indigenous, who worked hard and treated their livestock and their land properly. They respected him for the same reasons. He got to know quite a few non-Indigenous people, including some in government and education, and they respected him, too. It was my first experience of an Indigenous person being valued by people in the dominant culture.

Uncle Lawrence was gone for most of that morning. I was nervous the whole time. My mind was filled with worry that the officials would come back with him and take me then and there. But he came back alone, and he was smiling when he came in.

"Nephew," he said. "I got all the information I need to make sure you do not have to go back."

"Thank you, Uncle," I said. "What do I need to do?"

"You don't need to worry. I registered you in school with Tommy. You can start right away and it will be your job to work hard at your studies."

I nodded, but my uncle could tell I was still worried.

"Everything is set," said Uncle Lawrence. "You are good here."

My uncle was clearly confident things would work out. He and my aunt did everything they could over the next two days to calm me and make me feel at home. My aunt was busy, too, washing the clothes I was wearing when I left the school, and also finding nice things for me to wear from her son's closet. She made sure I got the best pieces of meat at dinner and the largest slice of dessert. My aunt and uncle cared for me like my own parents would have. It felt good to have someone making a fuss over me.

But I had experienced so many disappointments over the previous six years that I was still anxious. I kept waiting for the other shoe to drop.

And it did drop, on the third day, when I was sitting at the kitchen table finishing up another home-cooked breakfast. There was a loud knock at the door. Family and friends would have walked in without knocking, so right away everyone knew who was at the door.

"Nephew, don't move," Uncle Lawrence said in Cree. "Sit right there."

He walked over calmly, opened the door, and stood on the threshold as he asked in English, "How can I help you?"

"We understand there's a Robert Cree here," I heard one of them say.

"Yes, that is my nephew," Uncle Lawrence said. He kept standing in the doorway and did not invite them in. Usually, my people show hospitality when someone comes to our door and bring them right inside. Instead, my uncle blocked the entrance with his body while speaking in a tone so polite and nonconfrontational that he might have been commenting on the weather.

"Do you know where he is?" they asked.

"He is here," Uncle Lawrence said. "Why do you want to know?"

"He has to be in school."

"Of course he does. School is important."

"Get him ready to come with us. We will take him back so he can get on with his education."

"There's no need for that. I have put him in school here. In fact, he is getting ready for school right now."

"He needs to be supervised. We need to make sure that he attends."

"I am looking after that," my uncle said. "I am going to make sure that his grades are good. I think he's going to do very well in the local school."

Every time they asked him something, my uncle had an answer ready. He knew the things they would say and the arguments they would make. He never raised his voice, but he never budged from the doorway and they could not come in.

"We need to make sure Robert is okay," they said. "We can't leave until we know he is in good health and well cared for."

"Nephew, please come here," my uncle said. "Let them see that you are doing fine."

I was so nervous I was shaking, but I stood up and went to the door. They looked me over and could see I was dressed neat and tidy, face washed, hair combed. They could not deny that I looked good. They asked me how I was doing, and I said I was fine.

"Don't you want to come back to residential school?" they asked.

"No," I said. "I'm good here with my uncle."

My uncle told me to go sit back down at the table, and I did.

"He is going to turn eighteen in three years," my uncle said. "He would be out of your school then anyway. I will make sure he goes to high school and he will continue on even after his eighteenth birthday."

They tried a few more questions, but my uncle never budged. Eventually they had to leave, but they told my uncle they were going to go report to their superiors.

"Your supervisors can ask me any questions," Uncle Lawrence said. "But I guarantee that Robert will have good attendance at the local school. You don't need to concern yourselves with him anymore."

When they left, my uncle turned to where I was sitting at the kitchen table, still shaking.

"Nephew, everything is okay," he said in Cree. "You never have to go back. You're here to stay with us now."

"*Kinanaskomitin*," I said. "Thank you, Uncle."

I don't know if anyone from the residential school system contacted Uncle Lawrence further. They probably did, as they always had forms to be filled out and lists to be checked off. But he never mentioned anything. He never let me think for one minute that I would have to go back. He made me feel safe every day.

Uncle Lawrence also taught me the most useful lesson I'd learned since I was scooped up and taken to residential school. He was smart, brave, and confident, and used all three of those qualities to walk into the belly of the beast and meet face-to-face with my oppressors. He did not let people from the dominant culture intimidate him or confuse him with their complicated rules and regulations. He calmly and politely asked questions until he figured out the rules they played by. Then, still calm and polite, he gave them exactly what they said they wanted in a way that worked for me. He took control and outsmarted them at their own game.

And he freed me.

CHAPTER 17

I Laughed and Laughed

I stayed with Uncle Lawrence on his farm and for the first time in six years, I was in a place where I felt safe and loved. My parents would have been delighted if I could have gone home to live with them, but then we would have had to do the same work with the local government officials there to make sure I was not sent back to residential school. My parents did not have the same relationship with the dominant culture that my uncle did, so there was no guarantee that his approach would work for them. Everyone agreed I was safer staying on my uncle's farm.

My mother and father also knew there was not a better family in the world for me to live with if I could not be with them. I was lucky to make this transition at age fifteen and with a loving family around me. When most people aged out of residential school at eighteen, they were dropped off on a street corner in a city where they knew no one. They were left in a desperate situation and had to do desperate things to survive.

There were no more timetables, no more lineups, no more numbers for clothes and chairs and beds, no more random violence and cruelty. My aunt cooked delicious food and lots of it. I could eat what I wanted and have as many helpings as I needed. There was no more silence at mealtimes. We talked around the dinner table, and we spoke in Cree. It felt so good to speak my language again. I was a little rusty, having not been able to speak in full sentences for so long. No one in the family said anything about it, and I was soon speaking it comfortably again.

But I did not natter away like I had when I was *Napikan*, a chatterbox bursting with questions. Back then, my every thought, my deep curiosity about the physical and spiritual worlds, was on full display for everyone to hear and see. Every answer I got prompted me to ask four or five follow-up questions. I could talk all day, go to bed, and wake up with more questions.

But for six years I had to stay quiet and hide my thoughts and feelings. I was finding it hard to stop that behaviour. I could not shake the feeling that speaking up was risky and I shouldn't call attention to myself. It was one of the first signs for me that things were not going to magically return to the way they were before residential school, at least not overnight. I am sure my uncle and aunt were concerned about how quiet I was. But they did not question me, and the whole time I stayed with them we never spoke directly about residential school. In those days, people thought it was kinder to avoid reminding people about traumatic events, that it would hurt our attempts to get over it. But that doesn't mean they weren't thinking about it and the impact it had on me.

Though he was at ease with the dominant culture, my uncle was raised the same way as my father and was a very traditional man. Uncle Lawrence treated his family and his farm as Creator intended, as a loving steward. He would never have forced me to face my trauma when it was so fresh, and I had not had time to properly process it. Like the Elders, he knew a time would come when I had to deal with it, but he also knew this was not that time. He was well aware of that because he'd experienced leaving residential school himself. That is how he knew it was his work to make me feel safe enough to take my first steps back to the path Creator intended for me. I did not need to speak up for him to know what he had to do.

During the day, Tommy and I went to the same school. Like my uncle guaranteed the officials, my attendance was good and so were my grades. Every day I made an effort to do well, but I also stayed quiet and didn't cause trouble. This was the opposite of the way Tommy approached school. He thought rules were suggestions and studying was for people who weren't as smart as him. He was always in a bit of trouble — late on assignments, talking in class, that sort of thing. We must have been such an odd pair, me quiet and careful to follow the rules, Tommy cheerful and on the lookout for fun.

To be honest, even if I had wanted to say something out loud, Tommy made it hard to get a word in edgewise. Tommy was about the same age as me and had never set foot inside a residential school. I'm glad of that because Tommy was a real character and full of mischief. Residential school would have worked overtime to destroy a big spirit like his. Tommy would have been starved, beaten, or worse, until every last bit of his joy was snuffed out, even if they had to maim or kill him.

My aunt and uncle must have told Tommy not to bother me about residential school, but of course he asked me about it. I did not want to tell him the bad stuff because I didn't want him to see me differently. I liked that he didn't know what I had been through. Even with his terrific imagination, Tommy could not picture the hell I had been living through as Number 53, in constant fear of physical violence, starved of both food and affection. He treated me like just another person to hang out with and have fun. I was nowhere near ready to talk to anyone, let alone my cheerful cousin, about what had happened to me. I liked that. Around Tommy I could act as if nothing bad had happened.

Like I had with my mother, whenever Tommy asked a question about that school, I told him about the sports I had played. I described the gymnasium, hockey rink, swimming pool, and sports field, all things they did not have in his farming community. I told him about the medals I won and the competitions with other schools that my friends and I travelled to by bus. I bragged about how well our team did against schools from the dominant culture. Because of that, he was always challenging me to some kind of physical competition. Tommy was always thinking up new ways to compete. It was always fun, and most of his challenges were silly.

I remember one beautiful fall day when we were walking along a side road and getting up to some serious shenanigans. We were not supposed to smoke, but Tommy had figured out a way to get hold of some cigarettes and shared them with me. We were walking away from the farm so my uncle would not catch us smoking, but I was getting nervous at the idea of breaking such a big rule.

"Are you sure we won't get caught?" I asked Tommy.

"I'm sure," he said. "No one will see us."

"But what if we do?" I asked. "What will Uncle do if he finds out?"

"Don't worry," Tommy said. "I never get into trouble."

I knew that was not true because Tommy was always in trouble. He was forever getting caught at some sort of tomfoolery. He usually got a good scolding, and my uncle would assign him a punishment, usually extra chores. Sometimes he didn't even finish the punishment because my aunt had a very soft heart when it came to Tommy's monkeyshines and would let him off. But I did not like the idea of disappointing my uncle, and the idea of punishment unsettled me. It was hard to stop feeling the fear that had been my constant companion for so long. But I did not want Tommy to see me fearful, so I kept walking with him down the road. It was a familiar feeling of dread in the pit of my stomach, and my anxiety was building when Tommy stopped in his tracks.

"Now what, Tommy?" I asked.

"We're going to challenge each other," he said.

"What kind of a challenge?"

"A physical fitness challenge. You say you won all those medals, so let's see how you do."

"Okay," I said. I was pretty sure I could beat him, no matter what the challenge was.

"We are going to bet on who wins," Tommy said.

"What are we going to bet?"

"I will put two cigarettes here," he said, crouching and putting them down on the ground. "Now you put two of yours right next to them."

As I laid two of my cigarettes beside his, I was thinking that this was just like Tommy. The cigarettes had been his in the first place and he'd generously shared them with me. Now he was acting like they were mine all along and he was going to win them from me. Material things did not mean as much to Tommy as the fun you could have with them.

"Whoever wins," Tommy said as he got back up to his feet, "gets those cigarettes."

"What are we going to do for the challenge?" I asked.

Tommy looked down at a big irrigation ditch that ran alongside the road. It was a cold day, and there was a layer of ice across the water in it. We saw that ditch every day, but Tommy could always see things in a new light and make up a game on the spot.

"Cousin, you see that ice?" he asked me.

"I see it," I said.

"We're going to jump across that ice."

"Oh yeah?"

It was a very wide ditch, several feet across. I was already starting to visualize my jump in my mind. I could see that the banks of the ditch were covered in frost and looked slippery. It might be hard to get a foothold for a good leap. I said, "Who's going first?"

"I'm not going first," Tommy said. "You are the athlete, you go first."

"It's your idea," I said. "You should go first."

We argued back and forth for a bit, and then Tommy picked up a stick from the ground.

"I'm going to throw this stick up in the air," he said. "The person it points to goes first."

"Okay," I said.

Tommy gave it a great heave, throwing the stick way up, and it came down and pointed right at him.

"There you go," I said. "I guess you go first."

Tommy took his time working up to the jump. He looked at that ditch from every angle. He took off his jacket. He walked back a ways and jogged towards the ditch. When he got up close to it, he stopped and then walked even farther back. He ran towards it a little faster, stopping again in front of the ditch. Then he walked all the way to the other side of the road, as far as he could get from it. He crouched down a bit and got ready, then started running fast. When he got to the edge of the ditch, he tripped and fell headfirst through the thin sheet of ice into the shallow water. He jumped up, and I stared at him hoping he had not seriously hurt himself. He stood there sputtering, mud and dead grass smeared across his face, trying to catch his breath.

"This water is cold," he said.

For the first time in six long years, I started laughing. Once I started, I could not control it and it just rolled out of me.

"That's not cool!" Tommy said. "Don't laugh at me!"

He looked indignant as he stood up in the ditch. He was trying to wipe off the dirt and leaves that covered him head to toe, but he was only making a bigger mess. I laughed so hard that I fell over on the ground. I kept laughing and could not stand back up. I could barely catch my breath. I could not remember the last time anything made me laugh like that, and it was quite a while before I got hold of myself. I should have helped Tommy out of the ditch, but by then he had climbed out himself. He stood beside me dripping wet, with his hands on his hips, as I got back to my feet.

"Your turn now," he said. "Come on. Let's see how you jump that ditch."

"I give up," I said. "You win the challenge. You can have those cigarettes."

The surprised look on Tommy's face set me off again, and boy, did I ever laugh. I let myself go, giving in completely to the humour of the situation. I felt joy with every breath, and at the same time I felt myself growing lighter. Tommy gave me a great gift that day. He reconnected me with my sense of humour, a side of myself I might have lost forever.

Tommy wasn't happy with me for all the laughing, but he didn't hold a grudge. Nothing could keep Tommy down. Every day, in any situation, he would come up with something new. His mind was always churning out the next challenge, no matter how hard we were working on the farm. I enjoyed it, but despite Tommy's best attempts, it was not all fun and games. My uncle and aunt had high expectations for Tommy and me. They expected us to work hard, whether it was studying at school or doing chores on the farm. They also had high standards for how we should treat ourselves and each other. They were very clear about it. We always had to behave with respect, like the traditional teachings said. It was inevitable that one day Tommy was going to push things too far beyond the boundaries that had been set for us. I will never forget the day that it happened.

One evening after dinner, my uncle told Tommy and me that, early the next morning, the three of us would head out to the bush in his truck. He had his own trapline out there, and for extra money he cut down trees and sold logs to other farmers to use for fence posts. It was a big production because the bush was dense and the trees were big and heavy. My uncle needed his tractor for most of the work, but where the ground was too uneven or the trees too thick, he used a team of horses to haul out the logs. He wanted one of us to drive the tractor back to the farm, and the other would bring home the horses and wagon. Uncle Lawrence would drive his truck back.

Things started out fine. We were up bright and early for another of my aunt's delicious breakfasts. As soon as we were finished, Uncle drove us out to the site. He started up the tractor and checked it over to make sure it was running okay. Tommy and I harnessed the two horses to the wagon. Uncle Lawrence had good horses, fast and well trained. He took great care of them and was proud of them. After he got the tractor going, he checked over the harness to make sure we did a good job hitching up the team. The horses were well rested and ready to go, jostling around in their traces and eager for some exercise. Everything looked good, so he jumped in his vehicle. Before his truck was out of sight, Tommy came up with another competition.

"Do you want to take the horses or the tractor?" Tommy said.

"I don't care which one," I said. "It's up to you."

"I'll take the horses," Tommy said. "You take the tractor, and let's see who gets home first."

"Are you sure? The tractor should beat the horses."

"You're going to have to go along the road. I'm going to take a shortcut," Tommy said. "I am going to cut across some fields."

"I don't think that will be enough to beat the tractor."

"I think I can do it," he said.

"Okay," I said, but I was starting to get that anxious feeling again. Uncle would not want us racing. When he taught me to drive the tractor he said there was always a danger of it turning over and seriously injuring or even killing the driver. I also knew he never raced his horses because he saw them as having an important job to do on the farm. But Tommy could not be talked out of it. I also thought I could easily beat him, so I pushed down my worry and agreed to the race.

"Let's get ready to start at the same time," said Tommy. "I will do a countdown."

"You go first because I know this tractor is going to fly," I said. "I will give you a head start."

Tommy took off, and I let him get quite far before I started. Once I hit the gravel road, I put it in third gear and flew along. I kept watching for Tommy but I could not see him anywhere. Soon I passed where his shortcut should have brought him out to the road, but I still could not see him. I figured he was way the heck behind me. Sure enough, I got home first, and Uncle Lawrence walked out into the farmyard when he heard the tractor engine.

"Oh, you made it," he said.

"Yeah," I said. I was nervous because I knew Uncle Lawrence would be unhappy with what we had done. Even though my uncle had never scolded me or lifted a hand against me, my brain was expecting a severe punishment. I knew in the core of my being that my uncle was not the sort of person to send me back to residential school or kick me out of his house. But the message was not getting to my brain, which was sounding alarm bells in expectation of something horrible. I associated breaking the rules with horrible, brutal, painful punishment. I could not imagine another way to deal with someone who did something wrong.

"Where's your cousin?" my uncle asked.

"He must be close by now," I said. "If you want to go back inside, I'll let you know when he gets here."

Uncle had just gone back in the house when I saw Tommy flying down the road. The horses were running hard, and Tommy was slapping the lines on their backs to get them to go even faster. I ran out and flagged him down so that he could pull up the team before he got into the farmyard. White, foamy sweat lathered the horses and coated the leather harness. The horses stood with their heads down and gasping in deep breaths of air. It was obvious they had been driven hard.

"Drive the wagon around back," I said. "You don't want Uncle to see the horses like this. He's going to give you a good strap for that."

"Oh, don't worry about that," Tommy said. "He won't say anything."

He went ahead and drove the wagon into the front yard, and Uncle Lawrence was standing outside. He took one look at his horses and shouted, "Tommy!"

"What?"

"What did you do to my horses? They're all lathered up!"

"Nothing."

"It looks like these horses have been going full speed from the moment they left the trapline," Uncle said. "You must have made them run all the way. What the hell is wrong with you?"

Uh-oh, I thought. *Here we go.*

I saw my uncle start towards the wagon and Tommy hopping off it, hitting the ground at a run. He was going fast, but my uncle was right behind him, and he was going pretty fast, too. It took a lot to get my uncle to lose his temper, but there was no way he could stand for what had been done to those horses. He chased Tommy around the farmyard while my fear and anxiety kept growing as I stood rooted to the spot. Uncle kept yelling and Tommy kept running until my aunt stepped out onto the porch to see what the racket was about. Tommy made straight for her, and once he got there, his dad really chewed him out — deservedly so — for treating the horses so badly.

But that was it. No strap. No beating. Even though it must have been obvious to Uncle Lawrence that Tommy and I were racing, Uncle never said a word to me about it. The entire time I stayed with him, Uncle Lawrence never said one harsh word or raised his voice to me. But even though Tommy did not get a big punishment, I didn't think the incident with the horses was over. It was too big a violation, and we had stepped too far over the line. I was also sick at the thought that I'd disappointed Uncle Lawrence after he was so good to me. I knew he needed to teach us a lesson and could see he was deliberating on how to do that. Once again, I waited anxiously for the other shoe to drop, and, again, it didn't take long.

Soon Uncle Lawrence came home with a beautiful colt that needed to be trained. My uncle said he would get us whatever supplies we needed, but it was up to Tommy and me to train the young horse so that he could work on the farm. How we did it was up to us.

The colt, which Tommy named Joker, was smart, high-spirited, and easily spooked. He hopped around a lot, put his ears back, and swished his tail non-stop. Tommy and I decided to start out slow and let him get used to his new home. For the next few days, right after breakfast, we rushed out to see Joker. We fed him, brushed him, and talked to him so that he could get to know us. We led him around the farmyard as he adjusted to his surroundings and seemed happy to see us coming, probably because we gave him apples and carrots. Then we got down to the business of training him.

The first thing we did was build a stone boat, a type of sledge with a flat bottom that a horse drags across the ground. It is good for moving heavy objects that might break an undercarriage, like the big stones farmers pick out of their fields to prevent damage to their ploughs. My uncle got us the wood we needed, and Tommy and I nailed boards together for the bottom. Then we put posts across the front and bolted down big metal hoops for attaching the harness. We needed the stone boat to be solid enough that we could stand on it while Joker pulled it around.

My uncle gave us lots of time to train Joker to wear the harness and pull the stone boat. I would hold Joker as Tommy tried to carefully slide the harness over his back. Joker jumped all over the place trying to get away and shake it off. I liked calming Joker, talking to him, and stroking his neck until he settled down. When we finally got the harness on his back and properly buckled up, Joker got nervous again. He kept looking all over the place and dancing around, and I kept stroking him and talking to him. We did the same thing over and over for days. We always rewarded him for being a good horse. We were proud of how smart he was, how quickly he understood what we were trying to get him to do. All he knew from us was affection and respect.

When Joker finally settled back down, we trained him to listen. He learned what *whoa* meant. To get him moving we made a clicking noise with our tongues. It did not take long before he knew the sounds and what was expected of him. It was a very big day when we put the harness on Joker, attached it to the stone boat, and stepped on for our first ride. Tommy had to hold the reins, of course. It was very exciting the first time Joker leaned into the harness, and we started moving forward. We would never forget the feeling of accomplishment, as well as our pride in Joker and what we had trained him to do.

I told you my uncle was a very smart man. Instead of hitting or punishing us, he offered Tommy and me the chance to follow the traditional teaching of respect for an animal that Creator gave us and the purpose it served. My uncle trusted us to figure it out, and without even realizing it, we trained Joker according to the traditional teachings. We praised and thanked him when he did something good, and when he made a mistake, instead of whipping him we found a new way to teach him. We learned, too. We would never again treat a horse badly to win a silly bet.

It was good to be living in a place where every day I was surrounded by traditional teachings. I had almost forgotten how wonderful it felt. I felt that part of my brain, my connection to the wisdom of the ancestors, start to wake up. I still had a lot of work to do to get back to my true path. But I was learning again. Thanks to Tommy, I was also starting to see things in the world around me that brought laughter and joy.

CHAPTER 18

For Their Own Good

I n 1973, I was a young man of twenty in the beginning stages of recovering from my traumatic experiences. Now I know about post-traumatic stress disorder and that you can't wish away pain. Back then, I was still trying to process what had happened to me, and the same questions kept running through my mind. Why did people of the dominant culture believe they could "take the Indian out of the child"? Why did they think they had the power to take away Creator's gifts? How could they believe they were more powerful than Creator? Who did they think they were?

To find the answers I needed, I moved to Edmonton, Alberta's capital city, more than 430 kilometres south of my people's traditional territory. Back then, it had a population of half a million, making it one of the largest cities in Canada. The city was in the early days of an international oil boom. Buildings were springing up everywhere — stores, restaurants, schools, houses. Jobs were plentiful. I did all kinds of construction work, including pouring concrete, shingling roofs, and building scaffolds. I kept my eyes and ears open, learning everything I could about the dominant culture.

The first thing I noticed was that it was noisy. As a boy, I was taught to listen. I could recognize the change of season from a bird call or find a moose by hearing antlers scratching against tree bark. In the city, men shouted and swore as they dug holes and pounded nails. Bulldozer engines roared, digging up so much of the land that residents called their hometown Dirt City.

For the next two years I worked on all kinds of construction sites. I made good money. I also learned about building codes and construction standards, things that came in handy a few years later when I built homes for my people. But I still did not understand how the dominant culture made its decisions. I decided to find a job where I would see first-hand how its values compared to ours. I went to work at an industrial tannery where moosehides were processed into leather. I knew a lot about moose, one of Creator's greatest gifts. Seeing how the dominant culture treated moose would help me compare the differences. I would be a spy in their midst, watching and learning how they operated.

On my first day of work, I had no idea what I was walking into. They ordered me into the processing area in the basement. I walked down filthy, rickety stairs into a windowless concrete room lit by naked lightbulbs dangling overhead. As I stepped off the last stair, a sickening stench made me stagger. My knees grew weak as I fought the urge to vomit. *This is a dungeon*, I thought. *I will be a prisoner*. Every instinct told me to run back up the stairs.

But three men, my new co-workers, were already at work. I didn't want to look weak in front of them, so I pulled myself together. Still, I couldn't help gagging when they showed me the trap door in the ceiling. It was directly over a vat full of dyes and preservatives, the source of the horrible stink. Behind the trap door was a giant wheel connected to an outdoor loading bay. When I heard the wheel start turning, I was to open the trap door and jump back as fast as I could. If I was too slow, I'd be splashed when moosehides plunged into the chemical vat. The first time I wasn't fast enough, and the other men laughed when I was splattered with stinking liquid. As the hides steeped in the chemicals, we placed wooden sawhorses next to the vat. When the hides finished soaking, we plunged our bare hands into the rotten brew, dragged out soaked hides, and stacked them on the sawhorses. We dragged the laden sawhorses to the freight elevator, shoved them in, and sent them upstairs. That was to be my job, all day long.

After a few days, the dyes stained my hands a rainbow of colours, but I was getting used to the smell. I never breathed fresh air, not even when I went outside to the loading bay to inspect the tightly wrapped bundles of moose pelts delivered by truck. The first time I opened one, the stench of rotting flesh hit me like a slap. Maggots had chewed every inch of the hide, and it crumbled to pieces when I tried to lift it. I had not known maggots could bite, but they bit my hands while I worked. I barely choked back my own vomit as I rewrapped the bundle and tossed it in the dumpster. As the days turned to weeks, I found the hides were always covered with maggots. If I thought a hide was salvageable, I would salt and rewrap it, leaving it to cure and, best of all, kill the maggots. If the hide was too far gone, I threw it in the dumpster and asked myself how anyone could think this was a good way to do business.

After two months, my co-workers were assigned to other duties. I was all alone in that stinking room with the dangling electric lights and creaking wheel. Every night when I took my seat on the bus home, the other passengers hurried away as if I were a monster with my wildly dyed hands and disgusting tannery stink. And every night as I sat by myself on that bus, I asked myself if I was in my right mind to keep at this stinking work.

Why did I feel like a prisoner? I didn't feel trapped when I worked in construction. But that work was outdoors, where the sun told me the time of day and which way the wind blew. I watched summer turn to autumn and then winter. There was a natural rhythm to the work, too. I saw buildings come together, each piece a part of the whole. In the tannery, I put the hides on the elevator and they disappeared. It was the same every day, as if I was stuck on my own creaky wheel.

I told myself I had survived worse. I could escape any time, and each week I got a paycheque. Then I started thinking about that paycheque. I was one of the few people mentally and physically strong enough to cope with the working conditions. I was doing work that previously required four men. The owner of the tannery made a tidy profit paying one person instead of four, but he didn't offer me any financial recognition. I deserved more compensation, but clearly I was going to have to speak up to get it.

I mulled that over. My childhood terror of the repercussions of speaking out, drummed into me at residential school, held me back for a moment.

But, I told myself, *I am a grown man now. No one has that power over me. I have the power to meet face-to-face with the tannery owner and ask for a pay raise.* Finally, this was my chance to see first-hand how the top man made a business decision. He could not stop me from watching and learning.

The next day, at the end of my shift, I climbed the two flights of stairs to the owner's second-floor office and knocked on his door.

"Come in, Robert," said the owner. "What can I do for you?"

I was standing in front of his desk and looking him right in the eye. This was the opposite of what my parents had taught me. They said it was impolite to stare at someone while they spoke. You respectfully looked away and listened carefully until the person finished speaking. But the dominant culture communicated differently. I knew how the owner expected me to interact. I got right to the point, too. No one from his culture began a conversation by asking how I was or showing an interest in my family. They considered that a waste of time. They wanted to know what you could do for them.

"There were three other men working in the basement when I started here," I said. "Now I'm doing all the work myself."

"Yes," said the owner. "You caught on fast, Robert. You're doing a good job."

"I think I deserve a raise in pay," I said.

"How about two dollars an hour?" replied the owner. "Starting tomorrow?"

I felt great when I left the owner's office. I had figured out how to talk to him on his own level. I asked for what I deserved and got it, no questions asked. The owner did not even think about it.

But as I got on the bus and the other passengers scrambled away from me, I thought about why the owner agreed so quickly. I was making two more dollars an hour, but I still smelled like rotting moosehide. The tannery owner had a nice office away from the stench of the work floor. He had a shiny vehicle he drove to work and parked in a special spot no one else could use. I realized that the extra two dollars was nothing compared to the wages of three other men, and that his profits paid for his perks. He could instantly decide to make a small investment in me because my work made a much larger profit. He was concentrating on what I had heard called a "profit margin." *Clearly*, I told myself, *I need to learn more about that.*

On my way home each night, I read the business pages of the newspaper. I paid attention to words like profit margins, balance sheets, and cash flow. On the weekends — after I had heard about plans to extract oil from our traditional land — I went to the public library and read business magazines and books, devouring every scrap of information I could find about the oil industry. There was no internet in those days, and a lot of people I knew did not even have a landline telephone. I talked to friends and family in person about the engineers and geologists showing up on our land, and what they were saying to our people. I was able to cobble together enough information to realize that the plans for extracting oil from my people's land were much bigger than I had originally expected. New corporations were being founded across the world to mine Indigenous land. I read about the economic benefits, well-paying jobs, nice houses, and well-equipped schools. There were no articles about the impact oil development would have on my people's traditional land.

I needed answers for myself and for my community because we were facing our biggest challenge yet: Geologists had "discovered" oil on our traditional land. My people already knew about the sticky, tar-like residue that seeped from the ground. The Elders called it *kuskatew pimee* — black grease. My people had used *kuskatew pimee* for centuries to waterproof our canoes. It was another of Creator's gifts. We took only the *kuskatew pimee* we needed and thanked Creator. The oil people called it bitumen and planned to extract it from huge open pits. They would use it for many things, like fuel for vehicles and the plastic products that were becoming a part of everyday life. They told my people this was a great economic opportunity. It would be "for our own good."

Everything I read about the oil business mentioned the "bottom line." I thought that was the perfect description of how they made decisions. Their thinking had nothing to do with Creator. It was the same at the tannery. A moose was just another item, like a bag of cement or a truckload of gravel. It had no other value, no connection to anything else. This was the exact opposite of my people's teachings.

I had learned a lot after I willingly walked into my own spiritual prison at the tannery. Day after day, I forced myself into a dank, dark industrial basement that looked and smelled like a medieval dungeon. I toiled alone in a tannery, doing the hard physical labor of processing moosehide into leather. Over and over, I did work that dishonoured what my people consider one of Creator's greatest gifts. At the end of each workday, I felt and looked like a monster. It was one of the lowest points in my life, testing the limits of my physical and spiritual endurance. I did it because I was a spy, infiltrating the dominant culture to figure out how it operated. I had to do it to learn what I needed to save myself and my people from a catastrophic threat to our way of life.

Just like my experience at the river on that summer break from residential school, the spirits were letting me know that I was in a bad place. Warning signs were all around me: the maggoty moosehides, the horrific stench, the people shunning me on the bus. I felt trapped in a dungeon because everything I did there violated my people's traditional teachings. I saw it as a spiritual prison — but the dominant culture did not. They had not learned our traditional teachings, so they did not know how to read the signs. They thought it was okay to allow maggots to destroy Creator's gift as long as they made money. No one taught them to use the whole moose, the delicious meat, the tough sinews that bound baskets, the bones that made strong sewing needles. They did not know there was a way to respect Creator's gifts and still make a profit. Someone needed to show them.

I could be that someone.

As soon as I realized that, my road opened in front of me. I realized everything I had endured the last few years had been building to this.

Creator made my people the stewards of the land. It was, and is, our duty to protect it. Everything that lived on the ground and in the rivers, everything that sprouted and seeped, including *kuskatew pimee*, was under our care. My people made good decisions because our values were based on what was good for the land. But what values did the dominant culture use to decide things? How could my people deal with them if we didn't know that?

We would apply those teachings to the business world. We would speak the language of the balance sheet and sit down as equals in industry boardrooms. Our bottom line would be the physical and spiritual wellness of our people and our traditional land. We would start our own companies, which would operate according to centuries-old values, not what happened in the last fiscal quarter. We could show the oil people there was a profitable way to do business while respecting the gifts of Creator.

Why would I take on this mission? The odds were tremendously stacked against me. I was a traumatized twenty-three-year-old from a small, poverty-stricken Indigenous First Nation in the remote north. How could I convince hard-nosed international executives with business diplomas and huge bank accounts that there was a better way to operate?

That is how much I believe in the power of our teachings. I had no doubt they would give me the power to walk into boardrooms, look corporate executives in the eye, and get to the point. And the teachings also gave me a simple, perfect three-point plan.

I would seek out Indigenous mentors, business people, and political leaders who engaged with the dominant culture on behalf of our people. They would show me how to navigate the boardrooms, just like my father and uncles had taught me how to read the bush.

I would also build a team of people — hard workers with expertise. Our entrepreneurs, accountants, and labourers would honour traditional values in their work. They would do their jobs the right way, the same way my mother and aunties used every part of the moose to feed and clothe our community.

But first, and most importantly, I needed the support of the Elders. After all I had endured, I had to strengthen myself spiritually for the challenge ahead. I needed to return to our traditional land and fortify myself with the knowledge and wisdom of the Elders. Their teachings had to form the bedrock of my people's relationship with the industry coming to our land.

I could not achieve my vision alone. But with a community of Elders, mentors, and experts, I would take my people's traditional values into corporate boardrooms and show the oil people there was a right way to do things.

I would make them see it was for their own good.

CHAPTER 19

A Long Way from Here

When I was twenty-three years old, I began thinking about becoming a leader in my community. I didn't go about it the way young people do now. I did not set a goal of achieving the position of Chief and map out a five-year plan with a series of steps like taking leadership courses and jobs with increasing responsibility. Networking was not a word people used back then, and I did not set out to build a group of people who supported me. That is how people in the dominant culture approach leadership, by focusing on themselves and developing their skills and relationships in service of their personal goal. It is an inwardly focused approach to making yourself into a leader, creating an identity you can present to the people you want to support you.

That is not the traditional way my people approach leadership. We expect our leaders to do important mental, emotional, and spiritual work to prepare themselves for the difficult task ahead. We want our leaders to be healthy and balanced so that they can make healthy and balanced decisions. That is where the Elders come in. They use their knowledge and wisdom to assess the important issues our people are facing. Then they consider who in the community has the ability to tackle them. The Elders then approach those people and start praying with them to see if they are ready to take on such an important role. If they think someone is not ready, the Elders let that person know and advise them on what they need to do to prepare. Helping develop our leaders is one of the most important things Elders do.

I moved back to my home reserve looking for a role I could play for the benefit of our community. I knew the oil industry was coming and that it would bring jobs and money. I knew it would bring environmental challenges that endangered our traditional lands. I also knew I wanted to have a role in this new reality, both for myself and my community. But I didn't know how I was going to go about it. To find that out, I did the same thing that helped me survive residential school. I focused on the traditional teachings and let them guide me towards the right actions.

I started by doing what my father would have done, taking gifts to Elders and sharing what I was concerned about. The Elders already knew that the oil industry was coming. They pay attention to everything that has to do with the land and our people. They had many of the same questions I had, and we prayed together for our community's future.

People think Elders are primarily focused on the past because of their role as Knowledge Keepers, keeping the traditional teachings alive for the next generation. That is an important part of their work, but their most important role is using that knowledge as a foundation for our community's future. That is how our people have always made important decisions, by trusting the wisdom of the ancestors and applying it to our choices, making sure our future reflects the learnings of the past.

Because their role is so important, Elders cannot be rushed. They took their time to consider answers to my questions and to consider me, too. Elders only share their wisdom when they know you are ready for it. If they do not think you are ready, they do not give you an answer and there is nothing you can do to speed them up. It is a process of discerning, and that process takes time.

As I went through that process with the Elders, I could feel the spirituality I learned as a boy starting to develop to a new level. The Elders were sending me down a path of deepening spiritual awareness, which might or might not lead to leadership. They were guiding me, but they were also testing me to see if I had the spiritual strength to be a leader during a particularly important time for our community.

I was twenty-five years old when an Elder took me aside and told me I needed to think about running for election to the Band Council that governed our community. He advised me to pray on it, and I did. I realized he was right, that this was how I could make a difference. I was young and had the energy for this demanding role. I had the knowledge I had gained about the dominant culture during my time in Edmonton, as well as residential school. Most importantly, I had the traditional teachings and the support of the Elders. I felt ready to take on the challenge of leadership. During the next election I put my name forward, and with the help and blessing of the Elders, I was elected to a two-year term as a Band Councillor for my Nation. I spent those two years learning everything I could.

I had all the confidence of youth, but I was also at the beginning of a big learning curve. I knew our leaders had to work with the local Indian Agent as well as the federal department of Indian Affairs, which oversaw everything on our reserve. I did not know how their decisions got carried out. Back then, in the mid-1970s, there was no training for this type of role in our communities, no Indigenous governance courses or books, no internet to look things up.

Our governance system seemed confusing and overwhelming because it had nothing to do with traditional teachings. Because of colonization, the way Indigenous communities are governed and the way we traditionally governed ourselves are very far apart. A Band Council is a concept the Canadian government came up with, a governance structure it created under the power of the federal Indian Act. First passed on April 12, 1876, the Indian Act was the law through which the federal government controlled First Nations governments, land, money, and every other aspect of our lives. It even set out rules to determine who had "Indian status," meaning who was and was not a member of our community. It was a racist, discriminatory, greedy law that authorized the Canadian government to manage our day-to-day lives as if we were children. It gave the government complete control over us — including the right to take me from my loving family and hold me captive in residential school. It also took control of the rights of my people to practise our culture and traditions, which was why my father hid his sweat lodge and practised much of his spirituality in secret.

The Indian Act was the foundation for the government's attempt to destroy the cultural, social, economic, and political traditions of Indigenous Peoples and force us into mainstream Canadian life and values. Elements of the Indian Act have changed over the years, but it is still in effect today, and its legacy hangs over my people like a shroud.

The Act blocked the passing down of our oral history and our values. It also destroyed the respected forms of government we developed for ourselves, as the government refused to believe that an oral form of government without written codes could work. First Nations people had developed a system that not only worked but also helped us thrive for generations. We respected one another. We made decisions that benefited ourselves and the land. We lived a good life. But the Indian Act took that away from us. It established a form of local government called a Band Council with limited decision-making powers that replaced all First Nations traditional governance systems, whether they were Cree, Dene, Mohawk, whatever. A Band Council had to operate according to the Indian Act or the federal government would withhold money and services, even what was owed to us under our treaties.

A Band Council was, and still is in most First Nations, made up of a Chief and Councillors elected by the members of the First Nation. In some ways a Band Council is like a municipal government, and the election process resembles the one for mayor and council. But, especially back when I was young, a Band Council had extremely limited powers. Unlike a municipality, it could not do things like pass its own zoning bylaws, leaving overall control of the land out of our grasp. We were extremely restricted in what we could and could not do.

In the late 1970s, the Indian Act was a century old and completely entrenched in everything we did as Indigenous people. We had almost no say in the decisions that affected us. That meant I had a huge challenge ahead of me. I had to figure out a way to work within a racist and paternalistic system to get what my people needed. Serving on a Band Council governed by the Indian Act was what I had in front of me. I knew it, and the Elders knew it. The Elders wanted me to take it on and work within the system, so I needed to figure out a way to do that. I got to work learning everything I could.

To carry out the Act, the federal government made up a lot of rules it expected us to follow. If I learned one thing about the dominant culture while I was in residential school, it was that they are deadly serious about enforcing their rules. If I did not know the rules of the Act, they would stop me in my tracks and I would not get much done. But if I educated myself on the rules, I could try to find a way to use them for the benefit of our people, just like my uncle figured out how to use them to make sure I did not have to go back to residential school.

I knew it would take me a while to figure out how I could be true to my traditional values while working within the racist system imposed upon us. But my uncle had done it, and so could I. I needed to learn from the ground up, and as the Elders suggested, the best way to do that was to start as a Band Councillor and learn from the inside how things operated.

For two years I listened, watched, and learned about agendas, meeting minutes, budgets, audits, contracts, policies, and procedures. I read every official document that came my way and asked every question I thought of. I also talked to every federal bureaucrat I could, which was not easy in those days when our roads were rugged and often unpassable, and when our community shared just one satellite phone. But whenever I had the chance, I made sure to ask what was set in stone and what we could work around.

One or two government officials shared information freely with me, but most were not happy that an Indigenous man in his mid-twenties had the nerve to question them. I did not let that stop me. Whenever I needed to know something, I kept digging until I got to the bottom of things. I knew what it felt like to be on the receiving end of official decisions, and now I was getting a close-up look at the process of making them. I learned all sorts of things about governance, accountability, and transparency.

I also learned about the importance of Band Council Resolutions, known as BCRs. A BCR is an official motion passed by the Band's Chief and Council, and this decision is officially recorded in accordance with the Indian Act. A BCR directly reflects the wishes of a First Nation's leaders, and therefore has a lot of power and authority. Even when the federal system prevented us from controlling our own resources, a BCR let us voice a direction and a commitment because, according to their own rules, the bureaucrats had to read all of our BCRs. I filed pieces of information like that away in my brain, ready to use them in the future. The time would come, I hoped, when I could use BCRs to advance our traditional values.

BCRs are even more important now, more than four decades later, as the federal government is working with First Nations who want to transcend the Indian Act and develop a system of self-government. This is still a long, drawn-out, complicated process, but it means we are moving to a system of self-governance with broad decision-making powers that include making our own laws.

Back when I served as a Band Councillor, self-governance was a dream. I knuckled down to the task before me, learning to work with the system so that I could someday challenge it. I kept working with the Elders for the entire two years I was a Band Councillor. I told them the things I was learning and heard their suggestions for what needed to be done. I always got their views on any issue affecting our community. My two years in that role flew by as I dedicated myself to learning things I hoped would help move our community forward.

As my term as Councillor was coming to a close, the Elders let me know they thought that I should run for Chief. It seemed liked a very big thing for me to take on at twenty-seven years old, but I was confident I would succeed. I have never, ever felt I would fail at anything I put my mind to. It was because of the teachings of the Elders that I had left residential school feeling that so strongly.

"You will fail at everything you try," the nuns told me over and over, the whole time I was imprisoned in their school. They said it to everyone, but to me in particular. I learned to never say anything out loud that could earn me a punch or worse, but they seemed to sense that I was keeping the traditional part of myself alive, that they had not been able to transform me on the inside. That meant, in their view, I was doomed to a life of failure.

"You'll never amount to anything," the nuns said to me time and again.

Just watch me, I thought.

My traditional learning told me they were wrong in everything they said and did, so I kept believing in myself.

They don't know me, I told myself. *I know how I am supposed to do things. I will succeed.*

I never thought I was a failure. Not once. They could beat me all they wanted, but I refused to let the concept of failure take root in my brain. I kept alive my knowledge that Creator had already instilled in me everything I needed to succeed, and that the traditional teachings would show me the right way to use those gifts. Residential school tried to take that from me. It failed. In fact, if those nuns were alive today to see what I have accomplished, they would take credit for it — and in one way they might be right. I was driven to show them they were wrong about me, my people, and everything they did to us. Everything I have done since I left residential school, everything for the past fifty years, was partly so I could prove them wrong.

But that was not the only thing residential school did to me. In 1980, I was twenty-seven years old and had been out of the residential school system for more than a decade. I was running to be the Chief of my community with the support of the Elders. Everything seemed to be going my way. I could not admit to myself that the system had left a dark mark on me. But the Elders saw it. Many of them had been to residential school and they recognized it from their own experience. Even as they encouraged me to run for Chief, even as they supported me through my election campaign, they knew I had not dealt with that negativity and it was weighing me down. When the campaign was over and I was elected Chief, they made sure to put that message in front of me.

My first step after I was elected was reaching out to a well-respected Elder. I followed the proper protocols that my father taught me. I presented the Elder a gift and asked him to consider sharing his wisdom with me as I prepared for this important leadership role. I knew that if he agreed, it would be a process, that he would share his wisdom with me when he felt I was ready for it. I also knew it would not be easy. But I was not prepared for how it went.

When we started, I told him about what I wanted to do as Chief. It was a long list of practical things like housing, education, jobs, water, electricity. I went on for quite a bit. He listened to me, and then he cut right through to the heart of things.

"If you want to build a future for yourself and for our community," he said to me, "you have to do it spiritually. You have to do it based on the wisdom of the ancestors. That includes what our ancestors negotiated in the treaties that will last as long as the sun shines, the water flows, and the grass grows."

"That was what I thought," I said. I was very young and it was good to hear an Elder say I was on the right track. But the Elder went on to warn me that I had just scratched the surface.

"There's so much happening in your life right now that you don't have time to think properly," the Elder said. "You have too many things going on. It is throwing you off course."

"My mind is very busy," I agreed.

"It's a long way from here to here," the Elder said, pointing to the centre of his torso and tracing a line to the top of his head. "The spirit that lives in the centre of your being sends messages and signals to your brain. But there is so much going on in your brain that those messages may not be able to get through."

"How can I work on that?" I asked.

"You need to meditate," the Elder said. "You have to make time if you want to make the right decisions. You have to learn to let everything go and open your mind. Listen for the signals coming from within. Something is going to tell you what to do."

I was young and raring to go. I wanted to do things, not meditate about them. But as soon as the Elder said it, I knew he was right. This is the thing about Elders. When you follow the proper protocols you can ask them any question, but you never get the answer you expect. I thought I was going to an Elder to learn traditional knowledge that would help me take action and be a better leader. But the Elder was telling me I was not looking in the right place and I had to slow down. I had to look inside myself, do some hard work on myself, before the learning could properly take root. From that day on, he started teaching me how to meditate, how to pause and open my mind.

That was when I really took the first steps back towards my road. They were baby steps, although I didn't realize that at the time. The Elder started me off where I needed to be. He was a residential school survivor, too, so he knew exactly what I was experiencing mentally, emotionally, and spiritually. He knew that I had a long and difficult road ahead of me, and that to face it I needed to heal myself of trauma. He could tell I wasn't ready to absorb everything, and it was going to take a lot of time. Because he knew that, to truly heal myself, I was going to have to forgive my oppressors.

But I was not ready for that message. We met regularly, and I thought I was making progress praying and meditating. I felt myself opening up spiritually. But the first time he mentioned the idea of forgiving those who imprisoned me, beat me, starved me, and tried to destroy everything I was, I shut him down right away. Even though I had asked for his help, he did not judge me or abandon me when I rejected the idea. He could tell I was not ready for such a big step. If I had been able to forgive when he first mentioned it, I would have saved myself a lot of pain over the next few years.

CHAPTER 20

He Opens Things

The more I worked with the Elders, the more I realized I needed to build both my knowledge and my wisdom. That might sound confusing, but I believe knowledge and wisdom are two different things. Knowledge has to do with skills in the physical world, things like how to hunt, fish, fry bannock, and bead moccasins. Wisdom is related to the spiritual world and Creator, to our inner strength and our values. Knowledge and wisdom are strongly connected, and you need both to find balance and harmony. To be a good leader, both are essential.

As a twenty-seven-year-old, I clearly had a lot of room to grow in both areas. I had expanded my knowledge of governance and learned the Band Council system on the job as a Councillor. But as Chief, I could not make the right decisions based on knowledge alone. I needed wisdom to use my knowledge in the right way. Wisdom told me right from wrong. It told me if I was on the road that Creator intended for me.

In my work with the Elders, I found that some people have important knowledge to share, and others have great wisdom. Some special people have both. In my family, I had an ancestor who is still respected as a great leader to this day. He was known for having both important knowledge and great wisdom, and he was a particular inspiration to me. His name was

Sapotwkunum, and he was my great-great-great-grandfather. The English translation of his name is "He Opens Things." It means someone who can go anywhere and find his way past any obstacle, who can find a path through the thickest part of the bush. That was his gift, the one Creator gives us at birth so that we can help the people around us. He used his gift to lead our people during a particularly difficult time.

Growing up I heard many stories about *Sapotwkunum*, who was my mother's ancestor. In the late 1800s, he was the head man in charge of our community. This was when we chose our leaders in our traditional way, not the colonialized Band Council structure the federal government imposed on us. Our community members accepted *Sapotwkunum* as their leader because everyone recognized his knowledge and wisdom. He was particularly respected for his ability to communicate. He always set a clear mandate for what was going to happen next, and he explained carefully how things would unfold. That included decisions like moving our community from one area to another.

Before colonization, my community lived in camps anywhere from eighty to 160 kilometres in radius. For three or four years, we would stay in an area where there was plentiful wildlife to hunt and a river or lake with lots of fish. We also looked for a place rich with berries and herbs. We would find all we needed from the land in one place and stay there until we began to deplete those resources. Then we left that piece of land to replenish itself while we moved on to a new area.

Sapotwkunum's people lived according to the traditional teachings. They did their hunting, fishing, and gathering during the spring and summer seasons when the weather was warm and the sun shone for fourteen to sixteen hours a day. They worked hard to preserve their food. They hung the berries up high, where bears and other animals could not reach them, and away from the camp so that the animals would not attack the people. They did the same thing with the meat and fish they smoked and dried. They protected the food well and stored it for the winter months, when the sun only shines for five or six hours a day and temperatures can drop to minus forty degrees Celsius.

My people had a traditional way of packaging their food for storage in *Sapotwkunum*'s time. They wrapped the meat, fish, or berries in moss from the muskeg. The English word *muskeg* comes from the Cree word *maskek*. It is how we describe the boreal forest's wet, grassy areas, created when the glaciers were retreating north and the meltwater made large, flat, wet plains covered by a spongy layer of moss and grasses. After my people carefully wrapped food in the moss, they would dig down into the earth and bury it in the permafrost, the soil that stays frozen year-round in the north. The wrapping helped preserve the food, just like in a freezer, but better because no one was opening and closing the lid. When I was growing up, my mum still followed this tradition, using the permafrost as a natural freezer.

In *Sapotwkunum*'s time, our people also stored food this way in our traditional hunting grounds. They marked the food caches by taking logs, tying them together, and arranging them over the caches in a way that made them easy to spot. If a hunter was hungry or in trouble, he would look for these markers. When he found one, he would dig up the earth and there, buried so deep that bears and other animals couldn't find it, healthy and delicious food was waiting for him. It didn't matter if the hunter belonged to our community. The signs could be recognized by anyone. The food was there for anyone who needed it.

My people passed down this traditional knowledge through the centuries so that following generations knew how to do it. But how did they come up with this in the first place? Why did they invent something that helped not just their own community's members but also everyone? It was because they knew Creator had gifted them with everything they needed to live a good life, including the wisdom to share what they knew for the good of everyone. In the days of my great-great-great grandfather *Sapotwkunum*, our wisdom was about community. Our wisdom told us it was a good thing to share our knowledge and the gifts from Creator. We shared those gifts freely with one another. Our belief in the importance of the proper way to use Creator's gifts was so strong that we shared it with everyone, including the colonizers who came to our traditional lands. Then they set off in the canoes we showed them how to build, nourished by the food we showed them how to hunt and prepare, up rivers we helped them navigate. But, as we found out, they were not interested in sharing Creator's bounty with us. They wanted those gifts for themselves.

In June of 1899, *Sapotwkunum* signed Treaty 8 with "the Crown," meaning the dominant culture's government. It was an agreement between the Crown and our community. Other First Nations also signed Treaty 8, which is the largest treaty area in Canada — and most of it is in the boreal forest. It covers more than 800,000 square kilometres of our traditional lands in northern Alberta and northwest Saskatchewan, as well as parts of the Northwest Territories and British Columbia. It remains in effect to this day and has a big impact on the lives of my community. It affects all of our dealings with the federal government, including how we care for our vulnerable people and, of course, our traditional lands.

As I worked hard at becoming a good leader, I thought a lot about *Sapotwkunum* and the treaty. He always considered every angle of an important decision, and he must have thought this was the best he could do for the good of his community. He must have been hoping that, in the same way his people cached food for others who might need it, he was doing something that could have a benefit in the future, as long as the sun shone and the grass grew.

Because this was so strong in my mind, I was not surprised on the day I found one of our people's early campsites. The Elders had suggested I spend more time in the bush, especially when I needed to calm my mind. One day I was following their advice when I came across a hidden trail. It was almost completely grown over, so thick I could barely see it. But once I realized it was there, I followed it along, the bush getting thicker and thicker, until I suddenly came to a clearing.

It was a beautiful place, surrounded by trees, the ground cushioned with green grass. I heard the murmur of the nearby river. Birds were singing. I saw a special plant growing: buffalo sage, a sacred herb that can be wound into bundles and burned as smudge to purify places and things. I didn't expect to find sage out in the middle of the bush, because it needed lots of sun to thrive. Then I saw other traditional herbs, sweetgrass and the like, and I knew this was an important place.

I sat down to meditate. I crossed my legs, straightened my back, and sat very still. I slowly closed and opened my eyes, over and over. I focused on the sound of the water flowing in the river. As my breathing slowed and my mind cleared, I transcended to a different place, where time seemed suspended. I felt myself connecting with others who walked that patch of earth hundreds of years before. I sat there for a long time, smelling things, hearing things, tasting things, feeling things. When I finally stood up, I knew one thing for sure: It was time to consult an Elder.

I didn't put it off. I headed right away to see an Elder who was respected for his knowledge of spiritual practices. I knocked on his door, and he invited me right in.

"Hello," he said. "You look like you have something to ask me."

"I do," I said. "I have found something in the bush. I would like you to see it."

"Okay," said the Elder. He could tell I needed him to come right away. "Let's go."

He got his coat and hat, and together we walked out to the spot I had found. When we arrived, the Elder didn't say anything. He took his time walking around the little clearing, stopping to take in all the things that were there. I stood in silence while he checked everything out.

"Do you know what this place is?" he finally asked.

"I have an idea," I said.

"This is a very spiritual place," he said. "It was used for prayers and meditation."

"That's what I thought," I said, "because when I found it, I felt that was what I should do."

"Our people created special spaces like this for different spiritual purposes," he said. "For prayers, for meditation, for connecting with the ancestors. It is for when we need to find space to connect with Creator."

There was a long pause. I didn't say anything as I waited for him to form his next thought.

"Our people always used the land for every need, not just hunting or berry picking or medicine," he said. "We used it for spiritual and emotional healing. We left the herbs growing in places like this so that our people could find it when they needed it. When they came upon it, they could pray and meditate."

We left the clearing as we found it. I have thought a lot about that sacred site. It was created generations before, but I found it when I needed it.

I knew most people coming across such a place would not recognize it for what it was. The oil people arriving with their surveyors and geologists would not recognize it as sacred ground. They did not have the knowledge to understand what they were seeing, despite their engineering and science degrees. Because you cannot learn this in a book or at a university. You can only learn it from traditional Knowledge Keepers, who received this gift from the previous generation.

I wondered if *Sapotwkunum* was thinking about this when he signed the treaty. For generations, the government used the treaty against us. They passed laws that allowed them to run every aspect of my people's lives. But was there something cached inside this treaty that *Sapotwkunum* had signed? Was there something buried within in it that we could use for our survival? I would dedicate the next decade of my life to figuring out where to dig.

CHAPTER 21

We Will Not Walk This Path

At twenty-seven years old, I was one of the youngest Chiefs in Canada. During my previous two years as a Band Councillor, I had grown spiritually and mentally as I immersed myself in both the traditional Indigenous teachings and the workings of the colonialist-based governance system. But now I had an even bigger learning curve ahead and I needed to figure things out fast, because our Nation was in a desperate situation.

Residential school left generations of our people with deep and lasting post-traumatic stress. All of us residential school survivors suffer emotional and spiritual anguish from having been separated from our families and traditional land. Many of us are still in constant physical pain from the severe beatings and sexual assaults that occurred. Children were taken at such an early age that they could not remember what day-to-day life was like in the arms of a loving family, so too many of our people left residential school with no knowledge of what family life was supposed to be. Because so many of our survivors did not know how to parent their own children, the residential school curse was passed on, and intergenerational trauma became deep-rooted and ever-present.

All First Nations reserves were — and still are — struggling with the devastating legacy of residential school. Other harsh realities resulting from colonialism also continued to disrupt our traditional way of life. The fur trade long ago depleted the supply of fur-bearing animals, removing one of the few ways we were able to trade and earn money. At the same time, our people found it harder to live off the land as pollution contaminated our water and food sources.

When I became Chief, our traditional lifestyle was being destroyed, but we had none of the modern conveniences the dominant culture enjoyed. We had no electricity, no running water, no sewage systems. There was no indoor plumbing — imagine using a wooden outhouse at minus thirty degrees Celsius. We had a severe housing shortage, and it was not unusual to find more than a dozen people sharing a house that was nothing more than four uninsulated walls and a roof. We had no access to health care, education, social services, or any of the things the federal government had promised under our treaty.

Our poverty was directly related to the fact that the federal government was not honouring our treaties. All First Nations across Canada were asking the government to provide the things it promised, but it could turn a deaf ear because it had all the power under the Indian Act. It was easier to call us lazy and treat us like children than to work with us.

Things were even more bleak for my Nation. We were facing an overwhelming challenge unique to our location in the bitumen-rich oil sands of the boreal forest. The international oil industry was coming to our traditional lands, whether we wanted them to or not. They were after our naturally abundant supplies of bitumen and, despite the treaty, the federal government was listening only to them. The politicians wanted the millions of dollars of royalties that the energy industry would generate, royalties based on the amount of bitumen scooped out from the earth under our reserve. But compensating us for those natural resource was not on anyone's radar. As far as the government was concerned, they would decide what we needed and how we would get it.

The stakes could not have been higher, and the odds were completely stacked against me. As a leader, I had to find a way to create a better quality of life for my people. I had to find a way to get a distant, uncaring federal government to live up to its treaty obligations. I had to find a way to protect our lands from devastation by the multinational oil industry. I had to find the path forward for our community, and for myself as a leader.

I still had confidence in myself. My work with the Elders reinforced my belief that I could meet this challenge head-on. After rededicating myself to the traditional teachings, I was even more convinced of their power and confident that they could carry our people through. If I relied on Indigenous values to tell me what was right and made my decisions accordingly, I could not go wrong. Every day I prayed to Creator in gratitude for the gift of the traditional teachings. I also prayed that Creator would help me find the wisdom and knowledge to get the dominant culture to listen to me and see the sense of what I was saying.

Luckily for me, Creator made sure I connected with a brilliant mentor who helped me along this path. Creator knew I needed a guide who was wise, knowledgeable, and committed to our people. Someone who knew federal laws and politics inside out, and also recognized that traditional teachings were much stronger. I was not long into my new job as Chief before I met that exact person.

Part of my job as Chief was to represent our community at meetings of Indigenous associations where leaders gathered to work together on important issues. I needed all of my self-confidence when I started attending those meetings because I was always the youngest person in the room. At every big meeting, there would be a bunch of older Chiefs sitting around the table. I would walk in and sit down with them, and everyone would look surprised at seeing such a young person. Someone would introduce me as Chief Cree, and the older Chiefs would look at me with a smile. Sometimes there were jokes. Sometimes they tried to talk over me. But I did not shy away. I always stood my ground. I wanted to make changes and I wanted to find a new way to achieve them. There were people who noticed what I wanted to do and saw I could not be rattled, and they wanted to work with me. Luckily for me, one of those people was Harold Cardinal, who was with the Indian Association of Alberta, known as the IAA.

The IAA was a very important and long-standing Indigenous political organization. It had been founded in 1939 to help Alberta's First Nations work together for our people. At that time, founding such an organization was a very big deal because the Indian Act forbade our people from joining together to form political organizations. The Indigenous people of Alberta were determined to start working together and refused to back down. Our people defiantly formed the IAA in spite of the legal prohibition.

The federal government could not stop us, and it wasn't long before they recognized there were advantages to dealing with Indigenous Peoples through an official organization rather than with each Nation individually. For one thing, it cut down on meetings and saved them time. For another, it gave them a structure they could use to connect with us about the programming or decisions they were imposing on us, as well as a way to coordinate the response through one group. If the IAA could save the government time and trouble, the government was fine with it. But the IAA was never the government's lapdog. It worked hard over the decades lobbying for Indigenous rights, especially recognizing and respecting our Treaty Rights. It also wanted the federal government to treat us as the equals we were under the treaty.

The IAA had some successes over the decades, but things really heated up in 1969, when the federal government released what it called the "White Paper." It spelled out procedures that would bring Indigenous people into mainstream Canadian society. It included eliminating the federal First Nations reserves and the loss of specific rights for Indigenous people. In other words, goodbye Treaty Rights. The federal government would keep everything they took from us without giving us what they agreed to in exchange. They might have gotten away with it, but the IAA fought back with everything it had. It rallied opposition across Canada and never let up, and the government was finally forced to drop the White Paper in 1971.

This was a huge win for our people, and the person who led the IAA to that victory was Harold Cardinal. Harold was only twenty-four years old and had just been elected president of the IAA the year before, but he organized a national challenge to what the politicians in Ottawa were planning to do to our treaties. It was Harold who stood up to the government and told them, "We will not walk this path."

Harold started by writing the IAA's official response to the White Paper, which he titled "Citizens Plus," although it was better known as the "Red

Paper." Harold proposed that the federal government recognize Indigenous Peoples as Citizens Plus by giving us the same rights and duties as all Canadians, with additional rights based on our treaties. Harold argued that the treaty was an agreement made by the Crown and Indigenous Peoples as equals and could not be eliminated. He also presented a strong argument for our right to self-government under the treaty.

From the very beginning Harold was extremely clear about how he saw the government's White Paper. He did not mince words, calling it an outline for cultural genocide. His words were a rallying cry to First Nations across the country. He showed us what our rights were under our treaties and how the government was not honouring them. He demanded we be treated with respect and dignity as the original Nations of this land. He explained all this in great detail in a book called *The Unjust Society* (1969), which shocked the government even more, especially when it became a national bestseller, followed by *The Rebirth of Canada's Indians* (1977).

At that time, no one thought that we Indigenous people could write our own books or that we had our own legal arguments and our own view of history. But Harold showed everyone that Indigenous people have their own voices. We could tell the government what we thought and what we wanted. He kept writing and he got attention across the country with more bestselling books. He forever changed the way the government worked with us.

Harold's approach might have astonished the government, but it did not surprise the people who knew him. He was a well-educated man. He went to Harvard University in the United States to get his master's degree in law. He got his doctorate in law from the University of British Columbia, where he studied both Cree law and Canadian law and how those justice systems could work together. Harold knew federal law inside and out, and he also knew our traditional teachings. He was certain that the two could exist together.

Harold was one of the first of our leaders to publicly say that Indigenous people could hold on to our traditional teachings while living in the modern world. He believed with all his being in the traditional teachings and the wisdom of the Elders. He wanted the dominant culture to see our Elders as "public intellectuals." He felt that their knowledge and wisdom were of great value to everyone, and that balance and harmony were not only the essential components of a good life but also the way forward for our two cultures. Harold wanted Indigenous communities and the dominant culture to respect each other and to live balanced lives together. He wanted to change the way our cultures related to each other and build bridges so that we could communicate. Most of all, he wanted mutual understanding.

As part of building that understanding, Harold focused on the "truth" part of what is now called Truth and Reconciliation. Back in the late 1970s and early 1980s, reconciliation was just a dream, but we thought we could make progress on telling our truth. Harold was at the forefront of our battle to get the federal government to acknowledge its many transgressions against us, things that needed to be recognized before we could even consider what reconciliation would look like. Harold took our truth right to the seat of power on Ottawa's Parliament Hill. It was my honour to join him for some of that truth-telling.

When I became Chief, Harold had already moved on from his role as IAA president, a position he held from 1968 to 1977, but he continued on as the association's main advisor. He had already made the government back down from its White Paper, and that success made him work harder than ever at taking on the powers that be in Ottawa. He was looking for Chiefs who would support and help him in his work. Harold was only a few years older than me, so it seemed natural that we could work together as young men in senior leadership positions.

When I joined the table at the IAA, Harold noticed right away the type of questions I was asking and the things I wanted to do. He sought me out and kept asking me to meet with him. I already knew Harold because he belonged to the Sucker Creek First Nation in northern Alberta, where some of my friends were members. But I was so busy in my first few months as Chief that I took my time getting back to him. Finally, when I was in Sucker Creek visiting, I walked over to his house to see if he was home.

I think that was when and where Creator wanted me to sit down with Harold for our first one-on-one conversation. I already knew that Harold was extremely intelligent and well educated. I knew he read the dominant culture's legal documents, the Indian Act, and the treaties, and knew exactly what was going on. I knew he was an expert at understanding how the government interpreted its legal language and how it differed from how we read it as Indigenous people. But on that day, I also immediately recognized Harold's traditional wisdom and felt his deep spiritual power.

As soon as Harold opened the door of his home to me, I felt that spiritual power rolling out from him. Whenever he had a big decision to make, Harold turned to the sweat lodge and the Elders to help him find his direction. When he opened the door, I could see he was glowing with the relaxed, open clarity that comes to you during a sweat. I knew that sometimes you need time to process after a sweat and I offered to come back later.

"No, no, no, Robert," he said. "This is the perfect time. I am very glad to see you, come on in."

"If you are sure," I said.

"I am sure," said Harold. "I will put on some coffee, and we can have a good talk."

He brought me right into his kitchen and we sat down at the table. He made us coffee, and we talked a bit about what I wanted to do for my community, how I wanted to get access to the programs and funding promised us under the treaty. My ideas lined up well with Harold's. He told me he needed to bring together Chiefs who supported his ideas and felt it was possible to work side by side with the dominant culture. Harold asked me to travel with him to Ottawa to talk about our treaties and things that were ours by right. I agreed right away. I could already tell that Harold was going to be an incredible mentor and teach me things I needed to know to be a good leader. I also realized that Harold and I were on the same path, and Creator wanted us to walk it together.

One of the first things Harold shared with me as we sat at his kitchen table was that if the politicians and government decision-makers would not come to us, we would go to them. This was something he learned from his father, who had been a Chief and who would take Harold on multi-day train trips from northern Alberta to Ottawa to get in front of people with power.

"We are equal signatories on our treaty, and they have to meet with us," Harold said.

Right away I saw the sense of what Harold was saying. I liked the idea of sitting face to face with people who had never set foot in our communities but made decisions on our behalf. I agreed it was the only way we could make them understand what was happening in our communities, and I said so to Harold.

"We need to get that message across," Harold said, "but we can't walk in and start blustering and swearing and pounding our fists on the table. That is the kind of thing they want us to do, so they can dismiss us."

I knew Harold was right. With all the power on their side, we could not out-shout or out-bully them. More importantly, that type of angry behaviour — justified as it may be by the horrible wrongs done to us — was not in keeping with the teachings of the ancestors about respect and balance. If we did not model the proper behaviour in our own actions, how were we ever going to teach it to the dominant culture? I had known since I worked in the tannery that we needed to apply our rules to their game, and Harold had figured out how to do it.

"There is a lot more to it than showing up with a message," he told me. "We have to prepare carefully and be ready for what they are going to throw at us."

"How do we know what they will say?" I said.

"It's all there in their paperwork," Harold said. "They love their paper-work and their rules and regulations. We have to know that material inside out, so when they start waving their papers at us we are ready for them."

This made sense to me, and I knew we would be successful at it. Harold knew their documents backwards and forwards. He was more familiar with their paperwork than most of the people we would meet with. Then Harold explained we also had to manage our own expectations about what we could accomplish in one meeting and plan accordingly. At every meeting we would ask for something specific and not leave until they agreed.

"We won't take no for an answer," said Harold. "We need to leave the meeting with an agreement on what is going to happen next. The next steps have to be spelled out in detail for both sides. It can't be a vague promise of something in the future. Our people have had enough of those promises."

"Then what?" I asked.

"Then we hold them to it," he said. "We have to set a timeline they can meet. Then we let them know we will be tracking everything and we will be back if there is no action. They have to know we will hold them to account."

On our early visits to Ottawa, I sat back and watched Harold work. He did exactly what he said he would. I listened to him speak to cabinet ministers and senior government officials. They listened to what he said, but at the same time I could tell by their confident body language and condescending tone of voice that they were completely convinced of their superiority. Even though this attitude was clear, and they often said things that were uninformed or racist, Harold never had any outbursts. He stayed professional and self-assured at all times.

I paid particular attention to how he used his words. He did not talk to the dominant culture using their own methods, and he never exaggerated, threatened, or bluffed. I never heard Harold use any vulgar language whatsoever. He always communicated respectfully but strongly according to the traditional teachings, always well-mannered and serious. The words he chose were clear and powerful and made people understand, which was especially important at the senior political level. They clearly thought they were superior, but traditional wisdom told Harold when he was right and he never backed down. Sure enough, for the most part people treated him the same way he treated them, with respect and dignity, as Creator intended us to interact with other people.

The other thing Harold taught me was to never be afraid to ask any question. He made me aware that the more someone acted like I was asking a stupid question, the more important that question probably was.

"Listen very carefully to their answers," Harold said. "They are not going to tell us everything and give away their advantage over us. But you can tell things by what they are not saying. Pay attention to that because if you can figure out what is really going on behind their words, you will be onto something. If you can get enough information, you can see how they are planning to manipulate us into going along with things."

Harold said the dominant culture's own beliefs and expectations were our secret weapon. He was wise to the kind of tricks the government had used in the past to distract and divide us.

"They are going to underestimate us. They can't believe we would be smart enough to figure out what they are doing," Harold told me. "Pay attention when they offer us something different from what we are asking for. They will dangle money in front of us for a program here and there, something a lot smaller than what we are asking for. They want us to focus on that instead of what we came in asking for."

Harold was right. They often dangled things in front of us, things that would make it look like we had won something and were bringing program dollars back to our communities. Time and again, whenever he was getting somewhere on the big picture, they would offer him something — an employment training program, some housing money, a new study of this or that. Harold never fell for it. He always kept his eye on the prize. He did not have the time to spend on things that were specific to a single First Nation. Harold felt those matters were rightfully a decision for the Chief of each Nation, who would know best what would work for the community members who had elected them. They would know if they needed to train carpenters or plumbers, or build a new road, or drill a well. Harold had bigger goals that went right to the heart of things. He wanted us Indigenous people to have full control over our own lives.

"Our meetings are always about the treaties and the fact that we are equals under it, and our right to govern ourselves," he told me.

Harold was always two steps ahead, but at the same time he operated in a way that would let everyone on both sides of the negotiations get credit for successes, even when he had to fight every step of the way. I only saw Harold show his anger once, at one of the most absurd meetings we ever had.

We had been meeting for months with senior officials on the idea of transferring funding directly to Nations so that we could set up and operate our own programs. We did not have to be treated like children. We could look after our own reserves and decide on our own services. Harold argued that this was money guaranteed to us in the treaties and that we could oversee the outcomes ourselves. After some early progress, we found ourselves stalled in the office of a cabinet minister. We had a few meetings where he seemed to be working with us, but nothing was happening, and none of the next steps we asked for were being taken. Finally, Harold had had enough.

"Tell us exactly what the holdup is," he said.

"Look, there is no way the government is ever going to give you that money," the cabinet minister said. "You might as well stop trying now."

We weren't surprised by that. If the money promised in the treaties was shared directly with every First Nation in Canada, it would have amounted to millions of dollars, even back then. There would be no need for the huge bureaucracy that made up the Department of Indian Affairs. No politician was going to give up that power and control without a fight.

"Tell us why," said Harold. "We have showed to you that we can do a better job of managing our resources and do more for our people. What is the holdup?"

We were ready for a big argument, but we were shocked by the answer the minister gave us.

"If we give you that much money, you can use it to raise your own army," the minister said. "Then you can march on Ottawa and try to overthrow the Canadian government."

That was so far away from what we were trying to do that Harold lost it.

"That is ridiculous," Harold said. "There is absolutely nothing to back up that claim. You are scared, but not of an armed revolution. You are afraid of losing money and power. There are millions of dollars at stake, and that money is very securely under your control. You don't want to lose that, so you are making up stupid excuses. We came here to work with you respectfully and you wasted our time. You clearly have no intention of working properly with us. Shame on you."

After he put the cabinet minister in his place, Harold and I quietly stood up and walked out, making it clear that his actions were beneath us. But as soon as we were out the door, Harold was back to his usual self, planning how he was going to continue the fight.

Today I often think of Harold's words when I hear people talking about how much government money goes to First Nations. What they don't know is how much of the total budget is spent before we get a penny. When I was Chief in the 1980s, the Alberta office of the federal Department of

Indian Affairs leased six floors of office space in the best part of Edmonton, including the top floor of the building. They filled the floors with staff, but there were no Indigenous people working there. The staff were all from the dominant culture. They all had vehicles and large expense accounts. The administration was fully funded, and millions of dollars went into the operation of the regional office. The money left over was doled out to us in drips, like they were doing us a favour and it was not part of the treaty. What would happen to their vast Indian Affairs bureaucracy if First Nations people had control over their own governance? What would happen to all those jobs, with all those perks, if that money went directly to First Nations?

The federal bureaucrats were not going to give that up without a fight, and they dragged out the battle as long as possible. But Harold was no quitter, although he did not know that another forty years would pass before his vision started to become reality.

Harold was very free in sharing his knowledge and wisdom, and worked tirelessly to lay the foundation for where we are today. He was a great man, and I have always felt he gave himself up for the Indigenous people. He kept studying the traditional teachings with the Elders and kept up his spiritual connections. But he also faced enormous pressures and disappointments. His important work came at a high personal cost. Harold gave up his physical, mental, and spiritual health, his own balance and harmony, to keep working for the Indigenous people. I truly believe he sacrificed for us all. He passed away of cancer in 2006, when he was just sixty years old.

He taught me a lot, Harold did, as he travelled with me along my path. Along the way he taught me that, for First Nations to be effective dealing with government, we needed to know how they operated. They played by their own rules, and Harold made it his business to know those rules inside and out, the same way my uncle used the education authority's rules to keep me from having to go back to residential school. But Harold went even further. My uncle made sure he was in compliance with the rules so that he could keep me safe. Harold questioned every rule that was not in keeping with traditional values — and that was almost all of them.

Harold fought his battle long and hard, and while he did not see self-government in his lifetime, he had a lot of success. His efforts laid the groundwork for today's Assembly of First Nations, what we call the AFN. It is a very powerful national organization for First Nations that is modelled on the United Nations General Assembly and made up of First Nations Chiefs working to advance Treaty Rights. Today the AFN National Chief is a very important person in Canadian politics, treated as a peer with the prime minister and other leaders. They are a leading voice in today's steps towards real First Nations self-government.

Harold knew it was possible to give power back to First Nations and make us responsible for ourselves. He also knew we could bring the federal government to account for all the wrongs done to us, and that the truth would come out. He made us confident in ourselves and got us First Nations people working together and focused on our rights under treaties like the one that my great-great-great-grandfather *Sapotwkunum* signed in 1899.

I also believe that Harold's work in telling the truth to the Canadian public, as well as the people in positions of power, laid the groundwork for the federal government's Truth and Reconciliation Commission.

Harold had a vision all those years ago when I first sat down with him at his kitchen table, and I wish he was alive today to see what he accomplished, how so many of his dreams are becoming reality. The AFN is consulted respectfully by prime ministers. The Indian Act is widely acknowledged as racist and brutal. People across Canada are becoming more aware of the truth about residential schools. Truth and Reconciliation is honoured by an official day with people across the country taking time to inform themselves, and wearing orange shirts in acknowledgement of that truth.

If Harold was alive today, he would be one of our great Elders. He would also be going over the ninety-four recommendations in the Truth and Reconciliation Commission's final report with a fine-toothed comb. He would be grilling federal officials on how they planned to make reconciliation a reality, and he'd want it laid out step by step for everyone to see.

I think that today Harold does not get the credit he deserves or recognition for his sacrifices. But I know the ancestors welcomed Harold with great honour and respect for the work he did for our people.

Sometimes when I am praying, I say, "*Kinanaskomitin*, Harold. I thank Creator for all the work you did for the Indigenous people. I am grateful."

CHAPTER 22

You Work for Us

One of the things that Harold helped me figure out early on was that the government always had a plan and a budget in place for the money they were supposed to give us. They already knew how they would distribute it and what it was for. Everything was limited by that plan, which they always made without consulting us. That meant what we received usually did not help because it was based on policies and procedures developed by bureaucrats in faraway offices who had never been to our reserves.

When I was in Edmonton after residential school, I worked on all kinds of construction projects with very professional people — electricians, plumbers, all the trades — and I learned about all the parts that were needed. The homes we built were perfect, and the people living in them were safe and happy. I thought about that a lot after I went home to our reserve and our living conditions. Our people had absolutely nothing in their homes, just four walls and a roof. Housing was my top priority as Chief, and I wanted to get started right away.

"Well, here's some money for you, Chief," one government representative told me. "You can train your people in carpentry so you can build houses."

"But we can't build houses with just carpenters," I said. "We need to train electricians, plumbers, roofers, scaffolders, everyone."

"This program is only for carpentry," he said. "Train carpenters or you get nothing."

So, we did the program and at the end we had twelve people trained in carpentry, but no plumbers or electricians. I still do not know where the government got the idea a carpentry program would be helpful to First Nations, ignoring the bigger picture. I can imagine them on the top floor of their office tower saying, "Well, carpenters might work for them. Let's give it a whirl."

I learned a lot from that experience and others like it. I learned the government would always say, "This is how the treaty money is going to be used and there will be no questions asked." But Harold had showed me I *could* ask questions and have an impact on how decisions were made. I started using Harold's lessons in my work as Chief with the local district office that had been set up to serve the First Nations in our northern region. I started asking a lot of questions and I would not take no for an answer. I knew I was getting the hang of it when one of the other local Chiefs came to me about a problem with a bureaucrat.

"That Indian Affairs manager is giving me heck," he said. "Every time I try to see him, he tells me off. He doesn't want to work with me."

"What?" I said. "There must be something wrong. Maybe you misunderstood him."

"No, no, no. He swore at me, too."

"Well, I'll go there with you," I said. "We'll go meet with him together."

We went to the district office in Fort McMurray and walked right into the manager's office.

"Come on in and sit down, Chiefs," he said. He was a huge guy and had a big, booming voice. "How can I help you?"

"I hear that you were not talking in the right tone when you met with my friend," I said. "He wanted to ask you a few questions, but you weren't happy to see him."

"Why did he go to you?" the manager said. I noticed right away that he did not deny his behaviour. He seemed much more concerned that the two of us were working together.

"Do you know why you're here?" I asked him.

"What do you mean?"

"Do you know why the government sent you here? Do you know what your job is?"

"Of course I do."

"So you know the government put you here at this district office to help out the First Nations in this area. Whatever our needs are, you are here to assist us."

"I think I know my job."

"Then you know you work for us," I said. "Don't ever forget that. We do not work for you. If you think you are higher up in the hierarchy than we are, if you can't get rid of that negativity, you might as well go home now. That is not the way we work around here."

He did not like me telling him that. His booming voice got louder, and he seemed to puff up larger. He told me he was there to tell us what was what, and not the other way around.

"If that is the way you see it, there's no point in continuing here," I said. "We will be taking this to a higher level. We don't want to go to your director, but that is our next step." I nodded at the other Chief, and we started to stand up to leave.

"Oh no! You don't have to do that," he said, his tone of voice becoming much less aggressive. "Let's start over."

"Okay," I said, and the other Chief and I sat down again.

"What do you want me to do?" he said.

"I want you to apologize to my friend," I said. "Do that, and it will stay right here at this level."

"I'm sorry," he said. "It's just a misunderstanding."

I had straightened him out right there, and we did not have any issues going forward. It is often just a matter of making people understand where you're coming from. It is also a matter of not bluffing. When I said I would go over his head, I meant it, and he knew I meant it.

But I was not always able to resolve things so quickly, especially when I was dealing with people who were not based in our communities. Once I had a major issue with one of the senior bureaucrats, the regional director who oversaw our area from his office in Edmonton, four hundred kilometres away.

Communication was another one of our challenges in those days. At that time, we did not have the cellphone coverage we do today. We did not even have land lines. My community had only one telephone, a big satellite-type model. There was a special phone number for calling the Edmonton office, and an operator then had to dial the number of the person we wanted to speak to.

To get any major requests across, we had to travel to Edmonton and meet the bureaucrats in person. They certainly were not going to come to see us. Back in the 1980s we did not have the paved and well-maintained four-lane highways we do now. It was a long trip down a very bumpy two-lane road that became infamous for the high number of horrible accidents that occurred every year. In the winter, when we always had several feet of snow, it was never properly ploughed. But if something was important, off we went to see the people who controlled our lives from so far away.

One winter day, I travelled down that road to meet with the regional director about my plan to manage our social and economic programs from our reserve. It was a long, cold drive. When I finally walked into the meeting, I got right to the point, the way I knew these people liked to communicate. I would have been shocked if any of them had taken the time to ask me how my community was doing, or even if I had a good drive down.

"I want to start my own program office," I told him. "I want to oversee our reserve's programs from where they will operate."

"Why?" he asked.

"You're managing everything my community needs from too far away and it's making it difficult for me to make sure they run properly. We can look after our own funding and our own programs."

"That won't work. It is much more efficient to run all the programs for the region from here. It saves a lot of time and money."

"Efficient for who?" I said. "I have to drive hours every time I want to see you. Every time I have to do that, I think what a waste of time that is."

We talked back and forth about it for quite a while, but he would not budge. It was apparent right from the start what his real concern was. If my people took that work on ourselves, a big part of his work was gone. He did not want to give up any control of the programs or the big budgets behind them.

When he insisted I could not do this, I simply said, "Watch me," and got up and walked out the door.

I had a lot of time to think on the drive back. As soon as I got back to our offices, I went to see the band manager, who oversaw our day-to-day operations, and told him what I needed.

"I want you to write a plan to bring the management of our programs and services here to the reserve," I said. "Education, jobs, housing, every bit of it."

"Can we do that?" he asked.

"Of course we can. It's time we took over our own future."

The band manager and I worked hard to create that plan. It included a detailed work proposal, a budget, and a feasibility study to make sure that it was going to be successful. It was a very strong plan, and I knew it would work. I made the long drive back to Edmonton and personally handed it to the regional director. He was not happy. He said some angry and inappropriate things in a very loud voice.

"Hold on. I am the Chief here. You are not," I said. "You're a regional director. You're supposed to work with me. You have to listen to what I tell you."

But he would not listen and got carried away, using more strong, abusive language.

"That desk you're sitting behind is because of us," I said. "The money that you get paid with is the Indigenous funding negotiated under our treaties. Quit trying to act like there is a hierarchy here. You are not above us. You work for us."

But he made it clear that he was not going to do anything to move our plan forward.

"You're wasting my time and your time," I said, and got up and left. I knew I was going to have to make some pretty strong political moves to pull this off, and I was ready for that. As soon as I got back to our community, I went back to our band manager.

"I want you to write up a Band Council Resolution saying we want that director relieved of his duties from the regional office," I said.

"Can we do that?" he asked again.

"Of course we can. This is an official directive from the Chief and Band Council. He refuses to work with us, and we need someone in that role who will."

Once again, I was not bluffing. I was going to set a precedent by calling for his removal because that was the only way we could move forward. We drafted up a BCR calling for the removal of the director and sent it to his boss in Edmonton. I also copied the federal Minister of Indian Affairs, the person at the very top of the organization. As it turned out, the minister saw the letter before anyone else, and he used the satellite phone to contact me right away.

"Chief, what are you doing?" he said. "You can't fire my staff."

"Your staff?" I said. "Since when are they your staff? Those people are reporting to you, but they are working for me. They are my staff, not yours."

But this time, I wasn't berated, threatened or abused. There was a long pause while the minister thought about what I had said. Then, finally, I got the answer I wanted.

"I see your point," the minister said. "Tell me more."

I explained our work plan and told him I was ready to take ownership of our money and oversee the services in our community. I explained everything we had considered and all the areas covered by the plan.

"I'm really happy for you, Chief," the minister said. "You're taking a huge step forward. I think you'll be able to do it. You have the ability to move it forward."

Two weeks later I walked into the regional office in Edmonton, and boy, was their change in attitude obvious when they greeted me at the door. Suddenly everyone had a lot to say, but they were talking in a completely different way.

"Hello, sir. Chief, would you like a coffee?" That was how they started. Then they said, "The new regional director is waiting for you."

That was that. It did not take us long to work out the details to transfer program management to our community. We ended up with a big cheque for the funding, and then our band manager came to me with an idea. He was a well-educated person and had been to university to learn about finance and business. He had also been watching how I was trying to find new ways of taking things forward for our people. He had put together a plan for what we could do next.

"You know, Chief, we can double our money," he said.

"How would we do that?"

"This large amount of funding gives us the opportunity to start working differently with the bank. Now that we have some capital, we can leverage it to get a loan."

"We could do a lot with a bank working alongside us," I said. "Let's do it."

We set up a meeting with some senior bank officials. We told them we wanted to open a new account with our big government cheque, and they certainly liked the sound of that. Now, we told them, we needed additional money to help our community. We described our plan to them, that we were opening an office to bring in all of our different programs. We were going to hire experienced people to run things. We were going to build our own housing, expand our electrical grid, and build our own water and sewer capacity. We were also going to build roads to help bring in supplies. We had big goals, but we also had a feasibility plan, work plans, and the budget numbers to show we could make it work.

"We have to go talk to our bosses about this," the bank officials said.

Here we go, I thought. I started getting ready for another big round of convincing people that we knew what we were doing, that we had what we needed to carry things through. But that was when I found out business operates very differently from government.

"No problem," the bank bosses said. "We have read your plan and it is a good one. We will give you what you need."

Boy, from there we just took off. We built forty-four new homes and the services they needed. Roads. Electricity. Water and sewer. Everything fit together. Everybody was happy. Our people had a nice place to live. Our people were working. That was how we started, and that was just the beginning.

This process taught me some important lessons. I had stuck to our traditional values while dealing with the dominant culture, but I had put things in terms they could understand. I had overseen the development of a plan that was so clear that everyone could see it would work. I walked into the offices of powerful people, looked them in the eye, and laid things out. I spoke calmly and clearly, but I did not take any abuse. When they raised their voices and said vulgar things, I did not descend to their level. It had worked. I achieved what I had wanted for my people.

And I learned another important lesson: Power was about money. Whoever controlled the money controlled the future of our community. That raised another set of challenges. Because even if we got every cent owed to us from our treaties, it would not be enough to battle the big industry that was heading our way. The international oil industry wanted the bitumen that was underneath our reserve. Money was power, and they had lots of it. If my people did not figure out a way to meet them head-on, we would not be able to safeguard our traditional way of life. Like we had with government, we had to take them on face to face at the boardroom table.

CHAPTER 23

When the Train Stops, Get on It

The entire time I worked with Harold Cardinal, he always made sure nothing distracted him from his battle with the federal government over Treaty Rights. He knew that meaningful change for our people was only going to come when the government started living up to the treaties it made with us. Because of that, when it came to demands on his time Harold was always clear about drawing a line between what the individual Chiefs should do for their Nations versus his role at the national level.

At the same time, Harold was always free with his advice to anyone who needed it. That was why I brought my concerns to him about the oil industry mining my Nation's land. Harold was the first person who encouraged me to take a leading role in addressing the issue of protecting traditional land and balancing that with our people's desperate need for a stable economic future.

In the 1980s, the idea of economic reconciliation between mainstream Canada and Indigenous Peoples was not on the radar. There were so many ongoing issues, so much racism, paternalism, and colonialism, that reconciliation of any kind seemed almost out of reach. Indigenous people were living in extreme poverty and we knew we had to find ways of supporting ourselves, especially with the federal government not living up to our expectations regarding the treaties. But we had few options for earning money. The fur trade was gone, and the remote geographic locations of our Nations severely limited the type and number of jobs we had access to. In addition, on top of severely traumatizing our people, the residential school system did nothing to educate us for the mainstream workforce. The only thing we had going for us was the natural resources on our land — and that came with enormous risks to the environment as well as to the health of our people, who breathed the air, drank the water, and ate locally harvested food. The biggest challenges of my leadership were to figure out what to do about the oil industry and how we could steward the land while finding a way to control our economic destiny.

It is important to remember that Indigenous people did not invite the fossil fuel industry to our communities. But it came anyway. When the oil people arrived on our bitumen-rich land in the late 1970s and early '80s, we had no way to place checks and balances on them. The federal and provincial governments were eager to let the energy industry put mining operations where they wanted because that would generate millions of dollars in taxes and royalties. But Indigenous people got nothing, and it seemed we had no power to effect change.

From the moment First Nations signed our treaties, the government excluded us from decisions about ourselves and our land. What we thought was an agreement between Nations, the federal government saw as a way to exercise their paternalistic, racist, and greedy policies. They passed their own laws to control every aspect of our lives. There were no consultations and no information about what being excluded meant.

The government had the same approach to the oil industry coming to Indigenous land. It was our traditional land, given to us by Creator to steward. Government and industry refused to recognize that, and they believed we had zero power to influence how they raked in massive profits. They did not think they needed to allow us a seat at the table.

But I learned a lot from Harold Cardinal. He never asked the government's permission to sit at their table. He called a meeting, showed up with paperwork at the ready, and told them how it was going to go. He was undeterred by distractions they tried to put in his path and he never stopped moving things forward. Harold and I had been working together in this way for some time when I first talked to him about issues with the oil sands operations in our region.

"They are using our land any way they want without our input, and everyone is making money except us," I said. "We need a seat at the table. Can you help?"

"You are absolutely right, Robert. Something has to be done," Harold said to me. "But you don't need me. You can lead this yourself. You have the vision and the energy to make this happen. Take the initiative."

Right on the spot, the first time I had mentioned this enormous problem, Harold saw me as leading the solution! I was excited that Harold thought I was ready to spearhead something this big and important. He didn't have to tell me twice. He and I quickly outlined a first step to get this moving quickly.

"You draw up a proposal and present it to the IAA board for endorsement," Harold said. "Then we can give the federal and provincial governments a document equivalent to a BCR. We need to show them the Chiefs in your region want action on this issue and every Chief in Alberta is behind them."

Right away I started developing my proposal and, of course, I began in the traditional way. If I was going to take traditional values into industry and government boardrooms, I needed to be sure I was practising them myself. My first step was to consult with my own Nation, both Elders and other members. I consulted people individually and in group engagement sessions. I listened carefully and quickly found out there was a lot of agreement about what was happening.

Everyone could see that economic growth in our region was starting to move at an incredible pace. Some of the changes were aligned with what we wanted for our communities. New roads. New buildings. New water treatment and sewer systems. New electrical grid. New businesses. New jobs. The quality of life was ramping up everywhere in northern Alberta — but much less so on Indigenous reserves. As we discussed the challenges brought by this exponential growth and what it meant for us, I realized our people saw it breaking down into three main categories.

The first was stewardship of our land. Industry had started mining our natural resources, and we could already see an impact on the water we drank, the air we breathed, and the traditional migration routes of animals we hunted and trapped. We knew this would have an impact on our land for generations. But we had no mechanism for bringing this forward to the government regulators, and no expectation we would be listened to.

The second issue everyone raised was that industry was not hiring Indigenous people. Well-paying jobs of all kinds had come to the region, but not for us. We were deliberately discriminated against by the racist hiring practices of an industry that would rather hire out-of-town workers from the dominant culture. These workers were paid to fly to our region and then return to homes in places far from the environmental impacts they were contributing to.

The third was that Indigenous entrepreneurs were starting up their own businesses and hiring our people, only to have bigger non-Indigenous players swallow up those businesses. As soon as a company changed hands, the new owners got rid of the Indigenous staff and hired their own people, again bringing in out-of-town workers. The new owners did not have traditional teachings to follow and were only concerned with the bottom line, which was bad for both our people and the land.

Once I had this consensus about what was happening, I met with the Elders again. I gave them tobacco and asked for their guidance. They clearly saw the challenges in front of us, both the environmental risk and economic opportunity. They recognized that our people lived in extreme poverty and needed health care, education, and social and community services. After taking all this into consideration, the Elders saw that our only chance to preserve our land and improve our quality of life was to work with the industry. The Elders were very clear about that. They compared the oil industry to a runaway freight train about to smash into us, destroying everything before continuing on down the track. We were powerless to stop it. They said we needed to turn it into a passenger train that would stop to pick us up and carry us to our destination.

"If we see the train coming, we need to wait for it," the Elders told me. "When it stops, we have to get on board. If we miss it, that's it. We're finished."

The Elders were right. We needed a ticket to board that train. To get that ticket, we needed something more powerful than the oil industry's money. Luckily, the Elders felt we had that in our traditional teachings. We would start by treating industry representatives with the respect that is part of our tradition, and make it clear we expected to be treated in the same way. Once we had their attention, we would explain why we needed them to do things a certain way. We would not use our knowledge as a weapon or a bargaining chip. We would share it with them as a gift and show them the proper path. Traditional wisdom was so powerful that industry people would want to follow that path as soon as it became clear to them. It was the obvious way forward.

So I had to find a way to make their vision a reality. The future of my people depended on it, and the first thing I needed to do was convince the other First Nations Chiefs in the oil sands that we had to work together towards the same goal.

I had learned on my trips to Ottawa with Harold that government officials were intimidated when First Nations Chiefs worked together to achieve shared goals. When they kept us isolated from one another, we had less power. It was easier for them to dangle little tidbits of money for much-needed programs we could take back individually to our impoverished home reserves. When my people were united, the government officials had to work harder and think bigger to find solutions that worked for everyone. I expected the oil people had the same divide-and-conquer game plan. They would try to separate us and pick us off individually, and they thought no one could stop them.

I had to get the ducks in a row before I took my proposal to the IAA. I personally called all the Chiefs in our region to outline my plan, and we had our first meeting with all the local leaders in attendance. Right away everyone got what I was proposing. We were all seeing the same things, and we talked about the environmental impacts we already saw in the water, land, and air. I also found out that Elders all around the region were saying the same things as the Elders in my community — they also advised getting on the train. The Chiefs agreed we needed to work together on common goals. We knew it was going to take us all working together to get a seat at the table.

"We all need to pull our socks up," I said at that first meeting. "We need to get our brains working together on how to deal with all this development.

If we don't do anything, we're going to lose out and we're going to lose out big. Now is the time to do it because there are huge businesses that are already here, and more are coming."

I outlined the plan I wanted to submit to the IAA. We needed to act together because that gave us more strength and momentum. We would do that by creating our own Indigenous-run economic agency to promote our interests. It would be a joint non-profit entity registered under the dominant culture's own laws, so they would have to officially recognize it. They would see how serious we were and know how we expected them to deal with us.

It was a radical idea at that time, that we would work together for our common interests under an incorporated umbrella agency and meet with industry as a united front. But collaboration was not a new idea to our people. I had seen what Harold Cardinal achieved through the IAA in presenting a united front to the federal government. But there was no guarantee that our plan would work.

"Why do you think that organization will be able to get the things we need for our land and our people?" the Chiefs asked. "We hear a lot of talk but so far it has not come to anything."

"That's because right now, we have nothing official," I said. "It's all just words hanging in the air. Nothing has been nailed down. What I'm planning to do with your support is negotiate an agreement on our behalf with the oil companies about the things that we need as Indigenous people.

"We need to get them to make agreements in writing so we can hold them to it," I went on. "If we don't do our work, if we don't get commitments down on paper, we're going to lose out. They are all about the paperwork, that is what holds power for them. We need our own paperwork to battle them with."

They all saw the sense in that, but there was still the question of how we could enforce the written agreement.

"We are going to get government to join the agreement, too," I said. "The federal and provincial governments need to be signing authorities because they regulate the oil companies, and the industry won't go against an agreement signed with them."

It was a pretty simple plan. There would be four signatories to the agreement: Our Indigenous non-profit, the oil industry, and the federal and provincial governments. It would not be divide and conquer because we would all be part of the same agreement. Everyone was going to get something, and everyone was going to give up something.

The Chiefs liked the sound of my proposal. They also liked the idea of trying something that would be the first of its kind. But they worried that it was a lot for us to pull off in the face of well-funded businesses and governments, and the many lawyers and other experts they had on staff.

"I think I can do it," I said. "Let me try."

The Chiefs knew we had nothing to lose. If we did not act, the train would crash into us at full speed. There was a unanimous vote to work together and formalize my plan. The Chiefs scraped up some seed money to get us started, and I was voted in as chairperson. I submitted my proposal to Harold, and the IAA passed it right away. We were off to a strong start, with all the local and provincial Chiefs backing us.

Things got off the ground quickly, and it did not take any time at all to create the Athabasca Native Development Council. It was a non-profit entity that we all referred to as the ANDC, and we were clear on its purpose and goals. It gave us a forum to speak to the oil companies as one voice. It was a place to share our concerns and work together to find solutions, and to get signed agreements to bring about those solutions. I hired consultants, including some excellent lawyers, who walked us through the various federal and provincial regulations and helped us decide how to register our non-profit. I also hired a chief executive officer to run the day-to-day administration while I focused on working with the other Chiefs, the industry executives, and the politicians.

For our first agreement we focused on two things. The first was getting the industry to agree that Indigenous people would make up a guaranteed percentage of their regional workforce. The second was that all proposals by Indigenous-owned businesses in the region would be given priority. As individual Nations, we could build up our own companies with our own workers, taking control of our economic prosperity as we applied Indigenous teachings to our decisions. We believed that once we had the first agreement in place and showed we were serious about working with them, oil companies would be motivated to do larger contracts that covered more things.

And that's exactly what happened. The first official participants in the ANDC were four local First Nations, but right from the get-go we designed our agreements to include all Indigenous people — First Nations, Métis, Inuit, anyone. That was one of the first things Harold and I talked about as I was putting the proposal together. It would have been easy for me to negotiate something for my own First Nation, but Harold helped me see the bigger picture. Even though he was a champion of Treaty Rights, Harold was also a champion of all Indigenous Peoples, not just those who had signed treaties.

"All Indigenous people are in this together," I heard Harold say many times. "First Nations, Métis, Inuit, the government sees us all as people to be divided up and marginalized. But Creator sees us all as stewards of the land and wants us to work together."

We had to work collaboratively on the issues that united us, Harold said. We had to be aware that Indigenous people have been so beaten down by colonization that it can be hard for us to work together. Colonization replaced our traditional collaborative behaviours with the dominant culture's adversarial way of working. We had to be aware of that inclination and put it aside to work together in the traditional way.

This was a very important message for me. If I was taking our traditional ways into the boardroom, I had to do it properly. People from all across Canada were coming to our region to work in the oil sands. There was no reason that we should exclude our Indigenous brothers and sisters from other regions. We were all facing the same economic challenges, and there was lots of work for everyone, so we should make them feel welcome.

As soon as I had the IAA endorsement, I asked to meet with industry representatives. I prepared for the first meeting the way I had seen Harold prepare to work with government. I started by putting together the paperwork and getting excellent legal advice. I also made sure to get industry decision-makers at the table for our first meeting so that we could start taking action right away. These steps showed I respected the dominant culture's commitment to paperwork and their leaders. Showing respect is one of our traditional values, but it also turned out to be a good business strategy, because it had an immediate impact.

The top industry people showed up at our first meeting and, of course, they brought their lawyers. We expected that. We knew we were going after a giant. We brought lawyers, too. But we also brought an Elder to start off the meeting with a traditional blessing for everyone in attendance, recognizing we all had a role to play for the good of the land. That blessing set the tone for the meeting by immediately uniting everyone — Indigenous and non-Indigenous — as one group with the same goal. In the four decades since that meeting, time and again I have seen a traditional Elder's blessing begin a meeting by focusing everyone in the room on the big picture and the important work we were there to do on behalf of Creator.

As soon as the blessing was over, I could see the impact it had on the industry representatives. I soon learned that business leaders are better listeners than government leaders. Their minds were open and they listened to me from the start. They wanted to see what vision I had, not only for getting involved in their business but also for helping my community. They looked at my work and my progress and saw how they could work with us, not how they could destroy us. Of course, I knew that was because they wanted us to help them get what they wanted. But we were trying to stop their freight train from rolling over us, and a traditional blessing was the first thing I had ever seen slow them down. Their faces changed when the blessing was happening, becoming more relaxed as the blessing took root in them. It took away their anxiety about why we had invited them to the table. It was a place to start, trying to establish mutually beneficial relationships that aligned with our traditional teachings. That was how the industry leaders looked at it then. I think that is how they still look at it today.

The industry people saw that we were serious about what we were undertaking, and right away I felt they respected me and my role. I could see they were surprised and excited that ANDC had a clear vison mapped out and was willing to do the hard work to see it through. I easily got a commitment to some outcomes by our next meeting.

After that, I made sure things kept moving along, and in the first twelve months we made great progress because it turned out that the oil industry was an easier party to negotiate with than the government. Business people are used to negotiating and the idea of giving something to get something. If they see something is in their best interest, they don't waste time. They saw right away that we were ready to do business in a professional way, and that everyone would profit from collaborating.

Business people cannot get stuck or they will soon be out of business. They are motivated to find a solution that works for everyone, to create a balance among the parties. You hear business people talk about "trade-offs" and "mutual benefit," and they love terms such as "joint venture partnerships" and "common ground." As I first found out when I worked in the tannery dungeon, they pay attention to what they call balance sheets. They did not see balance the same way Indigenous people did, of course, but at least there was a way to start the conversation.

The oil companies liked what we were doing because it made good business sense. It would save them time and money to work with an umbrella organization rather than individual Nations. We were also offering them a mechanism by which Indigenous people themselves determined what constituted an Indigenous-owned company, defining appropriate ownership and staffing levels. This process was beneficial to them, so they agreed to fund our process for setting it up. Right from the start, the business people came to the table in good faith looking for something that worked for both parties.

In less than a year the two sides had settled on some goals. Indigenous staff would make up 13 percent of the local industry workforce, and proposals from Indigenous-owned businesses would be given priority. ANDC would allow a predetermined but reasonable time limit to build up to that level.

The industry was also quick to recognize that we were the experts on our land and had important contributions to make to discussions about its use and the environment. We immediately began setting out a process for them to report to us on benchmarks for air and water quality. They also agreed to fund studies on animals' migration routes in our hunting grounds.

They had reasons of their own to like our proposal. It was better for their bottom line to hire local workers than to fly them in, house them, feed them, and fly them home. It also helped their image to be cooperating with us, and a good image also meant good business. The industry representatives were eager to sign the deal and get started. They had a clear channel for communicating with us, and we had the ability to pool resources to make sure everyone was getting something they needed. It was all about *balance*.

Once we had a draft agreement, we took it to the federal government officials. They were impressed with the progress we had made. They could see that the agreement was going to work because industry also wanted it to work, so the government was ready to sign, too. Very quickly, we had our development council, the industry, and the federal government at the same table.

CHAPTER 24

Screech Owls

Y ou are probably wondering how I thought I could pull off an agreement this big with the multinational oil industry and two different levels of government. You might think I was naive to walk into the lion's den with nothing but traditional values and good intentions. But I also had a secret weapon that I could use if I needed it. It is called public opinion, and it is another thing I learned from Harold Cardinal.

Harold would have been happy if the government read his research, acknowledged the points he made, and agreed to do what was right according to our treaties. But that had never happened in the history of our treaties, so he didn't count on it. He knew he needed more than the facts to influence the people who had been ruling our lives for more than a century. He also knew that whenever he showed up at a public meeting and confidently voiced his opinion to the government, the newspaper and television reporters in the room sat up and took notice. Harold recognized that this gave him leverage. He began to use the power of the dominant culture's own mainstream media to defeat the federal government's White Paper.

Harold was a great communicator, and he was always respectful and professional when talking to the press. He did not call government people profane names or make wild exaggerations or pound the table and shake his fist. He did not need to do those things. He got his point across the way he always did, with facts and traditional values. The reporters at the meetings could see Harold was making sense, so they kept reporting what he was saying and doing. They had a trusted source of information in Harold, who was always ready to provide documentation to prove his statements. When reporters checked his facts, they always found that he was correct. Because of Harold, the press started paying more attention to what had been done to Indigenous people across the country.

This was the first big wake-up call to the Canadian people, who even to this day are shocked to learn about what was done to us, particularly the horrors of residential school. Now it wasn't just Harold and Indigenous people asking questions and demanding answers. There were also mainstream Canadians who did not support how Indigenous people were treated. Our communities started organizing our own protests and sending out our own press releases. The newspapers and broadcasters were happy to hear from us. Public opinion was shifting in support of Indigenous people, and it put pressure on the federal government officials. They could no longer sweep things under the rug.

Politicians are experts in public opinion. It did not take long for them to figure out they could use this growing attention for their own purposes. They got positive media coverage every time they announced they were working with Indigenous people to solve a problem. As soon as the IAA endorsed my proposal, which also meant an endorsement from Harold, the federal government was prepared to work with us. They did not want the media backlash if they did not look supportive of Indigenous people trying to deal with issues like water and air pollution. They also wanted to look like they were helping us lift ourselves from poverty.

At the same time, government did not want us to make our own money. They put an arbitrary cap on how much we could earn with our own businesses. If our earnings went over their cap, they reduced their payments to us by a corresponding amount, even though their payments were bound by the treaties. When an Indigenous community invested every penny it earned back into its members and land, the government reduced what it paid us. At the same time, the amounts they were paying us kept us in extreme poverty. It was a cycle of poverty that the federal government would not allow us to climb out of. There was no way we could move forward if every time we made a penny, the government cut a penny.

I needed a way to make sure we could use the money we earned to improve the quality of life in our communities. If we did not get the government to officially agree to remove the cap, they would keep doing what they had always done. They would use our natural resources and keep most of the money for themselves, dribbling little portions to us as they saw fit. I needed to get them to remove the cap and sign the agreement so that we could start moving ahead on economic sustainability. It would be a first step to economic reconciliation, even if no one called it that at the time.

Once industry agreed to the terms of the agreement, the federal politicians realized a freight train was now headed right for *them*. If they refused to endorse a deal that saw us ready, willing, and able to work for money that would lift us out of poverty, public opinion was going to smash right into them. The deal was on the table. Harold and the IAA were backing it. The oil industry thought there was enough money for everyone. The media would love it. There was no excuse for delay, so it did not take long for the federal government to agree to remove the cap on our business revenue. The politicians were ready to sign — and to take the credit. Like Harold, I was happy to give everyone credit if it meant a good deal for our people. It looked like we would have everything signed, sealed, and delivered within a year.

But then we hit a roadblock with the provincial politicians, who started trying to slow us down. They used every trick in the book to pump the brakes. They started throwing minor bureaucratic obstacles in our way, digging up old government documents to review, some from decades in the past. They kept changing our meeting times, which was a big deal since I had to drive hours, a lot of it on dirt roads, to get there. When we did have a meeting, they would try to change the agenda and talk about something else. They also did the old trick of dangling easy dollars in front of me for things that would solve an immediate problem on my home reserve but do nothing to address our long-term economic sustainability.

Their behaviour reminded me of a traditional teaching I learned as a small boy. When my father and uncles were showing me how to find my way in the bush, they told me Creator put things there to help our people navigate. They taught me what to look for, like moss that grew only on the north side of a tree, so that you could tell what direction you were heading in.

My father also warned me that not everything in the world was there to help me. There were things that would try to confuse me and tempt me from my path. Yielding to temptation could be a fatal mistake, leaving me wandering alone and in the dark. My father said some of the biggest temptations came from screech owls. Under no circumstances was I to follow their calls. Those little birds would lead me in the wrong direction until I got completely turned around.

Screech owls are not the big brown-and-white owls that go *woo-woo*. They are smaller and darker, and make noises that pitch suddenly from high to low, trilling up and down. Sometimes they sound like a barking dog. Sometimes they sound like voices talking. Sometimes they sound like they are speaking Cree. Sometimes they moan and wail. Sometimes they join their voices together. They sound creepy and weird, especially when you are alone and trying to find your path.

My father told me that screech owls are the voices of bad spirits trapped on this Earth. These bad spirits are especially restless at night when screech owls are also most active. The bad spirits would try to get me to step off my path. They wanted me to get lost in the woods, travelling in circles, so I couldn't find my way out. If I followed them too far, I might never find my way back. If I couldn't avoid them, I had to be extra careful to see the path ahead. Never trust a screech owl, my father said.

I thought a lot about screech owls when I was trying to negotiate with the provincial government. I was not expecting things to be easy. Government is about policy and procedures, keeping the bureaucracy running, and, of course, getting politicians re-elected. There is no motivation to resolve anything. They got paid the same, their work went on the same, whether or not we came to a resolution.

At first I gave them the benefit of the doubt as I tried to get them to the table. I have always been willing to work with anyone who was willing to work with me in an open and transparent way. I played fair with everyone.

But if a group was not really working with us, if it was promising one thing and doing another, I would be honest about that, too.

Working with Harold Cardinal, I learned the power of being transparent and open. If you behave that way, others have to work with you that way, too. That is how to open doors. I was open with everyone about how well industry and the federal government were working with us. Sure enough, as we continued working on our agreement, the oil industry representatives started getting positive attention from the media. As soon as the positive coverage got out, even more companies started jockeying to work with us.

But I still could not make any headway with the province. It kept us in negotiations for a long time, refusing to nail down details and logistics. I knew they were deliberately trying to slow things down and discourage us. But I could not figure out why. There was no real reason why we were being treated the way we were. It dragged on so long that finally I decided to play hardball.

It was at a meeting in Edmonton, with everyone sitting around a big boardroom table. Every seat was filled. There were provincial officials and their lawyers, and I had my administrative team and my lawyers there, too. In front of everyone, I put my question to the lead provincial negotiator, who was a very senior public official.

"Tell me exactly what specific clause in this agreement you have a problem with so we can address it and move on," I said.

He wouldn't give me a specific answer and kept talking around it. I kept pressing him, asking the same question over and over until I got an answer.

"There's nothing wrong with the agreement itself," the senior official finally admitted. "We haven't got any objections to what you, the federal government, and industry have agreed to."

"So, are you going to sign?" I asked him.

"No. We are never going to sign that agreement."

"Why not?"

"We don't need to give our reasons."

"We have already publicly announced that the three other parties have agreed," I said. "So I hope you have your answer ready about why the province won't sign on."

"What do you mean?" the official replied. "Why would we have to say anything?"

"Because there are reporters from all over North America waiting for me downstairs," I said. "The moment I step out of this building, they'll want to do interviews. Newspapers, television, radio. They all want to hear about our historic agreement."

"What are you going to tell them?"

"I plan to say just one word. You're the one the press will want to hear details from. You represent the province, so you have to tell them why the province won't sign. I suggest you decide what you are going to say, because they are going to wait for you if it takes all day."

"You only plan to say one word?"

"Yes," I said. "Just one word."

"What word?"

"Discrimination."

Then I stood up and started walking out. But I never made it to the door because several of his support staff leapt up, grabbed my arm, and tried to push me back into my chair.

"Don't leave yet," the official said in a loud voice.

"Why would I stay?" I said. "I have no reason to meet with you anymore. I heard you. You said you were not going to sign."

"Well, maybe there is something else we can do," he said. "Let me bring in our top man, and I think you'll be happy with what he has to offer."

"Okay," I said. I sat back down.

One of the provincial people dashed out of the room and was back in record time with the top man.

"Chief, I want to talk to you," the top man said, after he had settled into a seat right across from me at the boardroom table. "But before we start, can we excuse your lawyer and your staff?"

"I'll tell you what," I said. "I'll excuse my lawyers and my team if you excuse your lawyers and your people. Then you and I will talk one-on-one."

"I can't do that," he said.

"Yes you can. If you want to talk to me alone, it is you and I alone, or I walk."

The top man asked everyone to leave and to close the door, and I asked my people to follow them out. We sat there alone while he looked at me for the longest time.

"I can't figure you out," he said.

"What's so hard to figure out?"

He got up and came around the table, sat next to me, and leaned forward as he spoke.

"Chief, I have something that will put you in a comfortable position," he said. "Very, very comfortable."

"What is that?"

"I have a friend waiting for my phone call at one of the businesses who contract with the oil companies," he said. "As soon as I call him, he's going to get the paperwork done up, and all you need to do is go over to his office today and sign your name, and you'll be a full partner. He's got one of the biggest contracts in the oil business. You'd never have to work again. You'll be very, very wealthy."

I was taken aback. I had never been put in that situation before. I knew this was going to be a test for me because he was pushing for the answer right there and then. I knew the kind of money he was talking about, too, and it was hard to walk away from. But I also realized that this had to be a company worried about losing business to Indigenous entrepreneurs when our contract was signed. I also realized, given how intense the top man was, that he had a lot of worried business people who thought our Indigenous companies would take contracts away from them. That was exactly what I was trying to do, get our people a share of the pie, and I was so close. But right in front of me, a screech owl was trying to get me to step away from my path.

"It's an interesting proposition," I said.

"It's a once-in-a-lifetime opportunity," he said. "You will be set for life."

"You know I can't take it."

"Why not? It's so easy. We can do this today, right now."

"The only reason I am here talking to you is because of the people back home. These people elected me. They put their trust in me, and I can't betray them. I would never forgive myself for it."

"Then what is it you want?" he asked me. "What will it take to make you happy?"

"I want you to sign that agreement. That's all I want. Just sign it."

"Okay," he said. "If it means that much to you, we'll do it."

I thanked him, got up, shook his hand, and went out and told the reporters we had a deal.

Later on, we had an official signing ceremony in Edmonton with all kinds of media present. All four partners to the agreement were there, taking credit in front of the television and newspaper cameras. Everyone spoke respectfully of one another. The media reports were all positive, calling it a landmark agreement that gave Indigenous people the opportunity to develop their own economic stability. There was all kinds of celebration and back-patting, and the politicians got lots of time in front of the microphones. The story made headlines all across the country.

Today oil companies regularly brag about the Indigenous partners they work with and how many First Nations people they hire. They hold big events and release annual reports that highlight their Indigenous partners with beautiful photographs of our land and our people. The provincial and federal governments attend these events and they brag, too, about mutual cooperation and the benefits for the economies of Canada and Alberta. Everyone is taking credit for the fact that we are all moving along the path to economic reconciliation.

Sometimes I think that, had it not been for me, they would not have anything to brag about. Our agreement was the first of many steps in the journey to where we are today. My idea is still working in non-profit Indigenous agencies that focus on job creation, training, and economic development. The oil companies continue to work closely with those groups, and so do governments. The First Nations communities in our region boast many locally owned companies in all kinds of sectors. Many of our youth grow up dreaming of being entrepreneurs, and they have mentors and programs to help them along that path. I look around me, and I am proud of what I helped achieve for my people.

I might start bragging more. I believe I own the bragging rights for what I have achieved.

CHAPTER 25

Their Way Is Not Our Way

ANDC's agreement with industry and government was groundbreaking, but we were still in the early stages of figuring out how to do business alongside the dominant culture. We were making progress, but as Chief I had to create a solid foundation for my own Nation's business operations, while also finding a productive way to communicate our traditional values to mainstream partners.

I knew oil people made their decisions based on the bottom line, but I also saw how they reacted when we opened our meetings with an Elder's blessing. They behaved deferentially and recognized that a respectful tone was being set. They also seemed genuinely engaged in discussions about our hunting grounds and the migratory paths of our animals. It confirmed what I had suspected since I worked in the Edmonton tannery, that the dominant culture did not have the traditional teachings to help guide them, so they did not know things that we considered essential. I always felt the teachings were so powerful that everyone who heard them would want to know more, and now these business people seemed genuinely interested in learning from us and were asking some of the right questions. It was a good start.

The next step for me was establishing a business arm for our Nation so that we could start reaping the benefits of the ANDC deal. I had put a lot of thought into how to do this while establishing the ANDC because I knew that rapid economic growth brought risks as well as opportunity. The environmental dangers were plain to see, but I was also concerned about what would happen when large amounts of industry money started flowing in and our quality of life began improving dramatically.

That kind of money comes with great temptation, especially when you have been living in extreme poverty. It would not take much for greed to take the wheel and for the almighty dollar to drown out the wisdom of the ancestors. We were only human, and we had to continually keep an eye out for screech owls who would try to tempt us away from our core values. If we devoted ourselves to chasing profits, if we turned our backs on traditional values to enrich ourselves as individuals ahead of community, that would have a devastating impact. If we adopted this behaviour so common in the mainstream business community, if we allowed it to rule our judgment, it could separate us from the wisdom of the ancestors almost as effectively as residential schools and the Indian Act had done. If we behaved like our colonizers, we would no longer be the people that Creator intended us to be.

Sure enough, as soon as we signed our deal, the screech owls started showing up. They came camouflaged as allies and tried to confuse me and get me to step off my path. I had many offers to go into business with companies that needed an Indigenous name on the masthead to qualify for contracts that gave priority to businesses owned by First Nations people. I was offered opportunities to serve on corporate boards and in advisory positions with high salaries, bonuses, and stock dividends. It was the kind of money that bought mansions, fancy cars, and extravagant trips to exotic places. I was offered rides on private planes to top-level golf courses, tickets to concerts and hockey games, expensive steak and seafood dinners, fancy gifts such as gold jewelry, designer clothing, pricey watches. A golden-paved road was laid out before me, and the screech owls did their best to get me to walk down it.

I would like to tell you it was easy to say no to temptation, but I am only human. As the temptations came at me thick and fast, I prayed to Creator for strength to dedicate myself to the task in front of me. Once again, Creator answered my prayer by sending a mentor to help me understand business culture in the context of traditional values, someone who had already figured out how to successfully navigate the world of business while following the wisdom of the ancestors.

That person was Joe Dion. Like Harold Cardinal, Joe had served as president of the Indian Association of Alberta. I got to know Joe when I was serving on the IAA board, and I saw right away that he was a very smart man. I also knew he came from a long line of respected leaders. Joe's father was a Chief, and his great-grandfather was *Mistahimaskwa*, Big Bear, the Cree Chief who in 1876 refused to sign Treaty 6. *Mistahimaskwa* foresaw that the government would violate the treaty's terms, keep his people in poverty, and destroy traditional ways. He tried to unite the Cree people in the fight for social and economic justice and advocated resistance through nonviolence. The federal government responded by starving his people, who were already facing famine because the dominant culture had hunted buffalo to near-extinction. After forcing *Mistahimaskwa* and his people onto reserves, the government imprisoned him as punishment for the violence of some of his followers. *Mistahimaskwa* is remembered by our people as a strong and spiritual Chief who suffered on behalf of his people for speaking the truth and standing up against the government's injustice.

Joe carried on his family's legacy of independent leadership based on traditional teachings. He served as the Grand Chief for the province of Alberta and, like *Mistahimaskwa* and Harold Cardinal, he came to national attention by speaking the truth. He was one of six Chiefs who went to London, England, in 1976 on the hundredth anniversary of Treaties 6 and 7 to ask Queen Elizabeth II to protect Indigenous rights.

Joe was also a successful business leader who believed economic sustainability was a key part of our people's path to self-determination. He saw business as a way for our communities to control our economic destiny. Joe wanted Indigenous people to have the opportunity to earn a decent wage and have a good quality of life. Most importantly, he wanted to do this in ways that respected our traditional teachings. When I first heard him speak about Indigenous business ownership, I was inspired by his belief that not only was it possible to live a traditional life and participate in the modern economy, but also we could thrive under this approach. Our own hard work could bring about prosperity for our people.

The first time I took Joe aside at an IAA meeting and told him what I was trying to achieve for our people with ANDC and our industry agreement, he understood right away. He was well along the path towards what decades later would be called economic reconciliation. He had worked to grow his business knowledge with a university education and hands-on professional experience. There was no one better to advise me on how to properly set up an Indigenous business that could work alongside the dominant culture, and I quickly hired him as the business consultant for the four First Nations involved in our agreement.

Right from the start, Joe convinced me that if we operated at a professional level, business people from other cultures would work with us. He saw business as having its own language. If you said the right things, if you talked knowledgeably about your business plan and knew your numbers inside and out, business people would start a conversation with you. Once you had the lines of communication open, you could start to make things happen.

Even more important than his ability to speak the language of business, Joe had great traditional wisdom, and not just from his father's side of the family. He was taught traditional ways by his mother, who was a very holy lady. Like my mother, she knew it was her job to help her son find a good path in life and stay on it. From Joe's birth, she immersed him in the teachings of the Medicine Wheel, preparing him to make good decisions and act the right way.

Joe lived the values of the Medicine Wheel in whatever he was doing, whether he was helping another Nation start a business or talking with the Queen of England. Because the first thing the Medicine Wheel teaches is that everything is interconnected, from the bitumen under the boreal forest to the throne in Buckingham Palace. If you don't understand that everything is connected, you don't understand anything. Joe understood it on the deepest level.

You might have seen images of the Medicine Wheel, which my people usually draw as a circle divided into four quadrants, like a pie cut into four big slices. Each slice represents one of the four elements Creator gave us to sustain life. One element is *askiy*, the earth, which gives us food and shelter. Another is *nipiy*, the water that quenches our thirst and cleanses us. *Utin* is wind, the air we breathe, the breeze that cools us. *Iskotew* is the fire that warms us and cooks our food. The Medicine Wheel teaches us that these four gifts from Creator must always be used in a way that keeps them in balance.

Four is a very powerful number to my people, and we call ourselves the *Niheyawak*, four-part people. We recognize the number four everywhere we look. There are the four directions: north, south, east, and west. There are four seasons: spring, summer, winter, and fall. There are four parts of life: baby, youth, adult, and Elder. There are four parts of our well-being: spiritual, emotional, physical, and mental. According to the Medicine Wheel, all of these things must be kept in balance to live a good life.

This is just a simple overview. The teachings of the Medicine Wheel are huge and all-encompassing, and you can devote your whole life to understanding it. There is so much to learn that even now, as an Elder, I find something new in it every day. But once you understand the most basic element of it, you will look at the world in a new way. Everything under the Medicine Wheel — which is everything in the world — must be in balance for true harmony and well-being.

One way to explain this is to tell you the traditional way my Uncle James made canoes. Canoes must balance or they won't work, and that is one reason my people build them by balancing the four elements. The first element my Uncle James used was *askiy*, the earth. He chose a good spot and dug a pit to match the size of the canoe. He inserted four sticks into the pit, two on each side, to hold the canoe frame in place and to represent the four elements. Then he cut small trees and shaped them into curved sticks with his axe to frame the canoe.

Next came *waskway*, birchbark, for the sides. My Uncle James always built his canoes in the spring, when the sap is running and the bark moist. That is the only time of year you can strip birchbark and the tree will still thrive. My uncle also needed *iskotew* and *nipiy* for this stage, building a fire next to the pit and setting a big kettle of water on it to boil. When steam rose, he used it to soften and shape the bark. Then — back to the earth element — he used stones to hold the bark in place along the frame.

Next he split a log and sliced the wood into ribs that he soaked in water until they were soft enough to shape. After the ribs were fitted, he used an awl to punch holes where he joined the pieces with deer sinew, smaller and finer than moose sinew. He used very thin pieces that tied nice and tight.

The last step was harvesting *peiko*, spruce gum, the same gum my father chewed for energy when hunting. My uncle boiled it until it was soft, then added deer tallow to make it tackier and watertight. Sometimes, instead of tallow, he mixed the spruce gum with bitumen. My uncle then brushed the sticky mixture along the seams and left the canoe to dry in the air. Everything set perfectly, the bark keeping its shape and the spruce gum mixture making it leak-proof.

My uncle always followed the proper protocols, which was another reason his canoes were strong. He acknowledged Creator's gifts with an offering of tobacco, giving thanks for the dirt, the trees, the stones, the bitumen, the deer sinew. He gave thanks for the fire and water that cooked his food and quenched his thirst, and for the breeze that kept him cool while he worked. He gave thanks that, if there was ever a hole in the canoe, he could easily find the elements for repairs.

That is the right way to build a canoe, so it is in balance with all the elements, as well as the physical and spiritual worlds. My people put in that effort because we needed canoes to feed and clothe our families.

In the 1980s, when I was starting my Nation's business development process, I had the Medicine Wheel teachings firmly in my mind. I wanted to figure out how to put up guardrails to protect our traditional teachings from being destroyed by business practices that did not respect balance. Joe had been in business much longer and had a deeper understanding. He knew the traditional teachings applied to everything in life, so that meant they applied to business, too. If we followed them properly, in the long run we would always be successful.

But Joe went even further. He felt our teachings gave us what the business people call a "competitive advantage" because anything made according to the Medicine Wheel was strong and built to last. This came up at one of our very first discussions, when he and I were discussing how we could build a team to work for us.

"The first thing you need to do is hire the best of the best," Joe told me. "Accountants, consultants, engineers, truck drivers, legal advisors. Whatever the position you need filled, find the top people."

"How can we compete with the oil industry for the best people?" I asked. "Why would they come to work for us?"

"First of all, we are going to pay them what they are worth," Joe said.

"Industry does that by the bottom line," I pointed out. "They pay people based on the profit they want to make."

"People are more important than the bottom line," Joe said. "We want the best and we are going to pay them for being the best. They are the ones who are going to make this happen for us."

"Why would they want to do that?"

"They are going to stay with us because we are going to show them we recognize their value. We will show them that we respect them. We are going to treat everyone, no matter their background, according to the sacred teachings. They are going to want to work for us because of that."

"Won't industry just offer them more money? They will always have deeper pockets than we do."

"They won't be here just for the money," Joe said. "They will be here because they want to be part of something important, and because they are respected for what they are contributing."

As Joe urged me to be open to building up everyone on our team, not just our Indigenous members, it made me realize something that had been nagging at the back of my mind ever since residential school. It was also something I had seen in jobs like the one at the Edmonton tannery. In those places, people from the dominant culture used power to keep others down and take the best things for themselves.

"That is their way," said Joe. "Their way is not our way. Our way is better."

There it was. In two sentences Joe summed up our mission statement. We didn't just have a different way. We had a better way.

I did not want to use power to take things from people and keep them for myself. I wanted to create something good for our people that would let them enjoy a good life. That could not happen unless we treated everyone, Indigenous and non-Indigenous, with the dignity and respect Creator intended. If we were going to go head-to-head with industry and thrive, we needed to be true to who we were. We had to respect our non-Indigenous staff. We also had to respect our non-Indigenous business partners as we figured out where they were coming from. But we could not become them. We were not doing this just to make money. We were doing it to help our people and we needed to be true to our people's values.

I took Joe's word and hired the best of the best — people with the best education, best credentials, best experience. I hired people from all kinds of backgrounds, too: First Nations people, Métis people, settler Canadians, new immigrants from all over the world. We treated everyone equally with the respect Creator wants us to show everything. Things would be in balance, because we were balanced in our approach.

Before I hired somebody, I spent time talking with them. I would lay everything out, ensuring they understood what we were doing. When I hired them, I paid them well and made sure they knew our goals and values. On the few occasions when someone did not fit in, if it was just about the money for them, if they were cutting corners, if they were dishonest, I gave them their walking papers. When that happened, there was no big fuss, and I still treated the person with respect. Because of that, we attracted top people who knew their stuff and wanted to work with us.

That is how I was able to fulfill my leadership responsibilities, by keeping the best people I could find around me. They helped us get our big ideas off the ground, and that was partly because, as Joe had said, they spoke the language of industry. Whenever we had a meeting, they understood very clearly what was going on under the surface when the industry people spoke, what they really wanted, and why. They could clearly read those signals, and when we left the room after a meeting, the staff would let me know what they thought was really going on.

"Okay," I would say. "Let's figure out how we can work with them."

I learned that lots of things affect business, and they are not always obvious if you are not an insider. Sometimes it was share prices and profit margins. Sometimes it was public opinion, a court case, or a media issue. Sometimes a chief executive officer needed a new idea to impress his board. There were always a lot of things going on under the surface.

Another important thing Joe showed me was that we could easily take an idea from the dominant culture and put our own spin on it. The best example of this was Joe's recommendation that, rather than start from scratch, it made better business sense for us to buy an existing company that had contracts in place and brought revenue in from the get-go. This approach also addressed one of the issues brought to my attention during our engagements: non-Indigenous companies buying up our businesses. Joe advised us to turn that around and buy a non-Indigenous business. He and our staff drew up a business plan with details on what we were going to spend, what we were going to earn, and what bank loans we needed to make it happen.

This was a big first step for the region, and we structured it so that the four First Nations working together in ANDC were all balanced as equal partners sharing investments and revenues. The bank liked our proposal and gave us the loan we needed, which we could immediately start paying back with the revenue from existing contracts. When we made an offer to purchase, we had everything exactly right. We quickly negotiated a buyout of a heavy equipment and machinery company that was owned and operated by members of the dominant culture. By purchasing a going concern, our business could start operating immediately. That first company the four Nations bought together cost us $1.3 million. That was a lot of money back then. But we had our signed agreement with industry and government in place, we had our business plan, and we had a good relationship with the bank. We renamed the company *Neegan*, which in English means "front" or "first."

We grew *Neegan* every year because, with our ANDC agreement guarantee to review all proposals by local Indigenous contractors, the future was locked in. We ended up signing more contracts than the previous non-Indigenous owners. Joe made sure we knew how to write those contracts properly, that everything was spelled out in detail, with all the periods and commas, and that nothing was missing. Everything had to be perfect, and there could not be any surprises. He also made sure that all parties always had a clear understanding.

Clear channels of communication and joint understanding were important because Joe was also helping my Nation launch its own company, of which we were the sole owners. We got the right people and agreements in place and founded Christina River Enterprises. This was an arm's-length business wing for our First Nation, and under it we could run different operations such as janitorial, catering, and construction. Joe helped us set it up with the right pieces, the right board of directors, bylaws, financial statements, everything by the book. Of course, we also followed the principles of the Medicine Wheel. We had everything we needed for success.

Things immediately took off. I had one person at a desk in a corner who was doing business proposals all the time; as soon as one was sent off, a new proposal was started. I had another person doing research on the environment and what we needed from industry in terms of testing and reports. Another person was working on our relationships with the oil companies, making sure we stayed connected with higher-ups such as the presidents and chief executive officers. All of those people were taking our calls, and things were moving at top speed.

I had expected it to take forever to get things moving and for our community to see the benefits, but it did not take long. I always knew I was going to figure things out and we would make money. But once we started doing business properly, things took off like a rocket. We had money to invest in our community and companies right on our reserve that could do some of the work. We built houses and roads, put in sewage and water services, and started building up our social services. We also set up funds so that our young people could get different types of schooling. We hoped they would return to our reserve with their diplomas and degrees, and help keep up the cycle of prosperity.

The non-Indigenous staff we brought in to work alongside us were a big part of our success, just as Joe said they would be. When you look around our region today, you will see a lot of well-to-do Indigenous businesses. We are thriving, and that is in big part because of the help that we got from non-Indigenous people with the proper credentials and experience. They helped us get things off the ground, and I think we helped them, too, by sharing our Indigenous values.

It was my job as Chief to start this for our people. I now think that, in those early days, it was like I was in a busy kitchen preparing a banquet for my people. I filled platters with good food, set them on the table, and invited people to pull up a chair. Word started to spread, and more people began to join in. Before I knew it the banquet was in full swing, and there was always a new dish ready to be served up.

I was proud of what I was doing, but at the same time it was very hard work. There was always another problem to solve, another target to reach, another opportunity to follow up. More and more, I was getting pulled every which way. I was drifting away from the lessons I learned from the Elders about taking time to do things right, giving thanks, and finding balance.

CHAPTER 26

The Bottle Has a Spirit in It

I always enjoyed talking with my Uncle Victor, my mum's brother, who was known in our community as a great hunter. He was a good shot, so good that the Canadian military trained him to be a sniper. Victor and I used to talk a lot about hunting in the bush. One time, out of nowhere, he asked me a question.

"Nephew," he said, "have you ever gotten lost in the bush?"

"No," I said.

"Well, maybe one of these days you will. If you do, find an area where there is black poplar, and you'll see a growth on the north side of the tree."

"Is it there all year?"

"It grows there all the time. It doesn't matter where you go in the forest, there is always moss that grows on the north side of that type of tree. That's how you know your directions."

"*Kinanaskomitin*, Uncle," I said. "Thank you."

I always remembered what Uncle Victor told me, and it is a good thing because one time I did get lost in the bush. I was out hunting and had been walking a good part of the day. I was pretty far out when it suddenly got very cloudy and I could not tell directions by the sun. Right away, when I realized I did not know where I was, I remembered that most people panic when they get lost in the bush and start off in the wrong direction. Instead, I took off my pack and sat down. I used to smoke back then, so I pulled out a cigarette and smoked it. I listened carefully for anything — a car, a boat, a plane, running water — that would tell me where a road or a river or an airstrip was. But I heard nothing like that.

I took stock. It was not that cold. I had matches to use for a fire. I had my rifle so I could find game. Things were not too bad. All of a sudden, I remembered what Uncle Victor had told me and checked the trunk of a poplar tree. Then I checked a whole bunch of them, just to be sure. The moss was on the same side of every tree, so that was north. Okay, that meant south was the other way. I looked up and I could see the clouds were moving and the wind was blowing southwest. I headed straight south. While I was walking, I kept looking at the clouds, and every now and then I checked a poplar tree, too, to make sure I was going in a straight line.

As I walked along, I came to a marsh where I had been earlier and noticed some tracks. I knew they were mine because they were fresh and there was no one out there except me, and they went right around this marsh. Normally, when a person gets lost in the bush, they start following their own trail. They travel in circles and criss-cross their own tracks until they are completely disoriented. I ignored the tracks and kept going straight south until I came to a road. I was out. I was free.

After I had been Chief for ten years, I started feeling I was criss-crossing my own tracks. I was very proud of what I'd achieved during that decade — I still am. But it seemed like the work was always expanding, like a forest that kept stretching on and on in front of me.

Because of my work with government, and because of the successful economic development I led in our region, people all over Alberta started calling me and asking me to help their organizations. I sat on more committees. I was also travelling for business as the companies we started took off.

I was away from home all the time. I would just get back from one thing and would be getting ready to leave for another. I was always on the move, but it seemed to me that I was travelling in a big circle, going over the same territory again and again.

The entire time I was Chief, I worked day and night. Part of it was what I wanted to do for my people, the things that I knew could be accomplished to give us a better quality of life. There was always so much that needed to be done.

But there was also a dark side to my working all the time. The busier I was, the more I could avoid dealing with the childhood trauma of being taken from my family and forced into residential school. I did not have to think about the violence, the hunger, the horrible things they did to me. By working all the time, by being constantly on the move, I was trying to get away from the pain and suffering, to leave it behind me.

But it did not work. I had started using alcohol to dull my pain, and as the years went on I needed to drink more and more to get the same effect. I was getting in deeper and deeper, losing myself more and more. I was going down the wrong path, and I needed to find my way back to the right one.

I wanted to travel the road Creator intended for me. But residential school had erected a huge roadblock, and I refused to deal with it. In my younger days, when I lived in Edmonton and worked hard all week at different jobs, I would go out to blow off steam on the weekend. I used to party, go to dances, and have a few drinks. My thinking back then was that I was just having fun. But it was not fun for long. Addiction took hold of me pretty quickly and kept me in its grip. I was making progress in my role as Chief and putting my energy into my professional life. But I struggled every day with the trauma of residential school and was trying to ease the pain with more and more alcohol.

I wanted things for my people, but I wanted them for myself, too. I wanted a marriage like my parents had and I wanted a family. I got married young and I was so happy when my first child was born. I was over the moon. My first child was a girl, and it was so nice to have a little baby. Then we had a little boy, too. I spent a lot of time with them. I helped look after them, played with them, got them to school, took them all over the place. If I saw a friend, I was proud to introduce my kids to them. But my addiction and the trauma I had not dealt with got in the way of my being a good family man. I could not be the husband and father I needed to be, and that marriage ended.

A while later I was lucky to meet Tina, a wonderful woman who is the love of my life. We got married and started a family, and I was so happy when our children were born. But again I was not the husband and father I wanted and needed to be. I had not dealt with the things I needed to. If I did not smarten up, I was going to lose Tina and my children. My family was the most important thing in the world to me, and if I lost them I was not going to get another chance to get them back.

The Elders tried to warn me. They brought it up whenever they thought I might listen. One Elder told me that our people have our own way of seeing alcohol addiction. The Elders are not kidding when they call liquor "spirits."

"That bottle has a spirit in it," the Elder said. "When you pour from that bottle and drink it down, the spirit goes into you and takes over your body."

I knew what he meant. As soon as I took a drink, I felt different. I did not feel like myself.

"The spirit is not good at all and it will make you do stupid things that you would not normally do," the Elder said. "The spirit takes over your body and gets you in trouble."

I knew that, too. While I was under the influence of alcohol, I did things that were not good for me or the people around me, the people I loved and respected.

"The reason people have such a hangover the next day is because that spirit is getting ready to leave your body," said the Elder. "But it doesn't want to go. The spirit wants you to drink again so it can stay inside you. When the spirit leaves your system, your own spirit comes back and you feel better. You are more alert, more awake."

The Elder told me that is why we don't allow people to enter a sweat lodge if they have a hangover. They need to rest up for at least two or three days before they can enter to make sure it is their own spirit going in.

"They need to make sure that their spirit is back, that they are cleansed and spiritually connected," the Elder said. "Otherwise, the sweat is not going to help them. It won't work."

If you go into it correctly, if you follow the proper protocols, the sweat lodge can help you with your addiction. But it is only one part of your recovery. Once you have started down the path of addiction, you go down fast. It is a lot harder to keep the spirit out after you have started to let it in. There comes a time when you are just getting sicker, letting that spirit in and doing all kinds of things that keep you away from the gifts that Creator gave you.

Politics is not good for anyone struggling with addiction. It is a lot of pressure. People look for all kinds of ways to deal with that pressure, and they can go down a very unhealthy path. That is why sometimes the Elders meet with people who want to run for office, or somebody who is getting too old to be a politician, and tell them it is time to follow their path somewhere else. I understand that.

After ten years, I knew it was time to be more concerned about my family and my health than my work as a politician, so I let it go. I walked away and gave somebody else a chance to lead. I felt good about the things I had done for my community, but it was time to move on. As soon as I made that decision, I felt a lot of the pressure lift away — and I decided to celebrate that feeling with a few drinks.

"I wouldn't mind having a beer or two," I said to Tina. "I think I'll go and visit my uncle. I'm going to go and pick him up and have a beer with him."

"Go ahead," she said. I knew she was disappointed, but at that point she knew nothing she said would change my mind.

I got in my truck and went to pick up my uncle, who also drank hard. We bought some liquor and drove around the downtown, looking for a spot to park, until we came to one of the overpasses that spanned the main road.

"Drive under there," my uncle said. "That's where I usually drink."

I parked below the overpass, where we thought no one would see us. But I had not noticed there was a police officer watching us, and he followed in behind us.

"Oh, no," I said as soon as I saw him coming towards us. "This is it."

The officer made me blow into a breathalyzer and, of course, I failed. I was over the legal limit for alcohol while driving a car. I was embarrassed and ashamed. This was my big wake-up call. I was in major trouble and could no longer deny it. I had to act, or things were going to get steadily worse for me and my family.

The next day I knocked on the door of a Métis friend of mine. He told me to come in and sit down.

"I didn't come here for nothing," I said while he poured us some coffee. "I came here for a reason."

"Oh?" he said. "Is there something I can help you with?"

"I hope so. One time you told me you have twenty-seven years of sobriety."

"I do."

"I want to know how you did it. I need to know. I'm in the gutter right now and I need help to get out."

"I can't help you," he said.

If he was not able to help me, I didn't know where I was going to turn. Then he reconsidered. "Well, there is a chance if you are willing to try."

"I'm desperate," I said. "I will try anything."

"What we can do is pray," he said. "If the Higher Power is there to listen, things could change for you."

"I'd like to try."

"Okay," he said. He stood up and went into another room, and when he came back he had a briefcase.

Oh no, I thought. *He's going to pack up some things for me. I'm getting sent away to a treatment facility.*

He opened his briefcase, and there was a candle, sweetgrass, and a feather. There were a couple of rosary beads, too, and he gave me one.

"Here," he said. "This is yours."

Then he took the candle out and lit it.

"I've never seen Indigenous people pray like this before," I said. "With candles and rosaries."

"People pray differently," he said. "This is how I pray. You can pray whatever way works for you. The Higher Power listens to all kinds of prayers."

"Okay," I said.

"There's one more thing," he said. He got up and went back into the other room, and this time he came out with a jug. He put it down on the table and told me it held special water.

"My parents, my aunties, my uncles, all of them as far back as I can remember, have been using this water," he said. "They use it every time someone gets an ailment or is bothered by something."

"Oh?" I said.

"Yeah, I got it from Lac Ste. Anne," he said. "They have a pilgrimage there, and I go every year."

Back then, I did not know about Lac Ste. Anne. Since then, I have learned a lot about this holy site in southern Alberta. Every year for the past hundred years there has been a big pilgrimage there, and people come from all over. Many of the pilgrims are Catholic, but the lake is also sacred to my people. In Cree it is called *Manito Sahkahigan*, Spirit Lake. It has been a sacred place of healing to my people for generations.

When the settlers came, they called it Lac Ste. Anne and put a Catholic mission on the site. That is how powerful this site is — everyone recognized its spirituality. Now thousands of people, both Indigenous and non-Indigenous, come to the annual pilgrimage. There is a huge shrine where people can pray in whatever way works for them. Now I go every year, but back then I had never heard of it.

Healing water from that lake was in the jug, my friend said. "Would you like to try it out? Drink a little bit?"

"Sure," I said.

He poured some of the clear liquid, just an inch or two, in a glass.

"Here," he said, "drink it."

I grabbed it, drank it right up, and it burned all the way down. It felt and tasted like alcohol. I looked at my friend and thought, *I'm trying to quit and he's giving me a drink. Why is he doing that?* But I did not say anything to him, and he lit his sweetgrass and started to smudge everything in the room.

My father taught me about smudging. It involves medicines gathered from the earth, such as tobacco, sage, or sweetgrass. The medicine is lit on fire, and the smoke is used to purify the space. It is a sacred plant to my people and a powerful medicine. It has a beautiful smell and helps people slow down and become mindful and centred. It helps you to make connections and to ground yourself. Smudging, especially with sweetgrass, helps you let go of negativities, things that stop you from being balanced. It helps you feel calm and safe.

After my friend finished smudging, he sat down at the table with me and said, "Now we're going to start praying."

We started praying. We prayed and prayed and prayed.

"Okay, that's good," he finally said. "I think something good will come out of this."

Then he started telling me stories about his ways — how he used to trap in the bush with his dad, and things they used to do, things he had learned. We sat there and I listened to him until, finally, it got a little late, nearly eleven o'clock in the evening.

"I'm getting a little tired," I said. "I think I want to go home."

"Yeah, no problem," he said. "Everything is all done for today."

"Thank you for praying with me," I said.

"There's just one more thing," he said. "You'll need to remember this. Sometimes when people get angry, they think it is because someone has done something to them. But something else is pushing you into anger, something you're trying to beat. What is really angering you is your own negativity."

"How will I know?"

"Something will happen, and you will know. When it happens, I want you to stop and think about it in prayer. That's all you need to do."

"Okay," I said, then stood up and got ready to go.

"Would you like another drink?" he said, picking up the jug he had previously poured me a shot from.

"Why not?" I said. If, after all that praying and talking, he thought I still needed a drink, I was not going to say no.

He poured another inch or two from the jug and handed me the glass. I chucked it right down and waited for the booze to hit me. And there was nothing. It was pure. Clean. I could feel its healing power as it flowed through me, cleansing me. I looked at him and said, "So that was holy water?"

"Yeah," he said.

"It's good." I didn't say anything else and went home.

I sobered up for three months straight and I thought that was it. I had kicked it. But one day my wife and I got into a little spat. I got upset, jumped up, grabbed my hat and jacket and stomped out, slamming the door behind me. I was mad and I was walking towards town. I was heading for the closest bar.

There was a little trail that ran through the bush from our home into the downtown and I trudged along it, still furious. I was about halfway to town, right in the middle of the trail, when I heard someone say my name.

"Hello," I said, stopping where I was. "Who is there?"

But nobody answered. I turned around and saw some bushes. I went over to see if anyone was hiding and playing a joke on me. But there was nobody. I looked around a bit more, but I was all alone. I walked back to the path and was turning towards town when *ding!* — a bell rang in my head. I remembered what my friend had told me. You will know when your negativity is taking over, he'd said. So I stood there and did what he suggested. I said a prayer and asked the Higher Power to help me.

"I am angry because things aren't going the way I wanted them to," I prayed. "Please come and help me."

As I stood there, I felt something come down softly and brush the top of my head. I kept praying and it kept coming in a gentle wave that continued washing over me. It cleansed the negativity from me; all the anger was gone. I felt light. I felt peace.

Oh, geez, what am I doing on this trail? I thought to myself. *Why am I heading towards a bad place?*

I turned around and went straight home. It was early in the fall and a really nice evening for a walk. I looked around as I followed the path, enjoying the fine weather and the lovely scenery until I got back to my house. I went in through the door, closing it quietly. I hung up my jacket and my cap. I grabbed the coffee pot and made coffee, drank two cups, and then went upstairs to bed. I woke early the next morning and felt good. I thought about how many times I had woken up feeling terrible from a massive hangover. I thought, *This is great. This is what I want. This is how*

I always want to feel. This is how I want my wife and my children to see me every morning. That was when I made my real commitment to myself that I would never drink again. I felt so good. I felt alive.

I went downstairs and cooked a big breakfast for my family. Tina and our kids came down one at a time as I set the table. I put the food out, and we sat down. I said a prayer of gratitude for what we were about to share as a family, then we dug into the big breakfast. My wife and I started talking about the day ahead, and everything was good. When we were alone later, I told her the story of what had happened to me while I was walking along the trail towards town.

"That's good," she said. "Somebody's looking after you."

"Yeah," I said. "It was a miracle. I am going to remember it. I am not going back down that path of addiction. I never want our little guys to see me in that condition."

And they never did. I never touched alcohol after that day. I was thirty-eight years old and it was time for me to do the hard work of getting back on the road Creator intended. And I haven't stopped. I have been steadily following my road ever since.

CHAPTER 27

You'll Find Out

Now that I was no longer Chief, I needed to find a way to make my living. For a decade I had been Chief Cree. That was my identity, but it was also my job. When I stepped away from that role, I had not yet reached the age of forty and had a young family to support. I took a careful look around me as I thought about what to do next. I wanted to put the knowledge I had gained as Chief to work. I wanted to find a job that would allow me to remain committed to my traditional values. But I also needed money for all the usual things that a family needs.

I had a lot of prospects. Over the previous decade, I had built a reputation as a strong leader who could be trusted to do the best for his people. I had also made important connections with senior leaders in government, the oil industry, and Indigenous associations. The oil industry was exploding, and everyone wanted in on it. Companies wanted to hire me to help ease their way into the growing economy of northern Alberta.

There were a lot of people who wanted to put a price on my good name and use it for their own purposes. I was constantly being approached to sell Indigenous people on new plans for their traditional lands. This made me realize that the screech owls were still out there, trying to confuse me and get me to step off the road that Creator intended for me.

But they were lucrative offers, and I was sorely tempted. I wanted to shower my wife Tina with beautiful clothes, fancy jewelry, and luxurious vacations. She supported me in everything I did and had carried a heavy load looking after our family while I was focusing on my duties as Chief. Tina also stood by me as I dealt with my addiction. She deserved to quit the day job she worked so hard at. She deserved the best of everything. I would have loved to spoil my children, too, after spending so much time away from them when I was Chief. I wanted to give them the best education in the world and be able to set them up in their own businesses if that was what they wanted. There were a lot of things I could have done for the family I loved if I followed the screech owls down that path.

The temptations were powerful, but not as powerful as the traditional teachings or the people who so lovingly passed them on to me. My father always told me it takes years to build your reputation, and one split second to destroy it. He also warned me that it was easy to get distracted by screech owls but hard to find your way back once you step off your path. Every day of his life, he showed me through his words and actions that a good life was one led for the good of our community, according to the traditional teachings.

Companies kept courting me, trying to dazzle me with money so that I would help them improve their bottom line. But I had my own bottom line: I would never do anything against the teachings of the ancestors.

Ever since the incident with the *mekwenescuk* in the river, I had remained committed to what my parents taught me. They gave me a strong foundation and set clear expectations for how they expected me to behave. Their teachings helped me survive residential school and showed me how to help my people overcome racist governments and a greedy oil industry. After the teachings had led me through all that, how could I abandon them because temptation swirled around me? I would never feel right if I went against them. Like my family taught me, I prayed to Creator for the strength to stay on the right road and find the right work to do.

My prayer was answered when I was contacted by a friend I greatly respected. Elmer Ghostkeeper is from the Paddle Prairie Métis Settlement in Alberta. Today he is very well known as a Knowledge Keeper and for his dedicated work on Métis rights in Canada. He wrote a book called *Spirit Gifting* and has dedicated his life to helping Indigenous people steward the land.

Elmer is also a businessman, and at that time he worked for a forestry and logging company that held large contracts with the province. It was a lot like the oil industry in that they wanted to harvest natural resources on traditional land, and their work had the potential to create both big environmental risks and big economic opportunities. I could see it was a good fit for my knowledge and experience. But how would it work for me being on the other side of the fence, being part of the company trying to make the deal? Could I represent the company and remain true to traditional values? Would the company let me advise them on what was right for my people, or did they just want to use my good name to sell their plan?

I trusted Elmer, so I agreed to a meeting with the company's executive vice-president. As soon as I walked through the office's front door, the vice-president stopped what he was doing and came up to shake my hand.

"Welcome aboard," he said.

"I haven't accepted the job yet," I said. "I'm here to find out what you would like me to do."

"Well, that is up to you," he said. "We want you to advise us on how to work with the Indigenous communities."

I asked some questions, and all of his answers were about what I could do for Indigenous people. We took our time, and he seemed to listen to what I had to say. He told me the company was aware of my work as Chief. They saw that I always focused on the best possible outcome for all Indigenous people, and he said that was how his company wanted to work, too.

"We hope you will join us to help us make that happen," he said. "You are going to like it here because every person's opinion matters. We don't have hierarchies when it comes to information. We all get a say, and we are very interested in what you have to contribute to help us work better with Indigenous communities."

Elmer kept confirming everything his boss said, and I trusted him. It looked like this job might give me room to do what I felt was right. I decided to give it a try. I would see if I could put my knowledge to use with one foot in the business world and the other in the traditional world. The vice-president seemed to respect how I wanted to use my knowledge and experience, and he offered me a good wage for it. But the real test was going to be, "Would we be able to do the work we wanted?"

Right away, we started working on a plan for logging on the traditional land of one of the region's First Nations. It was not the one I had been Chief of, but I knew everyone involved. It was a major project that would have an impact on logging practices at all First Nations in our area, including my own. The company I was now working for had an agreement with the Alberta government to log all over the boreal forest. Elmer and I got to work developing an approach to Indigenous engagement that would set the precedent for how the company approached logging Indigenous land across the province, and eventually across Canada. My friend and I had to find a way to help the Indigenous people not only in our region but also everywhere. It was very important work, and I was excited to be part of it.

Up to that time, logging companies had given no thought to the Indigenous view of the boreal forest. They approached it the same way they approached a moose at the Edmonton tannery. They reduced everything down to the cost of a log and its impact on the profit margin. They never thought about the big picture and how everything in the boreal forest was related, not just the trees but also the animals, the plants, the water, and the air. They did not consider the boreal forest in terms of balance and harmony. It was not the lungs of the Earth to them. It was just a number on the bottom line of a balance sheet.

My new company had been clear-cutting before then. They would pick a spot, map out a huge square block, and go in and cut down all the trees. They left the devastated land behind, a scar on Mother Earth. When it comes to traditional values, there is nothing good about clear-cutting. Even beyond the obvious environmental impacts, the repercussions keep rippling out.

For example, Elmer and I found out early on that clear-cutting was having a direct impact on moose hunting. There had been logging along the moose migration path, and non-Indigenous hunters were taking advantage of the deforestation. They came from all over to sit and wait in the clear-cut area until a moose walked out of the protection of the forest. With no forest cover to shelter it, a moose stood out so clearly it might as well have had a bull's eye painted on it. We heard of "hunting parties" where six or eight moose were killed at once. Often the moose weren't harvested, so no meat went to feed a family. The antlers were cut off as trophies and the carcass was left to rot. It was the exact opposite of the respect and gratitude Creator intended for the moose. It wasn't hunting. It was a bloodbath.

The Indigenous communities were well aware of this travesty and the many other ways clear-cutting went against traditional values. Everyone was upset, especially the Elders, and they had made that known. Now the company was looking for a way to prevent this type of thing from happening. My first assignment was to find a way to ease the tension between my new employers and Indigenous communities.

I knew it was a big opportunity to spark change if we could get the logging company to recognize traditional teachings about the boreal forest. Elmer, who was now my boss, knew exactly where I was coming from because he followed traditional teachings, too. He showed me a picture of his father sitting outside his cabin. Just by looking at him, I could see Elmer's father was a traditional man who lived off the land. He had taught his son well, just like my father had taught me. The two of us started our work by talking about the teachings of the Medicine Wheel. We took our time and dug into that deeply, and by the time we were finished we had a plan that we knew could work if everyone was open to the idea

Our first step was to start educating the company staff. We built a sweat lodge so that the employees, who were mostly from the dominant culture, could experience it. We wanted them to see how our people prepared for major decisions, how we purified ourselves to be in the right frame of mind. We weren't sure how it would go over, but to my surprise the higher-ups agreed to the idea right away. They wanted everyone in the company to experience the sweat lodge, right up to the senior executives.

Much of my people's sweat lodge ceremony is private, so we only gave the company staff a basic introduction. Even if we had been able to share more, they were nowhere near the level of understanding they needed to participate to a greater degree. They were closer to the level I was at when

I was five years old and my father first introduced me to a sweat lodge. Some of them struggled with the heat, the darkness, and the length of the ceremony. But they all took it seriously. They said it was an eye-opener and were very appreciative of the opportunity. Afterwards, they talked excitedly about what they'd learned. They asked a lot of questions and wanted to learn more. That was when I knew we were going to be able to get some good things done.

Elmer and I went back to our planning, and we did a visual exercise. We drew a big circle and wrote down all the issues we could think of inside it. After we had everything down, we cut out a quarter of the circle like a big slice of pie. We labelled that quarter "technical." That was the science part: air and water monitoring, health-related studies, anything that was a technical matter related to science. Business people like numbers, so we put anything we could count and study in a scientific way into that category. Elmer and I both respected science, which we did not see as contradicting traditional teaching. We felt scientific findings would make the big bosses comfortable. It could tell them things in a way they understood, and we felt sure this would back up the traditional teachings.

The other three quarters were filled with cultural and traditional knowledge. We knew that First Nations cared deeply about traditional issues related to animals and their migration paths. The Elders were particularly focused on that, so we had to show them the company was not only taking traditional knowledge into consideration but also giving it primary importance. We looked at everything. Migration routes and the calving season for moose, deer, and caribou. The nesting season for eagles and hawks. Important medicinal plants that could not be disturbed. We used traditional knowledge to figure out what had to be protected at all costs. Once we knew that, we could figure out what could be used for logging and provide an economic benefit to the community.

We were careful to link the quarter of the pie that included scientific research to our traditional approach. We had scientists out in the field collecting and analyzing all sorts of data. We also hired local Indigenous people to help count different types of animals and birds. We counted different plants, too, as well as the trees we wanted to harvest. We counted animal dens and bird nests.

You name it, we counted it. We included all the numbers on detailed maps, so we knew exactly where everything was. Using this research, we mapped out a path for logging that would do the least damage, leaving the migration routes and breeding sites undisturbed.

The company supported our plan, and the staff worked hard to review and analyze the data. Keep in mind that back then, this was an entirely new way of thinking. Prior to that, all logging decisions were made according to the dominant culture's scientific facts and business needs. Elmer and I were proposing that the company give traditional learning the same if not more consideration in decision-making. We were also showing how science could not just work alongside traditional knowledge but actually support it.

There were millions of dollars at stake for the company and incredible pressure to pull off the plan. Elmer and I needed a huge success at the engagement session planned with the Elders. We were only going to get one kick at the can, and if we blew it and did not get the Elders' support, the company would be back to clear-cutting.

The company's senior executives took the engagement session seriously, and when the big day finally came, they flew north to attend it personally. Elmer and I picked them up at the airport, and they peppered us with questions as we drove north to the small community hall where the meeting was taking place. Elmer and I stayed positive, but I could see the business people were nervous. I was nervous, too. If, after all the work we had done, the Elders were still against the project, it would be impossible to convince the company to continue using traditional knowledge in their decision-making.

As soon as we walked into the meeting hall, we could tell the Elders were concerned. They were already in their seats, and they looked serious. They went silent as the company representatives — me, Elmer, and the senior executive team — walked in. The executives looked serious, too, as they went to the seats reserved for us. The hall stayed quiet as we all sat down. The plan was that I would get the ball rolling by speaking first, so I got up and went to the front of the room.

It is hard to warm up an audience that is sitting in stony silence, but I smiled and stayed relaxed. I wanted the Elders to think I had good news.

"*Tansi*," I said, greeting the Elders in Cree. I spoke in Cree for the rest of the meeting, too, because it was the language the Elders had spoken all their lives. When I introduced the executive team, they perked up when they recognized their own names, but that was the last thing they understood. Elmer got the gist of it as he was fluent in the traditional language of the Métis. But he and I had decided I would do the entire presentation in the language of my people. We upended the usual way these meetings were run — they would normally be conducted by the company managers, and in English, a language not all of the Elders understood. This time, it was the company managers who had no idea what was being said.

"Listen," I told the Elders. "You are in the driver's seat here. You get to decide where the logging is going to happen. You get to decide everything. You can decide what roads will be built and how the trucks will come in and out."

That had the Elders sitting up straight in their seats. I could see the executives were waiting for me to switch to English, because they were used to being the main focus of these meetings. But I kept going in Cree.

"You are going to see a presentation on the screen," I said. "I will tell you all about it in Cree. I will tell you right now that I have seen all the scientific facts they are putting forward, and I believe they are correct. But you can ask any questions you want, and I will make sure you get the right answers."

Now the Elders were nodding their heads.

"They really want to log this area," I said, "so they will pay you a lot of money to do that. They will also hire people from your community to work there. There will be jobs for your young people. It will be good economically."

Now the Elders were smiling. We started the presentation, and I translated every word into Cree. I made sure all the questions got answered. At the end of the meeting, the Elders were still smiling as they stood up and shook hands with the executives.

As we were leaving, one of the executives asked me, "What did you tell them?"

"Don't worry," I said. "You'll find out."

The deal worked out. Now you see Indigenous engagement models that focus on the community everywhere across Canada. Companies consult Elders about everything on their traditional lands, and they use interpreters who speak the community's language. First Nations communities also expect a high level of detailed and well-researched scientific information with any proposal. They insist on straightforward answers to their questions. They expect there will be good employment opportunities for their people. They demand that their traditional knowledge be respected and valued. I am very proud that I played a part in getting this model off the ground.

At the time, I was happy I had figured out a way to properly use the knowledge I had gained as Chief to help First Nations. My material needs and those of my family were being met, and I was still living by the traditional values of the ancestors. It was the right step forward on my path.

CHAPTER 28

Turtle Island

My work at the logging company was just one of my experiences dealing with detailed technical information. When the science is correct, I usually find it supports rather than contradicts traditional teachings. Over the years, I have come to see them as two ways of looking at the natural world. The main difference is that science parcels information into small factual packages of information to be digested. Traditional teachings are about the big picture and living by Indigenous values. To put it another way, science is about material things, while traditional knowledge is about spiritual connectivity. That does not mean one is right and the other is wrong, or that one cancels out the other. That is where wisdom comes in — seeing that these two things can exist at the same time and be connected. Like everything Creator gave us, the two can exist together if they are in balance.

Much of my work has involved reconciling the dominant culture's science with traditional teachings. I have always enjoyed science. I like working with numbers and statistics, and knowing about things like chemical interactions and soil composition. I am interested in how things work technically, how engineers continually find improvements to the operation of machines and processes. I feel the same about medicine. I had successful heart surgery when I needed it. I followed all my doctor's advice, and the issue with my heart was fixed. But I also strongly believe traditional medicine is important for me to continue to live a balanced life of well-being that helps keep me healthy and away from the surgeon's knife.

In my professional life, I have worked with many fine scientists and engineers. Many times, we find that we are saying the same things. We are just coming at it differently.

For centuries, in the middle of northern winters, my people have seen sparkling pillars of light that seem to come out of the darkest part of the boreal forest, glowing straight up into the sky. It is very dramatic, like someone in an invisible spaceship is beaming up thousands of droplets of light. My people have traditional stories about these sparkling pillars. We know that when they appear, it is a sign there will be extremely cold weather for the next few days. We get out our warmest coats, gloves, hats, and boots because we know we will need them.

Science can tell you that these light pillars are "atmospheric optics" visible because ice-filled clouds have dropped much closer than usual to the Earth's surface and the ice crystals are reflecting the moonlight. Science can tell you what temperature this phenomenon occurs at, how the ice crystals form, why they reflect moonlight, and other facts. After all this close study, scientists can tell you that it means it will be extremely cold for the next few days, so you should dress warmly. The scientists learned this by studying at university. I learned this from my parents and my grandparents. We learned the same thing but in two different ways.

In today's world, people think that science has all the answers, that you can boil everything down to numbers on a piece of paper. But that is not correct. There are many times when traditional knowledge has something to teach science. I have proven that more than once over the years in my meetings with scientists and engineers.

I recall one time I had an opportunity to work publicly with scientists on an issue where traditional knowledge proved more relevant than scientific research. It was a meeting about the oil industry's environmental water monitoring. There was a packed room of 350 people, Indigenous and non-Indigenous, listening to researchers who had been hired by the oil companies to tell us what was happening to the river that my mother had travelled by dogsled the night she gave birth to me.

I sat back and listened, watching them bring in documents that were thick and full of numbers. The scientists told us where they had collected their samples, which part of the river they went to, and at what time of year. They went over all the details, from the tiniest particle they collected and how they analyzed it to what they thought it meant. They said it showed that oil sands operations in the area were having a minimal environmental impact on the river. They claimed this applied along the watershed from the mountains in southwest Alberta all the way north to the Arctic Ocean. They were going to make the document public so that all the study details would be available. I listened to them, but what their numbers were saying did not make sense to me. Finally, after a few hours, I got tired of listening and put up my hand.

"Mr. Chairman," I said, "can I tell you something?"

"Yes, Mr. Cree," he said.

"I wouldn't distribute this document any further because it needs to be revamped. You need to get a more thorough study done so that people can have a better understanding of the river."

"Why?" they said. "We worked very hard to get all these facts. It is a very detailed study."

"But it's not accurate," I said.

"Our scientists say it is accurate," the chairman said.

"No," I said. "It's not."

They explained all the scientific research again and went over and over how they had collected their samples and analyzed them.

"All I can tell you is that what you are saying does not add up according to my traditional knowledge," I said. "The only way that I'm going to prove this to you is if you send these fellows back to do another study. Go five thousand metres from where they did the initial study, either farther north or south, and see if you get the same readings. Then come back and tell not only me but also everybody here."

That created a major debate. The scientists could not understand where I was coming from, why I would think that where they scooped up the water would make a difference to their information. But the biggest issue was money. Who was going to pay for the scientists to go back and do this additional research? We would have spent the whole day talking, but finally someone from the oil industry said they would commit to funding further study.

"You have to go farther out from where you initially did the study," I said to the scientists. "Don't miss anything. We need to know exact measurements so that everybody understands what I am telling you."

"Okay, don't worry," the scientists said. "We'll do that."

The scientists were happy because they had more money to do research. They went off to do their work. They returned two months later for another public meeting, and they were very quiet when they carried in their briefcases and their big reports. They avoided looking at me. I did not say anything. I just sat back. They stayed seated, too, and saying nothing. The chairman kept looking at me and then at the scientists. Finally, he said, "Well, give us the information. What were your findings when you went to the new spot?"

The scientists went up to the front of the room. They stood there uncomfortably, looking at one another and waiting for someone to start talking. Finally, one of them spoke up.

"I don't really know what to say," he said.

But the chairman kept at him, and finally he had to lay it all out.

"Mr. Cree was right," the scientist said. "In that new spot, we did not find a single measurement that matched the previous study. Everything was totally different. The weight of the particulate, the turbidity of the water, every organism produced different results."

They admitted that this meant they could not make claims about everything in the watershed from one set of measurements. They were going to have to do detailed analysis at a variety of places before they could make any claims about the environmental impact on the water.

After the meeting, one of the scientists came up to me. "How did you know that?" he asked. "What did you use? What type of instruments? What computer software?"

"First of all, I love science," I told him. "But science doesn't have all the answers. As a Knowledge Keeper, I fall back on my traditional learning. The Elders keep telling us the trees are alive, the land is alive, the water is alive. And do you know what happens to things that are alive?"

"No, what?" said the scientist.

"They move."

"The river moves?"

"The river moves constantly. That's why you see people get stuck on a sandbar when they're travelling in their boats. They are travelling along and all of a sudden, *boom*, they hit a sandbar in a place where there was nothing the year before. People think the current is always the same, but it is not. It moves. Every year it moves and goes from one place to another."

"But how did you know the readings would be different?"

"Think about it," I said. "When the current changes, everything in it moves and starts a new life. Everything in it is always changing. That is why you will never find the river to be all the same from A to B."

It was a matter of traditional knowledge and looking at the big picture. I did not question the science itself. The test results they had were probably accurate. But those technical results did not show the big picture. As a First Nations Knowledge Keeper, I can use my traditional knowledge to find the right answer because my people have been thinking about these things for centuries.

One of these days, the scientific community is going to accept the traditional knowledge we have to share. Some day, people will understand that for centuries human beings had knowledge that science has not found a way to explain. Think about how the pyramids were so perfectly built, but science cannot explain how the ancient Egyptians knew how to build them. It is the same with our traditional knowledge. Science may not be able to explain it, but it does not change the fact that we know these things about the land we call Turtle Island.

Years ago, I sat down with a very wise Elder and asked him why we call our land Turtle Island. We do not call it North America, or Canada, or the United States, or Mexico. We have always called it Turtle Island. I wanted to know why it had that name, so I took a gift to the Elder and followed the protocols. Then I asked my question. Of course, the Elders did not answer right away. Part of what the Elders teach is patience. It was quite a few days later when he talked to me.

"You asked me about Turtle Island," he said.

"Yes," I said. "I always wondered why our people call it that."

"Years ago, some of our people had a way to move around outside of our bodies. Their spirit was able to travel from one community to another, then come back to report how everybody was doing out there."

"How did they do that?"

"They would build a box out of logs and make it just big enough for somebody to lay down in it. Someone would lay inside the box and meditate. Eventually their breathing mellowed down to the point where they needed very little air to stay alive. That's when they went into a trance and their spirit left their body and took off travelling."

"How far could they go?"

"Mostly they would go to the next village and see what was happening, then come back and tell everyone. But one time there was a very great man who could travel like that and he could go farther than anyone else. One time, his spirit went up in the air, all the way to where the Earth's atmosphere ends. He looked down and he saw the turtle."

"Can we still see it?"

"Now we can see it through science," the Elder said. "When you have a chance, look at the map of North America and you'll see the turtle. The head is what the map-makers call the Arctic. The right front leg is what they call Labrador and Quebec. The right rear leg is Florida. The left rear leg is California and the front left leg Alaska. The tail is Mexico."

I went and checked a map. He was right. I could see it right away. It is very clearly a turtle. I went back to talk to the Elder again.

"Wow," I said. "How long were our people able to travel like this?"

"Centuries," he said. "There were a lot of things we were able to do when we were alone on our land, things that we have lost. We have to work our way back to them so we can do them again."

"You think we could still travel like that? Could we still find those things we lost?"

"Of course," the Elder said. "We all have a connection to Turtle Island, to its physical and its spiritual parts. All human beings have it, not only Indigenous people. Everyone who is part of Turtle Island is connected to it. Everyone can learn to use that connection in their spiritual life."

I liked the idea that we were all connected to Turtle Island. It made sense to me. The more I thought about it, the more I felt really, really good about it. We are all here together in this wonderful place. We can all improve our spiritual connection to it. We can all live together here in balance and harmony.

I once found a turtle in the boreal forest. I do not know how it got there. We are too far north and our winter is too cold for most turtles to survive. But I had heard years before about the time one of my uncles set a net on the Clearwater River, and when he checked it, there was a turtle in it. A big one. Somehow it travelled up our river, the river that is alive and always changing. Maybe it took a wrong turn somewhere, but it made it to my uncle's net and he caught it. He showed it to a lot of people before he let it go to continue its journey. I always thought about that turtle.

When I found my turtle, it was upside down. I was driving along a gravel road to pick up some groceries when I saw something flipped over on its back with its little legs waving around in the air. *That cannot be a turtle*, I thought. *How could it get way out here?* I pulled off the road and got out for a closer look, and sure enough, it was a turtle. I picked it up and turned it over to see if it was all right. It scratched my hand with its little claws, and I dropped it. Luckily, it did not get hurt. I picked it up again because I did not think I should leave it in the middle of nowhere so far from the water. I tucked it up all nice in a box I had in the back of the car and made sure it was comfortable. It settled right down, so I went on to the store, got a few things, and headed back home.

As I was driving along, I saw a couple of boys from our community walking along the road. It was a hot day, so I pulled over.

"Would you like a ride home?" I said.

"Yes, please," they said. "It's very hot today. We'd be happy for a lift."

"Hop in," I said.

They jumped in the back seat and started telling me stories about what they were up to. We were having a nice talk and then, all of a sudden, I heard one of them start screaming and hollering like I had never heard before. I pulled the car right over.

"What's wrong?" I said.

"Something is crawling up my back!" one of the boys said. "It's attacking me!"

The turtle had crawled up the rear of the passenger seat and was climbing onto the boy's shoulder. When the boy turned to look, he only saw the turtle's head. He thought a snake was biting him because he could feel pinpricks on his arm, but it was the turtle's little claws digging in as it tried to climb.

"That's just my turtle." I started laughing. "He won't hurt you."

"What? Where did you get a turtle?"

"I found it flipped over on the road. It must have been waiting for me to come along."

After I dropped the boys off, I took my turtle home to my wife and we laughed about how it scared the boys. We kept it around for a few days and it crawled around contentedly, eating and sunning itself. Finally, I talked to Tina about what should happen next.

"I don't know what I'm supposed to do with this turtle," I said.

"Just let it go," Tina said.

I carried the turtle to the shoreline in front of our home and set it down. Right away it started crawling towards the water. Pretty soon it was swimming, with its little head sticking up as high as it could go. It kept swimming in a straight line. It just kept going until it was out of sight.

The next summer, I heard somebody found a turtle on a sandy beach in an Indigenous community farther north up the river. The people upriver took a good look at the turtle that had swum so far. Then they put it back in the water and it swam off again, still going north. I have always wondered if it was the same turtle I found. Think of what it had to go through to get that far. Think of the strange currents and freezing water it had to swim through before it crawled up on a sunny beach. It must have been very determined to keep going.

Sometimes I think I am like that turtle. I wonder if that is why I was brought here to Earth, to see what I have seen, to experience what I have gone through, and to keep moving forward. I made my way through colonialism's cold and turbulent river and tasted its bitter waters. I tasted them quite well. Maybe I am supposed to bear witness to it all, because a lot of people got so hurt, so damaged, that they cannot bear to talk about it. Some of my friends could not survive it. They're gone with the spirits now.

If it was not for the Elders, I don't know where I would be today. I would have probably been buried years ago. With the Elders' help, I managed to survive so that I can bear witness to what happened to my people. When I tell my story, it no longer drags me down to an angry, desperate place. But it does get to me. All that sadness. All that pain. That is colonialism affecting me again, almost sixty years after the government tore me from my family and imprisoned me in residential school. The trauma is always there. Sometimes I am feeling great and then, out of nowhere, a little thing triggers it and it all comes back. I will never escape it. But I learned to survive it, to be true to myself, and to keep moving forward.

And now when I tell my story, a lot of people say, "Thank you for your wisdom. Thank you for your knowledge." It pumps me up when they say that. I feel good.

I am proud of the decade I was Chief of my community and the role I played in building a future for my people. When I look around, I see beautiful community buildings, good roads, all the things a thriving community needs. People have good jobs and run successful businesses. If my parents could see our community now, it would blow their minds. In my *Mooshum*'s day, only the wealthiest people had a home with running water. Now many in our community have a big, warm house with electricity, a nice kitchen to cook in, and two vehicles in the driveway.

I did my part to lay the foundation for that prosperity. And I have prospered, too. My grandfather would never have dreamt that I would do things like travel on vacation or play golf. My health is good. I have a beautiful family, a happy home, and my children and grandchildren have good futures. I know that my people still have a long, long way to go on their journey. There are many bends in the river ahead. But I am grateful for the many gifts Creator has given me.

Not long ago, I was sitting with my wife on the deck of our home. We were drinking coffee and looking out at the beautiful lake. Ducks were swimming around. The sun was shining. It was a really nice day.

"You know what, my dear?" I said.

"What?"

"I think sometimes we take things for granted. Do you know how many people would like to sit right where we are and enjoy this view?"

"We have been blessed," she said.

Sometimes when I look out at the shore, I remember that turtle. I still do not know where it came from or where it ended up. It must have been very powerful to make it to a peaceful shore to rest a while before the next part of its journey.

CHAPTER 29

Truth and Reconciliation

T hings were falling into place for me. I had a loving family, and my wife and children were happy and healthy. I was in recovery from my addiction. I had a job that paid me a good salary and allowed me to use my knowledge to help my people. I had everything I wanted in the material world. My life should have been perfect.

But I had a nagging feeling deep inside me. I realized that, as the Elders had told me, the spirit at the centre of my being was sending signals to my brain. Now that addiction and overwork were no longer jamming those signals, they were coming in clearly. I could no longer ignore them. The messages told me to pay attention, that something important was missing from my life. I wanted — I needed — to figure out what that was.

As always, I turned to the Elders. I followed the proper protocols, brought gifts, and asked for wisdom. The Elders asked me questions and listened carefully to my answers. They prayed with me. They meditated on my question. Finally, when they felt I was ready, they gently shared their answer. I had a problem, and it was a big one. I had never truly faced up to my residential school experience or what it had stolen from me. Although everything seemed good in my material world, I was suffering spiritually.

If I wanted to be spiritually healthy, I had to reconcile what had happened to me in the past with how I wanted to live in the present and the future.

"You will never be free," the Elders told me. "Not until you can forgive those people."

The Elders had hinted at this earlier, but at that time I was not in the right state to properly hear their message. This time, freeing myself from addiction and overwork made it easier for me to hear that painful truth. But the clock was ticking, the Elders warned. Hanging on to my anger and bitterness was dangerous. I was sober now, but the conditions that made me drink were still there. It was bad for my mental health and had already led me into addiction. The Elders felt my mental health was still at risk, and they were also concerned about my physical health. They warned that my negativity would contribute to heart disease, stroke, cancer, or any number of wellness issues. Even worse, the Elders said, it was affecting my spiritual health. In the same way someone under the influence of alcohol or drugs cannot absorb the healing power of a sweat lodge, my anger and bitterness kept me from fully embracing my spirituality. It was impeding the road Creator intended for me.

It was a huge message. I took a lot of time to pray and meditate on it, and with the help of the Elders, things started to get clearer. I thought about my road before residential school and remembered *Napikan*, the little boy eager to learn about spirituality. Creator meant me to be *Napikan* and walk a path of spiritual learning. But, at residential school, the spiritual part of me was what they most hated. Speaking in Cree was brutally punished. Praying in Cree could have got me killed. I truly believe that if I insisted on acting like *Napikan*, I would not have made it out alive. Because of my extreme fear for my physical safety, I compartmentalized myself and connected with *Napikan* only when it was safe. It was almost never safe, so *Napikan* only peeked out in the dark of night, when I lay in my bed and prayed silently.

I realized that when I left the school behind, I left *Napikan* behind, too. I was using traditional knowledge in my working life, but I was still compartmentalizing in my spiritual life. I had not fully reintegrated those parts of myself and I could not figure out why. But the Elders knew. They went to residential school, too, so they understood trauma. They knew that, to get on with my life, I kept my trauma tamped down in the deepest, darkest part of myself. It stayed there while I put one foot in front of the other and achieved the goals I set for myself in the material world. But the trauma was still inside me, ready to cause trouble at any moment. Until I dealt with it, my material and spiritual worlds would never be in harmony. I could not truly live the teachings of the Medicine Wheel. I could not walk my true road until I was a wholly integrated person. The Elders said I needed to face the truth and reconcile all the parts of myself.

Even back then, the Elders were thinking about reconciliation. It took everyone else a while to catch up. It was not until 2008, decades after I left residential school, that the government decided it needed a Truth and Reconciliation Commission to start the healing process between First Nations and the Canadian people.

The English word *reconciliation* was not new to me. I heard it a lot from business people, who use it when balancing financial accounts. Everything a company spends is recorded in one column and all the revenue in another. The two columns must reconcile, with money going out balanced by money coming in. If you cannot balance those two columns, you cannot tell if you are making or losing money. You don't know where you are.

Reconciliation is ingrained in Indigenous culture. My people see it as about balance, too, but in a much bigger way. We see it in terms of the Medicine Wheel. Our bottom line is that Creator meant for the world to be in balance and harmony. All of our traditional teachings centre around that. When I gave the Elders a gift and they gave me their wisdom, that was a balanced exchange. So was thanking Creator for the gift of a moose I harvested to feed my family. Everything in our culture is about finding balance. Something is taken, and something is given. It is reconciled. The more I prayed about it, the more I realized that the mentors who shared their wisdom with me were always working to find balance between the Indigenous world and the dominant culture.

My Uncle Lawrence was a farmer who sold his agricultural products to the dominant culture. He learned how that culture operated and used that knowledge to support his family, and to keep me from being sent back to residential school. While Uncle Lawrence participated fully in the larger economy, he treated his land and everything on it according to traditional values. He was able to balance two worlds, the traditional and the dominant culture, and stay true to the First Nations man he was.

Harold Cardinal took it even further. He never stopped urging the government to see Indigenous people as equal partners. Harold wanted the government to see us that way, but he wanted Indigenous people to see ourselves like that, too. He wanted us to realize that we were empowered by traditional teachings, that we had the knowledge and wisdom to change things for the better. He wanted us to be leaders, to share our traditional knowledge for the betterment of our people. But he also wanted us to share it for the betterment of the dominant culture, and the betterment of the world. Harold was always a big thinker. He knew the power of traditional teachings. He knew that if everyone lived by them, the world would be a better place for everyone. He wanted us to work together side by side in the spirit of respect and collaboration.

It was the same with Joe Dion when he advised me to bring in the best professional people, no matter what their cultural background was, to work together to build an economic future for my people. Joe knew that we needed experts like accountants and lawyers and engineers, that we needed their knowledge. But he was thinking about the big picture, too, when he said, "Their way is not our way." He did not want Indigenous people to adopt the behaviours of the dominant culture's business world. He wanted them to adopt ours. He wanted to show people from all cultures that the traditional teachings were a better way to do business — better for people, better for the environment, and better for the bottom line. He wanted to show everyone that the business world benefited from balance and harmony.

It was the same with Elmer Ghostkeeper, too, when he brought me into the logging company to provide an Indigenous-led solution that worked for everyone. We dug deep into the traditional teachings to come up with a plan that respected our culture and our land, but also helped the dominant culture. We introduced the non-Indigenous staff to concepts like the sweat lodge, and they were respectful and interested. They wanted to learn more and they asked good questions. We had opened the door, and people were willing to walk through and join us. We shared our knowledge in a transparent way, and everyone was the better for it.

I was lucky to find great mentors who guided me wisely. These very smart people were all, in their own ways, striving to reconcile traditional teachings with the dominant culture. The drive towards reconciliation was always there, whether I was working on my uncle's farm, holding government officials to account, or negotiating with business people. Without realizing it, I had been on a journey of reconciliation.

I was finally starting to figure out what Creator wanted me to do next. My people were not given the traditional teachings so we could hide them away. We were supposed to share them and teach others the path to balance and harmony. We were not supposed to force anyone onto that path. That was what the dominant culture did, but their way was not our way. Our way was to share our beautiful teachings peacefully and respectfully because they could help every single person on the planet.

This was why my spirit kept signaling my brain. I didn't see the dominant culture as part of Creator's world. I saw it as a problem to be solved, something to figure out to get a business contract or a bank loan. I also saw it as an oppressive force that stole me from my family to imprison, starve, and beat me. I did not see its members as people. But, in the eyes of Creator, they were human beings who needed the wisdom of the ancestors. To truly live Indigenous values and treat them as real people, I needed to fully embrace reconciliation and fill my heart with forgiveness.

I want to be clear about one thing. I am not talking about "forgive and forget." Reconciliation with the dominant culture doesn't mean Indigenous people forget what was done to us. The horrific violence, the inhuman sexual assaults, the vicious attacks on our culture, the greedy theft of our lands, the stolen children, and the missing women. Those things happened over generations, and some are still happening. My people still feel the deep impact of intergenerational trauma and will for a long time to come. There are many, many immense wrongs that must be properly addressed.

That is why we need the truth part of Truth and Reconciliation. I need to tell my truth, to bear witness to what I saw and felt. It needs to be on the public record, along with the testimonies of other residential school survivors, thousands of stories that fill up federal government archives. I thank Creator that I can tell my story, because many people can't. For some it is too horrific, too heartbreaking, too painful. They cannot speak about it without being overwhelmed. There are too many victims who can no longer tell their story because they passed over to the spiritual world, taken by addiction, violence, or suicide when their pain was too much to bear. It is partly in their honour that I tell my truth to you now. It is also because Creator wants me to help everyone know this truth.

That is not all Creator wants me to do. Creator wants me to pray for everyone, including people of the dominant culture, to find their way to a good life. By forgiving the dominant culture and trying to help them, I found my way to healing.

When I first realized what Creator was calling me to do, I was not ready. I had suffered too much for too long, and my pain was a part of me. But once again, I was lucky. My family had taught me that suffering and sacrifice were an important part of our spiritual traditions. I saw this as a little boy when our community held a Sun Dance, a powerful and sacred four-day ceremony for our people. The Sun Dance is deeply ingrained in our culture, an age-old tradition going all the way back to the ancestors from long before colonization. The entire community participates, and it can take a year for members to prepare for it. Different First Nations have different ceremonies and protocols, but it is always a powerful prayer for community healing.

The Sun Dance is so powerful that, of course, the dominant culture wanted to erase it from existence. The government banned the ceremony until two years before I was born, so for almost sixty years it was something my people did in secret. My father helped keep the tradition alive. He made sure to tell me all about it, too, so that I could pass along the knowledge when I was older. It involves gathering together to pray for healing, and individuals like my father make personal sacrifices on behalf of the group to reinforce the power of their prayer. When my community had its first "legal" Sun Dance in my father's lifetime, he went four days without food or drink, and offered up his suffering for our people. I could see the immense physical toll it took on him. As *Napikan*, I asked him why.

"It's not because I want to do it," he told me. "I do it because our community needs a very powerful prayer."

"But why does Creator want us to suffer?" I asked.

"Sometimes Creator wants us to put everything we have into a prayer," my father said. "Creator sees our suffering and knows our prayer is real and for a very important need."

"But why do *you* have to do it, Dad?"

"We all have to do it while we are on Earth in our physical form. Creator made it our job to help everyone and we have to do it now. Once we pass on, it is too late."

"Everyone? Or just our family?"

"We need to pray so everyone can be well and prosper," my dad said. "Not just our own family. All the families, all the kids, the parents, the grandparents, everybody. That's a very big prayer, and we need to put everything we have into it."

I thought a lot about the teaching my father shared with me. He didn't say Creator wants us to help some people and not others. He said Creator wants us to help everyone. Creator wants everyone to live in balance and harmony. If we can't pray for everyone to be part of that, we can't pray to be part of it ourselves.

My father saw his share of suffering when he was in residential school. But when he came home, he did not let negativity stop him from doing Creator's work. He gave himself over to helping others. Sometimes he did it physically, sharing moose meat and firewood with people who needed it. He also worked tirelessly to preserve the spiritual wisdom of the ancestors, no matter what the law said. He was always working to build up his spiritual strength, too, so that whenever the community needed him, he was ready.

I followed my father's example and began building up my own spiritual strength, and I took it very seriously. I concentrated on my breathing and my ability to meditate. I used plants and traditional medicine to maintain the purity of my health. I smudged with sage and buffalo grass to spiritually cleanse the spaces around me. I went into the bush to clear my mind. I spent all the time I could with the Elders, expanding my learning. I did everything the teachings said was necessary to improve the strength of my own prayers and make them powerful and authentic.

It took a long time, but finally, after a lot of dedication and commitment, I had a major breakthrough. I realized forgiving the people who oppressed me was in my power and my power alone. I controlled it. No one could force me. It was something I could do, not something that could be done to me. With that, I stopped clinging to my anger and bitterness, and instead put my power into a prayer for the people who had oppressed me. As I prayed, I felt the negativity leave my spirit and disappear. In its place, in every part of me, the physical, the emotional, and the spiritual, I was filled with a powerful light. I felt purified.

I carried that feeling with me the next time I participated in a sweat lodge. Because of all of the heavy spiritual work I had been doing to cleanse myself, I was well prepared for the ceremony. I felt powerful when I began the most important sweat lodge ceremony I have ever participated in. It was an incredibly intense experience that took me to deep levels of spiritual connection.

When the spirits entered the sweat lodge, right away they touched the top of my head to let me know they were there. They recognized me by all my names: Bobby Mountain, *Napikan*, Number 53, Chief Cree, Robert Cree. The spirits knew that the experiences connected to those names had led me to where I was that day. They knew it was time for me to integrate those names — my birth name, my traditional name, my number name, my leadership name — as stages in my journey. The names had important connections, too. My mother named me Bobby. My *Mooshum* named me *Napikan*. The government called me Number 53. My people called me Chief Cree. The business world called me Robert Cree. I had done the hard spiritual work and I had embraced all those parts of myself — child, spiritual seeker, victim, leader — and was able to reconcile them.

The spirits gave me a new name, my spiritual name, my true name, whispering it into my ear in Cree. It is a sacred name so powerful that I had to pray about whether it is appropriate to share with you. Through my prayers, I accepted that Creator wants me to share all of my story with you, including this name, so that I can fully share my message of healing. I am *Kisikowasha Ka' Ki Kkawat*, "The Person with the Holy Child Within." I try to live up to that name every day so that I can live the way Creator intended as I continue to walk a road of forgiveness.

It can be a challenging road to follow these days. The world is unbalanced and full of disharmony. Everywhere I hear people talking about their "righteous anger." My people's traditional ways teach there is nothing righteous about anger, which strips the balance from our lives. It makes us sick in mind, body, and spirit. It blinds us to the wisdom of the ancestors and the gifts of Creator. It takes us off our true road. We are meant to live in harmony and balance, and we get there through true reconciliation based on healing, understanding, and compassion. That is the way of my people, and that is how I live.

I am here to tell you, it is forgiveness that is righteous.

CHAPTER 30

A Spirit Gets Stuck

As I got older, I was able to spend more time with my family and do a lot more things related to our culture and traditions. One of those things was going to Powwows, which are a very important part of Indigenous culture. A Powwow is a gathering where we celebrate our traditions and learn from one another. There is music, dance, regalia, food, all sorts of things. People of all ages come, from babies to Elders, because it is one of the ways we pass on our knowledge and traditions to the next generation. Powwows are usually held in the summer and hosted by a First Nations community or organization, sometimes on reserves and sometimes in an urban setting. Relatives and friends travel from all over to participate.

In Canada, the Indian Act outlawed Powwows until 1951. When my father was young, he had to hide his participation in Powwows, the same way he had to hide his sweat lodges. People like my dad continued to have Powwows in secret, and we used them to celebrate our culture. Now Powwows are a big thing and getting bigger. We have opened them up to Métis and Inuit Peoples as well as First Nations. Non-Indigenous people come, too, and we are hospitable to them. It is a way to teach them about our culture.

Every year there is a Powwow held just north of Edmonton that is hosted by one of the premier Indigenous addiction treatment centres. It is organized by the treatment centre's staff and clients to help people look beyond their addictions and find strength in their culture and community. Every year my family and I go to this Powwow, which is held near the site of a former residential school.

One night, not too long after I left my role as Chief, my family and I drove to the Powwow in a great big car we had at the time. It was still early afternoon when we pulled into the camping area, and there were not many people around. After we unloaded the car and got everything set up, there was still lots of daylight left. We were planning to go into town the next day to pick up supplies, but my wife thought we could get it all done in one day.

"Let's go to the store now and get some groceries," Tina said. "We need some things for breakfast."

We drove to the grocery store and got what we needed. By the time we headed back to the campground, the sun was getting lower in the sky but there was still lots of light. We could clearly see the old residential school as we drove past it. It had been closed for years, and there were boards over the doors and windows, and signs warning people to keep away. We were almost past it when my wife shouted for me to stop.

"Why?" I asked.

"Stop!" Tina said.

I pulled off the road and stopped the car.

"I can see a kid standing in that upstairs window, three floors up," she said. "He is peeking through that window."

"There can't be anybody there," I said. "It's boarded up tight."

"I saw him. I saw a kid up there."

"There are fences all around the perimeter of this building, and all the entrances are boarded up. How could he get in there?"

"I don't know, but he's in there," Tina insisted. "What if he hurts himself? We have to do something."

I didn't know whether to believe her or not, but I backed up the car and pulled over in front of the building.

"Where did you see him?" I asked.

"Right there," she said, pointing to a third-floor window that was not boarded up.

"There's nobody there."

"I saw a kid there. I am sure of it."

I looked up at the window she was talking about. I looked and looked but I couldn't see anyone. She was so certain she had seen someone that I watched for a while until, all of a sudden, I saw a boy looking down at me. Sure enough, he was peeking out sideways from the third-floor window. When he saw me looking back, he hid fast. Too fast. So fast that I knew it was not a person.

"Oh," I said.

"What?"

"I've just seen him."

I was still in the driver's seat of our car, so I unbuckled my seat belt, opened the door, and got out. I walked towards the building to check it out. As I looked up, I saw the boy peeking out the window again. This time he was right in the centre of the window, and I got a good look at him as he stared down at me. He was not very tall, and he was very thin. He had a brush cut — the same kind they gave us when we arrived at residential school and chopped off our hair. He opened his eyes big and wide, wider than possible for a human being. Then I knew for sure that I was not looking at a living person. I felt the hair on the back of my head stand up, but I stayed still. He hid again, then came back out and opened his eyes wide again, trying to look menacing.

"You're not going to frighten me," I said. "Forget about trying that. I won't be scared."

He stopped and put his head down, so I knew I was communicating with him. I felt so many emotions pouring out from him. He was sad. He was frustrated. He was lost and confused. There was also a lot of fear, and all these emotions were mixed together and spilling out of him. I could see them in his features and his expression, but I could feel them, too.

"Why do you try to scare people?" I asked.

"That's the only thing I have left to do," he said. "It's the only thing I can do to amuse myself."

I was talking to him in English; I tried to switch over to Cree, but he was afraid to speak it. So I kept using English, and he kept sending me messages, and they came in very clearly. I had heard about telepathy before and thought it was a joke. But now I was putting things together spiritually, things I had learned from the Elders over the years. The Elders had told me that we can communicate with spirits and that it was nothing to be frightened of. They were right.

"You're not scaring me," I said to the boy. "I know what you are. You don't have to try to frighten me."

"I don't know what else I can do," he said. "I'm stuck here."

The Elders had told me that sometimes there are people whose spirits get stuck on our plane of existence and they do not want to leave. Something holds them back and they assume they can continue their life on Earth. But they are spiritual beings, so there's no physical thing they can touch. They are no longer of this Earth and do not belong here.

"I know where you are supposed to go," I said. "I'm here to help you get there."

"How can you help me?" he asked.

"I know how to help you see the path ahead. Let me get a few things ready and I will help you."

"Okay," said the boy.

I always carry some ceremonial tobacco. I dug a little hole in the ground and buried some of it to thank Creator for bringing me there to help. I made sure the boy could see and hear what I was doing, and then I spoke to him.

"I want you to listen to me," I said. "You have to move on. You've finished your life on Earth. You have to go."

The boy nodded.

"I'm going to pray for you," I said. "While I pray, I want you to be aware of what is going on around you. When you see a light behind you, that is the light coming to pick you up. When you see that, you go with it."

"Okay," he said.

I always carry sweetgrass with me, too, the same medicinal herb that my friend used to pray the night I stopped drinking. I lit it and used it to smudge the land in front of me. The smoke rose and drifted towards the residential school, and I started praying. The boy kept watching me. I could still feel emotions rolling out of him, but they started to change. The fear was going away, and he was feeling hope. As soon as I felt his hope, I started seeing right through him, like he was disintegrating. All of a sudden, there was a light behind him. It was so bright! I had never seen white like that. It cleansed the boy and gave him warmth. It did the same thing to me. It was a beautiful feeling — I felt purified. I saw the boy turn around and take a step into the brightness and disappear. I kept praying and thanking Creator for helping me with the things I cannot understand. When I finished praying, I went back to the car and got in the driver's seat.

"He's gone now," I told Tina. "He's moved on to the spirit world. No one will be seeing him again."

We do not have to be afraid of spirits. Most of the time they are stuck because no one has helped them try to move on. When I see a spirit, I do not scream or holler. I look at it and ask, "What are you doing here now?" They behave quite well when they know you don't have any fear. Once you show fear to them, they will do anything to scare you. But they need us to help them. They are stuck on this plane. They cannot do anything, not even pray for themselves. We can pray for them because we are still alive. We were given this physical being and we can use it to help out the spirit realm. It's very important work. Once you help out, you get a wonderful feeling of great joy. You feel calm and cleansed. Afterwards, you sleep just wonderfully. That's how you know you've done something good for that spirit.

Prayer is very, very powerful. At one time, prior to European contact, my people were very close to knowing what the spirit world is all about. Because of our prayers, our ceremonies, and our blessings, the spirits were there to help us. Then we were pulled away from them, and that knowledge was stripped from us. Now we are relearning those ways and are moving closer again. One day, we will be reconnected with the spirit world. It will take time to do it the right way. But we will get there.

CHAPTER 31

Elder Robert Cree

M any people think I automatically became an Elder when I turned a certain age. They think it was like becoming a senior citizen: The clock ticked down, I turned sixty-five, and *boom*! I was an Elder.

It is true that all Indigenous communities treat their oldest members with great respect for their knowledge, life experience, and seniority. But different groups have different processes for recognizing an Elder. In some Indigenous communities, an Elder is someone who has reached a certain age or has grandchildren. I was taught there is no specific age or experience that makes you an Elder. Someone in their thirties can be an Elder, and someone can be in their eighties and not be an Elder. Everyone who goes on a spiritual journey travels at their own pace, and not everyone's road is meant to lead them to becoming an Elder. Different people have different roads and purposes, as Creator intended. It is not better to be one thing than another. Everything Creator intends for us to do is important.

When it comes to being recognized as an Elder, I was taught it is up to the community's other Elders to study you while you are on your journey, observing the deepening of your learning as well as the decisions and the progress you make. They watch how you pray, both for your own spiritual strength and for the good of the community. They are looking for signs that you have properly grown your wisdom and that you are ready to share it with your community. When they think you are ready, they let you know.

Elders are able to give guidance and support to everyone who needs it. Sometimes they help individuals who present the proper protocols and ask for wisdom. Other times Elders voice their opinions without being asked because they think it is needed. For example, if they think the community's elected leaders are going down the wrong path, they can be very vocal in letting the community know. It works the other way, too. If they think the leaders are doing the right thing, they will reinforce that. Elders are not meant to keep neutral in political or cultural settings. They are there to help the community in whatever way they can, and sometimes that involves speaking up. There are many roles an Elder can play for the good of the community. They can be role models for youth, advisors to those making important decisions, and leaders when they have a concern they want addressed. Elders also help counsel those struggling with addiction or intergenerational trauma. That is why spiritual preparation is so important. It is a role that requires strength and stamina — you have to build up for it both physically and spiritually.

Elders are not born with wisdom. They are like everyone else. I was taught that, while Creator gives us different roads, we share many of the same life experiences right from the beginning. When you are a newborn, you are in your purest spiritual form because you are still connected to Creator. That's why it is the perfect time for a mother to bury her baby's umbilical cord in the bush. A baby is pure, exactly as Creator intended, and is wide open to the spiritual ceremony performed by the mother and the aunties. A baby can accept the gifts of Creator and the blessings of family with no obstacles or distractions.

In the normal course of life, as you grow up you get more distracted by the material world. As a youngster going to school, you are introduced to new people and new ideas, and you get a glimpse of the bigger world out there. New things start to get your attention, such as making friends, taking tests, and playing sports. Your own world starts to get bigger, and there are more distractions.

As a teenager, you get even more involved in the material world. You think about your appearance, your hair and clothes, first jobs, romance, learning to drive — all the heady things that come at that time. You are also exposed to drugs and alcohol and other negative temptations. Your road starts to zigzag as good and bad influences pull you back and forth, and it gets harder to make your way forward.

When you are a young person with a job and start your own family, you get very busy. There are so many decisions to be made and so much pressure in your day-to-day life that it is easy to start putting spiritual things aside until you think you will have time for them. It is easy to leave the straightforward path. No one is perfect, and everyone strays now and then. That is why the traditional teachings are important. If you live by them, you won't get too far from your path. If you do stray, they are always there when you start to look for your way back. There is good and bad everywhere in this world. When you're trying to walk a straight road in life, the bad is going to pull at you. But the good side pulls at you, too.

As you get older, your road starts to straighten. There are fewer distractions. This is partly because your life pressures start to ease. Your children are out of the house and entering the busy stage of their own lives. You are getting closer to retiring from your job. The lessening of distractions is one of the reasons Elders can focus on the important work of sharing wisdom and knowledge. They have gathered wisdom and knowledge throughout their lives, and now they have more time to share it. The zigzagging slows down and it gets easier to focus on what is important. Most importantly, you are also getting closer to returning to Creator. Just like when you were a baby, you are closer to that purity as you get ready for the next stage. You start to let go of material things and generally experience things differently.

I saw that when my mum was nearing the end of her physical life. She was in the hospital for special care, and my siblings and I were there every day as she moved towards Creator. She slept a lot, but when she was awake she talked to us about the past and the lessons she had taught us. She asked me if she had ever told me about the *mekwenescuk*, the little river people she had played with as a girl. I assured her that she had and that I remembered the story well. Most of the time, she wanted us to pray with her.

"I see a little boy," she said to me as I sat beside her bed.

"What is the little boy doing?" I asked. I wondered if it was a baby she had lost just after he was born. I knew she thought about him all the time.

"He is praying," she said. "He prays all the time. Pray, pray, pray."

"What is he praying for?"

"He's praying for me. He prays for our people too. He prays for everyone and everything on Earth."

"Would you like us to pray with him?" I asked her.

She nodded her head. My siblings and I stood around her bed and joined hands as we prayed with her and the little boy praying for us all.

My mother taught me important things about how to live a traditional life, how to find my road, and how to be a good person. With her last breath, she gave me her final teaching: We had to pray for everyone. I was very lucky to have such a wonderful mother. Many times, I have prayed in gratitude to Creator for the blessing of learning from her.

I think she would have been very proud on the day an Elder came to see me and offered me a gift of tobacco.

"Why are you giving me this gift?" I asked him. "It is for Elders."

"The other Elders and I have been discussing you," he said. "You have studied hard and worked hard. You are ready. It is time for you to share your knowledge and wisdom. You are now Elder Robert Cree."

It was one of the greatest moments of my life. It was a great honour for me to join the ranks of the Elders, to share my knowledge and wisdom, to try to help our community and its members. It was not the end of my story. It was a new beginning.

Just because you've become an Elder doesn't mean all the other issues in your life disappear. I am still learning and still need to make sure I am building myself up spiritually. There are still things that can knock me off my road. All the trauma I experienced is still there, and I still have to deal with it every day. Releasing the anger and bitterness freed my spirit, but my brain is still a computer, and sometimes a computer can have a glitch. Now I have the wisdom and knowledge to help me deal with those glitches. I pray every day, and I try to keep my spiritual strength up so that I am ready when challenges come.

One came not too long ago. I had gotten up in the middle of the night, not turning on a light because I didn't want to disturb my wife. In the dark I bashed my foot against something and tore off my toenail. Physically it was very painful. But emotionally it immediately took me back more than five decades to residential school. A memory popped right into my mind, with sights and sounds and smells as if I was still there. I was going through a growth spurt and getting too big for the shoes they had given me. But every item of our clothing was carefully rationed out, and their timetable said I was not yet due for a new pair of shoes. I kept wearing the ones I had, and they were getting tighter as my feet kept growing. I started limping around, and soon I was in pain with every step I took. I woke up every night with an unbearable pain in my toes. In the morning, I looked at my feet and saw they were raw and swollen. They were so tender I didn't want to touch them, but I kept putting those shoes back on. My toenails started to fall off and I bled into my shoes. Finally, someone noticed, and I was admitted to what they called the infirmary.

Every time somebody got sick, they were taken to the infirmary room on the fourth floor. It was not a hospital ward or anything like that. For one thing, there were no doctors. The nuns gave us a bed to lie on and, every few hours, one of them would come in and check on us. That was it. It was a let-the-body-heal-itself type of thing. They didn't do any kind of treatment for my feet — no antibiotics, no bandages, no creams, no medicines of any kind. I just lay there in pain until my toenails started growing back. Eventually the nuns felt I had healed enough to return to my regular place as Number 53. I was sent back to my regular bed, they gave me shoes that fit, and I returned to the everyday violence and abuse.

All of that trauma came flooding back to me just because I stubbed my toe. And that was just one thing I endured at that school. There was so much trauma that it can never totally leave me. It will always lurk inside me, ready to jump out whenever it gets a chance. That's what trauma does. But with the help of the Elders, I not only survived it, I flourished. I became a person with integrated physical, emotional, and spiritual health. I have the skills to keep up that health. I have the skills to help others. Now that I am an Elder, I know exactly what to do when my trauma leaps out from the darkness. I lean into my spirituality and I pray. I pray for myself, for my family, for my people.

And I pray for the people who made a little boy wear shoes that were too tight.

CHAPTER 32

Living in a Good Way

One morning in late summer, I sat on the deck with my wife drinking strong black coffee and watching the sun rise over the lake in front of our home. It was a perfect morning, bright and clear with just a hint of a cool fall breeze. The sun's rays sent pink and orange diamonds dancing over the smooth surface of the water while little wisps of morning mist gently drifted up into the air. We could hear a white-throated sparrow whistling on the edge of the boreal forest, happy that her work raising her young was done for the season.

We could also hear our reserve waking up around us. Dogs barked as their owners let them out. Vehicles, windows down and satellite radio playing, began to crunch along the gravel road that snakes behind our house. We heard the arrival of the big busses that transport some of our people to job sites around our community and our region. Transportation, that big word I first heard as a little boy, is still important to our people and our economic future.

As I sipped my coffee, I thought about what I was going to do that day. I was working as an addiction counsellor, and all that summer I was also doing my work as an Elder and Knowledge Keeper, teaching traditional ways to the youth in our community. I found that very rewarding, but that morning I was thinking about the way I share traditional knowledge and how it is different from the way it was shared with me.

When I was a boy called *Napikan*, my whole family lived together in the bush. My *Mooshum* was with me every day, sharing his traditional knowledge as we did our chores to help our family stay well-fed, warm, and comfortable. We spent most of our time outside on the land, which was my classroom as well as the source of our food and water. *Mooshum* taught me the entire time as we gathered the eggs of wild birds, trapped rabbits and squirrels, and collected plants to make tea. Every day I peppered him with questions, and I learned, as they used to say, at his knee. Knowledge sharing was embedded in our daily lives, woven into everything we said and did. Every time my grandfather taught me something, Creator's gifts were all around me to be seen, touched, scented, heard, and tasted. I was completely immersed in our land and our teachings. Our traditional ways were ingrained in every step I took on the land.

Things are different for our children today. Our people and our land are part of a larger, busier world. Everywhere I look, I see how things have changed. The Clearwater River that my mother and uncle travelled by dogsled on the night of my birth still freezes every winter, but now people ride all-terrain vehicles on it — some for traditional things like hunting and ice fishing, some for fun. It is no longer our main transportation route. Our people can get to town in half an hour on safe and well-maintained roads. They can travel to their jobs in any kind of weather. Those jobs pay well and include benefits and pensions, and that comes from the groundwork I laid decades ago when I was a young Chief negotiating that first Indigenous employment agreement with industry.

Our people come home to warm, comfortable homes, some of them in the cozy houses I built decades ago. They buy their children nice clothes, toys, and birthday cakes, and take them to hockey games and dance practices. There is a commercial airport not too far away, where our families leave their vehicles in the long-term parking lot to travel on vacations to Mexico, the Caribbean, and Europe. We also have resources in our community for health, education, and recreation, all in their own buildings with properly trained staff. We also have a Youth Council that gives our young people a voice in our community's decisions.

Our days of sharing a single satellite phone for the entire community are long in the past. Now our young people use their cellphones to watch movies from Japan and soccer games from Spain. They learn how to brew fancy teas from India and do the latest dance moves from Korea. Our youth know much more of the world than I did as a boy, and they seem to have unlimited access to information. But they do not have the access to traditional knowledge that I had when I spent my days at an Elders' knee, absorbing the teachings of our ancestors in every thought and action.

That was weighing on me on that peaceful morning as I watched the world wake up around me. It is my sacred responsibility as an Elder to pass on knowledge. I feel that deeply because we have so few Knowledge Keepers now. Too many members of my generation were robbed of the chance to learn the ways of our ancestors due to the residential school system. Because of this, I feel an even greater responsibility to pass along my knowledge, especially as the generation of Elders before me passes away. That is part of the reason I have written this book: to record important things so that they will not be lost. I wonder what my *Mooshum* would think about my having to record my knowledge in a printed book. He would have been astounded that I sometimes share traditional knowledge with an online community, where the learners are physically separated from one another, everyone inside in their own room looking at a computer screen.

All that summer, I tried to get our students, most of them teenagers on break from our on-reserve school, out onto the land. One day I took them to where medicinal herbs and plants grew, teaching them things like how to recognize rat root and brew it into a tea to fight a cold. I watched them take photos of rat root with their phones. They looked up its scientific name, *Acorus americanus*, and they read online information about its properties. They showed me how they could order rat root tea online and have it delivered right to their home — even though that rat root is a variety grown far away in Asia, not the same plant growing on their own traditional land.

When our youth feel a cold coming on, they buy a pharmaceutical cough medicine right in our community.

They were respectful of what I was teaching. But I could see that, in their own way, they were struggling to reconcile it with the science they studied in school and saw in movies about space travel, catching criminals, and miracle cures. They know about DNA, drug trials and, of course, pandemics. But while the cellphones always at their fingertips can give them scientific information, they don't tell the whole story. Their phones do not connect them to our ancestors' teachings and our traditional responsibility as stewards of the land we were gifted by Creator. As Indigenous youth, that was what they most needed to learn.

I told them science has great value. It can tell us the medicinal properties of rat root and why it relieves a specific condition. I also told them science and traditional teachings can respect and learn from each other. But I wanted them to know that traditional land-based teachings address the big picture, the spiritual and emotional aspects that must be in balance for our long-term health and wellness. I wanted them to feel the connection to the land that I have felt ever since my mother buried my umbilical cord deep in the bush. I wanted them to connect with the land and the important role Creator gave us as its stewards. I wanted them to know the sense of pride and self-esteem this stewardship brings. But I was struggling because they were too used to looking at their tiny screens, not the world around them.

As I watched them take selfies beside the traditional plants, I couldn't help but think of my cousin Tommy, now passed away, and how he approached the world when we were that age. Tommy's dad made sure he knew the serious business of stewarding the land and respecting Creator. But Tommy also saw the world around him as a wonderland of games and challenges. He saw the opportunity for delight everywhere, even in a muddy ditch of icy water. No matter how hard we worked for his father — chopping wood, bailing hay, training a horse — he found a way to make it fun. Tommy was so filled with joy at the gifts of Creator that he helped me free myself from the mental and emotional prison that residential school had built around me. Tommy showed me how an Indigenous boy could live joyfully in a world that Creator wanted him to experience to the fullest. I wanted the young people I was teaching to have beautiful memories of the sun warming their backs, the sight of ducks landing on a lake, the smell of fresh sweetgrass, and what it felt like to laugh so hard you could barely stand. I wanted these youth to be fully present in the moments when Creator's glory surrounded them, not seeing everything through a cellphone camera.

We made some progress as the summer went on. We walked our traditional land, and I worked hard to get them to connect with the ground beneath their feet. I showed them the moss on the north side of black poplar trees, warned them about screech owls, and shared teachings about plants and animals. They told me it reminded them of reality shows on television where survivalists are dropped into the wilderness and have to figure out how to survive.

"It is true," I said, "that once you know the things I am teaching, you can go any place in the bush and you'll never starve or freeze. But survival skills are not the most important thing."

"What is more important than survival?" one of them asked.

"It is not just about survival. It is much bigger," I said. "It is about our values and how to live our way of life whether you are in the bush or not. The ancestors passed these traditional things on to us so that we can live in a good way."

They were puzzled about how traditional teachings applied outside of the bush, but they were listening. I told them how our values developed through our sacred connection to the land, but applied everywhere — in the bush, in the classroom, in the boardroom. It does not matter whether you are on a trapline in the boreal forest or in a cabinet minister's office on Parliament Hill in Ottawa. It is all the same to Creator. Our values of balance and interconnectedness can help us live a good life wherever we go and whatever we do. If all of our actions are guided by the sacred teachings, we can never go wrong. It was the same message I gave to oil company executives and government bureaucrats, but sharing it with our youth is the most important work I have ever done.

It was a huge concept, and I could see them trying to wrap their heads around it. They started to grasp it when I warned them to be careful about information they shared online, to make sure it did not interfere with their duty to protect the land. I told them about a time I brought non-Indigenous people to a special spot to show them some medicinal herbs. When I returned to the site later, I found all the plants dug up, not a single one left behind to replenish the land.

"That is their way," I told the youth. "It is not our way. Our way is to make sure Creator's gifts are sustained for generations to come."

That made an impression. They were upset anyone would behave in such a wrong way on our land. But I had to get them to take the next step and make the spiritual connection between the land, their stewardship, and the bigger world around them. They saw it intellectually, and they were starting to feel it emotionally, but they still needed to feel the spiritual connection that led to the joy that came so naturally to Tommy.

I sat on the deck with Tina that morning and contemplated the day ahead, when I would teach my last lesson of the summer. I said a silent prayer to Creator, asking for help finding a way for the youth to see that spiritual connection with their eyes, feel it with their hands, hear it with their ears, taste it with their mouths, and smell it in the air.

Then my wife said, "What is that in the water?"

I looked where she was pointing and saw a huge bump sticking out of the calm lake. I could tell it wasn't a log or debris because it was making deliberate progress towards the shore opposite and sending out even ripples in its wake.

"It's a moose," I said, and stood up for a better look.

The moose was swimming steadily, moving its head left and right to scent the air as it travelled to the other side of the lake. Moose are most active around sunrise and sunset, so it was behaving as it was supposed to, starting off its day with a bit of travel. But my wife and I were surprised to see it. The wildfires that are becoming part of regular life in northern Alberta had burned a large swath of the boreal forest around our community, throwing moose off their traditional migration routes. The Elders and hunters in our community had been saying all summer that moose were staying deep in the bush and no one had spotted one close to our community. To see this one powering its way across the lake was very special, and I knew it was coming to help me.

"I know where it is going to come out of the water," I told my wife. "There is one place it can easily walk up on shore to feed on the grassy growth, and it looks like that is exactly where it is heading."

"You better hurry," said my wife.

She was right, and I rushed inside our house to get my gun, ammunition, hunting knife, rope, and tobacco. As soon as I gathered everything, I raced outside. When I was a boy hunting with my brother August, we would have run to the site on foot, but now I hopped into my pickup truck. Things have changed for me, too, as I've gotten older. I appreciated that I was driving a nice comfortable vehicle as I zoomed along the road.

I drove towards the water treatment plant and pulled in behind the building. As I stepped out of my vehicle, I carefully checked the wind direction. It was blowing off the lake towards me, which meant the moose could not detect me with its huge, soft nose. I stayed upwind, the way my brother taught me more than half a century earlier, as I loaded the ammunition into my gun. As I walked around the side of the building towards the shore, I carried my gun in the safe way August had first showed me, now the habit of a lifetime. When I got to the edge of the building, I crouched down beside it to watch the moose, feeling its energy as it swam straight towards me.

I could tell a lot about that moose even though most of it was underwater. I knew it was a male, because female moose do not have antlers. Bull moose shed their antlers each winter and sprout new ones in the spring. As they age, their new antlers grow larger and acquire more points. Bull moose antlers stop growing in size around the age of five, when the animal reaches its prime. After that, the number of points and size of the antlers decrease each year, and mishappen antlers are often a sign of old age. It was almost fall, so the annual growth was nearly complete, making it easy to tell the animal's age. I knew this was a male yearling because its antlers were smaller and had only three points on each side, and also by the power it showed as it swam steadily across the lake.

The moose drew closer to the shore until it was half walking and half swimming, its hard cloven hooves reaching to touch bottom. Soon it found its footing, and it was a majestic sight: a young moose rising up from the water on a clear morning, giving itself to me so that I could use it to teach young people the same way I had been taught. When it was finally close enough, the water now below its chest, I took careful aim. I took a deep breath, filling my lungs with the crisp morning air, exhaled slowly, and fired my gun. The moose gave a jerk and fell over, creating a huge splash that sent waves cascading across the calm water. They rippled towards me on the shore and also back out into the lake, tracing the route the moose had travelled.

Like my brother taught me all those years ago, I made sure I had done the job properly and that the moose was not suffering. Then I ran back to my pickup and drove to our band office, the administrative centre of our community, which was just opening for the day. I walked into the office of the chief administrative officer, who oversees the daily functions of our Nation. I told him I had a moose and would be taking the summer students out on a special field trip.

"A moose!" he said. "Finally! Congratulations Elder Robert, that is great news."

He nodded out his office window towards the students, who happened to be walking up to the steps of the band office.

"They are right there ready for you," he said. "Go show them what they need to know."

There were a dozen young people in the group, both boys and girls. They all looked up when I told them it was a big day, that I had a moose and needed their help. They had heard a lot of talk in the community about the scarcity of moose that summer, so they knew something important was happening. They got in the back of my truck, and I drove to where the moose was waiting. They hopped out of my vehicle, every one of them looking like they did not know what to expect.

"Where's the moose?" one of them asked.

"Do you see that big bump in the water there?" I pointed at the lake. "That's the moose. Go get it."

They looked out at the moose. It had rolled over onto its side and its spine was perpendicular to the shoreline. Its head and tail were underwater, the midsection sticking out of the water like a small, dark-brown island. They started firing off questions the way I had once pestered my *Mooshum*.

"How are we supposed to get that? How will we to get it to shore? What are we going to do with it?"

"First you have to get into the water with it," I said. "Then you can move it around easier."

"Easier?" one of them said. "That moose looks like it weighs a ton."

"It weighs about three-quarters of a ton," I said.

"You want us to move something that weighs three-quarters of a ton?"

"I could do it all by myself when I was your age," I said. They looked skeptical, but they carefully put their phones down on the shore, took off their expensive sneakers, and waded out into the lake. The moose was tall and had been in fairly deep water when it toppled sideways, so they were up to their waists when they got to it. They did not look happy. They were half-heartedly poking and prodding at it.

"It's heavy," one of them said.

"I know," I said. "That's why I need strong young people like you to help me. I need you to turn it around so the head is pointed towards the shore."

They started pushing it, but they were disorganized, pushing this way and that. Eventually, with the brute strength of youth and the buoyancy of the water, they got it turned around so that the head was pointing more or less towards shore.

"Now what?" one of them shouted to me.

I tossed them the rope. "Wrap it around the moose," I said. They looked at me like I was crazy. "Wrap it around the head, then tie the strongest knot you can."

"Then what?"

"Then you guys work together to drag it to the shore," I said.

That prompted another flurry of questions, but I just said, "I know you can figure it out."

I watched as they tried to wrap the rope around the moose's neck while the head, heavy and awkward because of the antlers, was still mostly underwater. It took them a while and they had a heated discussion among themselves, but at last they had the rope all the way around the neck and tied good and tight. Then they split up, some of them pulling on the rope and others pushing at the back of the moose. It wasn't long before they had that moose slowly drifting towards shore. That got them excited because they were making progress. Soon they were all at the front of the moose, walking backwards and pulling together on the rope until they half-floated, half-pulled the moose almost to the shoreline. When the moose's full body weight hit the bottom, buoyancy couldn't help them anymore. It was dead weight. They had dragged it as far as they could with their own strength, so after a few unsuccessful tries, they stopped and stood knee-deep in the water, looking at me.

"Give me the end of the rope," I said.

This time there were no questions. One of them brought the end of the rope up on shore. I made him stand to one side while I got back in my truck, turned it around, and backed down to the water's edge. Then I tied the rope to my trailer hitch and told everyone to stand back. I hopped back into the driver's seat, put the truck in gear, and inched forward. I kept one eye on my rear-view mirror as I eased the moose up onto the shore, pulling it completely out of the lake until there was enough room around it for us to start harvesting it.

"Now what?" one of them asked.

"Now we thank Creator for the gift," I said.

I took out the tobacco I'd brought, made an offering to Creator, and said a prayer in our Cree language. The young people stood respectfully as I thanked Creator for the four elements: the water that had brought the moose to us, the food it had grazed from the earth to fill its belly, the air that had filled its lungs, and the fire we would use when we cooked the meat. Then I thanked the moose for giving itself to us so that I could teach the youth of my community. Our young people now learn Cree at school, learning to count in Cree when they are in kindergarten. But few of them are fluent in it, so I repeated the prayer in English. It was a long prayer but they were quiet and listened to every bit, and I could see the meaning taking hold of them. At the end they joined me in saying *hiy hiy*.

While I was praying, something special was happening. Our chief administrative officer was telling people the good news about my moose, and word was spreading fast. Our youth are not the only ones with cellphones. Even Elders like me have them, and texts were going out with the exciting news. People were heading over to see the moose and join in the harvest.

One of the first to arrive was my older brother August, who had taken me on my first moose hunt all those years ago. That had been one of the best days of my life. I had been so excited to share the bounty of my hunt with everyone in our community that I smiled for days. Now my brother had a huge smile, his face lighting up when he saw the moose. August had brought his hunting knife and he jumped right in beside me to help with the meat. The youth gathered around, their full attention on my brother and me. Soon he was teaching them, too, showing them how to hold the knife and where to make the cuts, and telling them which the tastiest pieces of meat were. We let them take our knives and make their own cuts, and right away they had the same big smiles my brother and I had. It felt wonderful being there with my brother, sharing knowledge our father and grandfather had taught us, things they had been taught by their fathers and grandfathers, and their ancestors before that.

As we worked, I made sure to set aside the hide. It was beautiful, strong and unsoiled as Creator intended, not like the maggot-ridden abominations I saw when I worked at the tannery as a young man. I wanted to cure this hide myself in the traditional way to make a drum to use at ceremonies. I also made sure to set aside parts like the nose, tongue, and heart to use for delicacies to offer to the ancestors.

People kept arriving, everyone excited that this moose had come to our community. We gave away most of the meat, making sure the best cuts went to other Elders. My brother got some of the tender meat along the spine, and I cut up steaks and ribs to take home. The students were taking photos again, but they were also working with us to complete the tasks at hand, thrilled to be doing something that made our community so happy.

It felt wonderful to be working out in the morning sun, land-based learning happening at the right time in the right way, the whole community sharing Creator's gift. We were all there — Elders, youth, everyone.

We arrived in trucks and cars, wearing jeans and baseball caps, recording everything in photographs taken with the latest technology. But we were gathered in the same way our people had for generations to celebrate Creator's gift of a moose.

I see that morning's events as an act of reconciliation on the part of our community. We were reconciling technology we took from the dominant culture — vehicles, rifles, cellphones — by using it to practise our traditional values. This how our world works now. We share this world with that culture and we have to figure out a way to be in it while staying true to our traditional values. I do not find it hard to do. In my life I have seen great changes in things like technology and transportation. But traditional Indigenous values have not changed at all. The tools of the dominant culture are just that: instruments we can use. That day we used those tools to harvest the moose that gave itself to our community, and our Indigenous values were evident in every thought and action. We used every part of the moose. We shared with our community. We respected our Elders. We prayed in gratitude.

Ever since I was a boy living in the bush with my family, I have believed Indigenous people can live the good life Creator intended as long as we keep to our traditional values. I always had an unshakeable faith in the traditional teachings of the ancestors, and that has sustained me as I've lived under the different names this world has given me. That is also why those names are still alive in me, bringing me strength instead of bitterness. I am still Bobby Mountain following my mother through a world of wonder. I am also *Napikan*, thinking big thoughts and striving to be a great man in the eyes of Creator and my people. I am Number 53, following the brilliant light of traditional wisdom, a beacon on my darkest days. I am Chief Cree, using my skills and knowledge to benefit my community. I am Robert Cree, working with government and industry leaders who ask how we can heal the jagged wounds of the past. I am Elder Cree, immersed in the sacred spirituality of the ancestors and sharing the traditional teachings. All of my names are signposts along the road Creator intended for me. They are all part of the truth I have shared with you in this book.

Now that you know my truth, I hope you will join me on a journey of reconciliation. All people, Indigenous and non-Indigenous, must walk together on this path, respectfully sharing our knowledge, humbly striving for balance, and gratefully recognizing our interconnectedness. We must work together to take care of one another and our world. Because who are we if we can't exist in harmony on Turtle Island and on this magnificent planet Creator gave us?

Creator gave us everything we need to live a good life.

Now we have to live it.

Acknowledgements

Kinanaskomitin. Thank you.

There are many people I need to thank for joining me on the path that has led me here.

First, I want to thank the Chief, Council, and members of Fort McMurray 468 First Nation, who generously supported me in the writing of this book. Our Nation is a very special place on Turtle Island.

I offer my deepest thanks and loving gratitude to my wife Tina Cree, the most important person in my life. Thank you for the forty years of love and strength you have shared with me and our family. It is because of you that my story has the happiest of endings.

I want to thank my children Jacquline Berland, Robert Berland, Hope Stevenson, Jeffery Cree, Larissa Cree, and their families. I thank Creator for the blessings of my children and grandchildren, and the great joy they have brought to my life.

I acknowledge my early mentors Joe Dion, Elmer Ghostkeeper, and the late Harold Cardinal for generously sharing their wisdom and knowledge as we worked side by side for the benefit of our people.

I want to express my everlasting gratitude for the traditional teachings and loving guidance of my late mother Eva Cree, my late father Mike Mountain, and my late *Mooshum* Cree.

My life has been greatly blessed with many wonderful aunts and uncles who were always there to help guide and support me. I am eternally grateful to my late Uncle Lawrence Mountain, his late wife, and my cousins Philip Mountain and the late Tommy Mountain. They welcomed me into their home after residential school, and with their loving support I took my first steps towards healing.

I thank my father's other brothers, Isadore and Leo, and my mother's siblings Joe, Irene, Johnny, Flora, Norman, Albert, Freddy, Walter, and Jimmy. I also want to thank my brothers and sisters. I would not be here on this Earth today without the grounding in traditional values that my family so generously gifted to me.

I also want to thank the non-Indigenous people who embraced the spirit of reconciliation and encouraged me to tell my story in this book. I appreciate the deep respect they have shown for me and for my people's traditional teachings and protocols. Thank you to literary agent Claire Gerus and all the staff at ECW Press, especially Jack David, Kenna Barnes, and Lisa Frenette. Thank you to Sheri Anthony and the staff of the Wood Buffalo Regional Library for generously sharing their resources and for making it possible for me to do a blessing and smudging for this book project. Thank you to Steve Bonisteel for his technical support. Thank you to Therese Greenwood for suggesting I share my life story in a book and for collaborating with me to make it a reality.

I also want to acknowledge my lifelong gratitude to the many Elders and Knowledge Keepers who shared the wisdom of the ancestors with me. They started me on my path in the right way and gave me the traditional teachings I needed to survive residential school and heal from its abuses. Everything I accomplished in my life was because of the power of the traditional teachings and the wisdom and knowledge of the people who taught me.

Finally, I want to thank Creator for bringing all of these people into my life and for the many blessings bestowed upon me. *Kinanaskomitin.*

Entertainment. Writing. Culture. ─────────

ECW is a proudly independent, Canadian-owned book publisher. We know great writing can improve people's lives, and we're passionate about sharing original, exciting, and insightful writing across genres.

───────────────── **Thanks for reading along!**

We want our books not just to sustain our imaginations but to help con-   **Certified**
struct a healthier, more just world, and so we've become a certified
B Corporation, meaning we meet a high standard of social and environ-   (B)
mental responsibility — and we're going to keep aiming higher. We believe
books can drive change, but the way we make them can too.   **Corporation**

Being a B Corp means that the act of publishing this book should be a force for good — for the planet, for our communities, and for the people that worked to make this book. For example, everyone who worked on this book was paid at least a living wage. You can learn more at the Ontario Living Wage Network.

This book is also available as a Global Certified Accessible™ (GCA) ebook. ECW Press's ebooks are screen reader friendly and are built to meet the needs of those who are unable to read standard print due to blindness, low vision, dyslexia, or a physical disability.

This book is printed on FSC®-certified paper. It contains recycled materials, and other controlled sources, is processed chlorine free, and is manufactured using biogas energy.

FSC
www.fsc.org
MIX
Paper | Supporting
responsible forestry
FSC® C103567

ECW's office is situated on land that was the traditional territory of many nations, including the Wendat, the Anishinaabeg, Haudenosaunee, Chippewa, Métis, and current treaty holders the Mississaugas of the Credit. In the 1880s, the land was developed as part of a growing community around St. Matthew's Anglican and other churches. Starting in the 1950s, our neighbourhood was transformed by immigrants fleeing the Vietnam War and Chinese Canadians dispossessed by the building of Nathan Phillips Square and the subsequent rise in real estate value in other Chinatowns. We are grateful to those who cared for the land before us and are proud to be working amidst this mix of cultures.

ecwpress.com